Apocalypse South

Judgment, Cataclysm, and Resistance in the Regional Imaginary

Anthony Dyer Hoefer

THE OHIO STATE UNIVERSITY PRESS   •   COLUMBUS

Copyright © 2012 by The Ohio State University.
All rights reserved.

Library of Congress Cataloging in Publication Data
Hoefer, Anthony Dyer, 1978–
 Apocalypse south : judgment, cataclysm, and resistance in the regional imaginary / Anthony Dyer Hoefer. — (Literature, religion, and postsecular studies)
  p. cm.
 Includes bibliographical references and index.
 ISBN-13: 978-0-8142-1201-1 (cloth : alk. paper)
 ISBN-10: 0-8142-1201-8 (cloth : alk. paper)
 ISBN-13: 978-0-8142-9303-4 (cd-rom)
 1. Apocalyptic literature—History and criticism. 2. Apocalypse in literature. 3. American literature—Southern States—History and criticism. 4. Faulkner, William, 1897–1962—Criticism and interpretation. 5. Wright, Richard, 1908–1960—Criticism and interpretation. 6. Kenan, Randall—Criticism and interpretation. 7. Allison, Dorothy—Criticism and interpretation. I. Title. II. Series (Literature, religion, and postsecular studies)
 PS374.A65H64 2012
 813'.009353—dc23
                                        2012006529

Paper (ISBN: 978-0-8142-5644-2)

Cover design by James A. Baumann
Text design by Juliet Williams
Type set in Goudy Old Style

*In memory of John Cobb and Larry McGehee,
two great teachers who were there at the start.*

*And for Kate and Cora,
without whom I could not have gotten this far.*

Contents

Acknowledgments   vii

Introduction **Tracing the Apocalyptic Imaginary**   1

    A Note on Structure   14

PART I

Chapter 1   **Southern Jeremiad, American Jeremiad: Region, Nation, and Apocalypse in Faulkner's *Light in August***   21

    "A walking pollution in God's own face":
The Apocalyptic Logic of Blood, Contamination, and Purity   24

    The Apocalyptic Ritual of Lynching   37

    "Lincoln and the negro and Moses and the children of Israel":
American Millenarianism and the Burden Narrative   44

    Percy Grimm: Nationalizing the Southern Apocalyptic Imaginary   48

    Modernism, the Cataclysm of Meaning, and the Possibility of Revelation   51

Chapter 2   **"Tearing Down the Temple": Prophetic Time and Richard Wright's Eschatology of Resistance**   61

    "We git erlong widout time":
The Ahistorical Condition of Jim Crow   66

    Typology and the Apocalyptic Structure of *Uncle Tom's Children*   77

    Revising the Teleology:
The Possibility of Rupture, Revelation, and Rebirth   85

    Conclusion: Writing New Endings   95

PART II

Chapter 3   **"Some Say Ain't No Earthly Explanation":
Excavating the Apocalyptic Landscape of
Randall Kenan's Tims Creek**   101

         Tims Creek and the Eschatology of Place   104
         Apocalypse as Alternative Discursive Space   111
         The Possibility of Revelation: Excavating Apocalypse   120
         The Uses of the Past   128

Chapter 4   **"An't It Time the Lord Did Something?":
Vindication and the Practices of Place in
*Bastard Out of Carolina***   130

         The Limits and Restraints of Southern Spaces   133
         The Boatwrights' Attempts at Narrative Resistance   138
         The Alternative Narrative Space of Apocalypse   145

Epilogue   **Apocalypse South, *Redux*—
Searching for Meaning after the Flood**   154

         "Playing the Blame Game":
             Condemnation and Scapegoating after the Flood   156
         Katrina and the (African) American Jeremiad   160
         The Possibility of Revelation and Renewal   162
         Justice, Deliverance, and Resistance   168

Bibliography   173
Index   182

Acknowledgments

During the years that I've been thinking about the questions and problems addressed in this book, I've been fortunate to belong to several intellectually rich communities and to have the friendship, guidance, and support of many kind, smart people. Without their generosity, insight, advice, mentoring, feedback, poking, prodding, and cajoling, this book would not exist.

At Wofford College in Spartanburg, South Carolina: I owe particular debts to Bernie Dunlap and Talmage Skinner, as well as the late John Cobb and Larry McGehee. The department of American Studies at the University of Alabama helped begin my career as a scholar and teacher; in particular, Stacy Morgan is due much appreciation. At LSU, the members of my dissertation committee—Brannon Costello, Edward Henderson, Katherine Henninger, Jerry Kennedy, and Rick Moreland—provided exceptionally useful comments on the earliest versions of this project; thanks also to Anna Nardo, who did more to improve the quality of my writing than any one since elementary school. No dissertation advisor could have been more gracious with his time than John Lowe: over the last eight years, he has shepherded this project though all of its many stages, beginning with an essay written for his "Native Sons/Native Daughters" seminar in 2004. I'm also grateful for the support, friendship, and thoughtful discussion provided by all of my LSU colleagues and tailgate team—in particular, Courtney George, Scott Gage, and Scott Whiddon. From my time at Georgia Tech: thanks to my fellow Brittain Fellows Jürgen Grandt, Matt Paproth, Jen Parrott, and Nirmal Trivedi. Thanks also to the entire crew from Success Programs (now the Success Center), particularly Eric Moschella for his friendship and guidance.

For the last two years, I've had been humbled by the generosity, commitment, and vision of my colleagues in the Honors College at George Mason University—simply the best team I've ever joined. Particular thanks to our fearless leader and dean Zofia Burr, who took a chance on me and then made it possible for me to take this project across the finish line. Much appreciation to my great and wonderful students, who never cease to challenge and impress me.

I owe a singular and strange debt to my friend Mason Brown. Eight years ago, he made a compilation CD (when one still did such things), filled with strange and creepy blues, gospel, and folk tunes. He called it "Apocalypse Southern," and everything began when I played it.

Many thanks to the great team at The Ohio State University Press—Sandy Crooms, Eugene O'Connor, and Ed Hatton.

My greatest debts, of course, are owed to the members of my family; I was born into a family in which love, encouragement, and thoughtful discussion were the norm, and then, I had the good fortune to I marry into another one. Thanks to my parents, Nancy and Anthony, and my siblings, Paul and Emily, for supporting me throughout my career – and for not blinking when I told them I'd likely be in school for all of my 20s; thanks to my parents-in-law, John and Len, for their support – and for not blinking when their daughter brought home someone who'd been in school for all of his 20s. Finally: Kate, I could not have done this without your love, patience, and encouragement—I'm lucky and grateful to have you as my partner. Cora, I hope that one day you'll read this, understand what I was doing on my laptop all those nights, and maybe even enjoy it. In the meantime, though, please don't color in this book.

The Great Question before us is: Are we doomed? The Great Question before us is: Will the Past Release us? The Great Question before us is: Can we Change? In Time? And we all desire that Change will come.

—Tony Kushner, Angels in America, Part Two: Perestroika. Act I, Scene 1.

Introduction

Tracing the Apocalyptic Imaginary

> Fear the hearts of men are failing
> These our latter days we know
> The great depression now is spreading
> God's word declared it would be so
>
> I'm going where there's no depression
> To a better land that's free from care
> I'll leave this world of toil and trouble
> My home's in heaven
> I'm going there
>
> In this dark hour, midnight nearing
> The tribulation time will come
> The storms will hurl the midnight fear
> And sweep lost millions to their doom
>
> I'm going where there's no depression
> To a better land that's free from care
> I'll leave this world of toil and trouble
> My home's in heaven
> I'm going there
>
> I'm going where there's no depression
> To a better land that's free from care
> I'll leave this world of toil and trouble
> My home's in heaven
> I'm going there
>
> —The Carter Family, "No Depression (in Heaven)"

THE CARTER FAMILY recorded "No Depression (in Heaven)" in 1936, the same year that Dorothea Lange photographed "Migrant Mother" and that James Agee and Walker Evans first began the project that would become *Let Us Now Praise Famous Men*. Though the song was a selection from a popular shaped-note songbook rather than an original composition, it remains among their most notable and frequently covered.[1] But the Carters were no gospel act, and their professional aims did not include an evangelistic mission (Malone 93). Nonetheless "No Depression (in Heaven)" takes on a specifically religious theme: it employs the cosmology of evangelical and fundamentalist Protestantism in an effort to make some sense of an experience that is all but incomprehensible in its scope and complexity. Facing instability wrought by drought, foreclosure, plummeting tobacco and cotton prices,[2] and the early stages of the Great Migration of African Americans from the South,[3] the Carters' audience tuned their radios to 650 kHz and sought solace in a signal broadcasting from Nashville's WSM to homes across the South (and, at night, across the entire continent). By casting the contemporary crisis in the familiar words of Scripture, Carter Family songs like "No Depression (in Heaven)," "The World is Not My Home," and "Can the Circle Be Unbroken?" reconfigured chaos as the realization of prophecy. "The great depression now is spreading," they sang, "God's word declared it would be so." Such songs endow even the most awful consequences of this catastrophe with meaning, and they situate the current moment of suffering as the fulcrum upon which the future depends: the darkest moment—"midnight"—is upon them, and the coming storms of the Tribulation will "sweep lost millions to their doom." Their suffering, however, will be redeemed because it is a necessary step in the progression toward ultimate deliverance—a point in the journey toward "a better land that's free from care." Crucially, that deliverance is configured in two ways. The most immediate and singular of these is death, when the *individual* "leave[s] this world of toil and trouble" for his or her heavenly home. However, the invocation of the "tribulation times" evokes

---

1. Over the last two decades or so, the song has held a seminal position within the genre variously referred to as "alternative-country," "Americana," and "roots music." The alternative-country group Uncle Tupelo recorded it for their 1990 album, *No Depression*, and that truncated title was appropriated for the bimonthly magazine devoted to the genre.

2. The 1920s and '30s were a time of rapid economic expansion in southern cities, as well as growth in the textile, mining, and steel industries. However, as Roger Biles notes, the bulk of the South's population could be found in rural areas and did not experience this prosperity; rather, for "southern farmers . . . the Great Depression immediately meant more misery and deprivation" following the collapse of cotton prices in 1920–21, the Great Mississippi Flood of 1927, and the drought of 1930–31" (18). According to Biles, "From 1929 to 1932, the value of cotton sales dropped from $1.5 billion to $45 million, and income from the cigarette tobacco crop declined by two-thirds."

3. For instance, fully 14 percent of Mississippi's population of black men between 15 and 34 years old left the state during the 1920s (Godden 11).

the *collective, communal* deliverance promised by the millennial return of Christ.

"No Depression (in Heaven)" offers hope to an audience in a hopeless moment, reminding them of the promise of imminent deliverance from worldly misery. In doing so, it deploys the *other*worldly historical vision of Apocalypse to explain the experiences of *this* world; this apocalyptic vision promises justice in the face of oppression and suffering. However, this invocation is only one possible permutation of Apocalypse, and often the uses of Apocalypse seem to be at cross-purposes: though the Carters' song offers hope to the oppressed and the dispossessed via a prophecy of deliverance and justice, the rhetoric of God's judgment is powerful tool of marginalization when it is invoked to condemn those who might violate the prevailing social order. Examples of this second category are not difficult to find. For instance, George C. Wallace supported his famous declaration with unmistakably apocalyptic rhetoric in the address following his first inauguration as governor of Alabama in 1963. Speaking of racial progress, he told the audience

> Not so long ago men stood in marvel and awe at the cities, the buildings, the schools, the autobahns that the government of Hitler's Germany had built . . . just as centuries before they stood in wonder of Rome's building . . . but it could not stand . . . for the system that built it had rotted the souls of the builders . . . and in turn . . . rotted the foundation of what God meant that men should be. Today that same system on an international scale is sweeping the world. It is the "changing world" of which we are told. . . . [I]t is called "new" and "liberal." It is as old as the oldest dictator. It is degenerate and decadent. (Wallace, Inaugural Address)

The implications of this rhetoric would be obvious to the Alabamans listening. Wallace's references to Rome and Germany do not simply recall a secular, worldly history of collapsing empires, but rather, fit into a prophetic vision of history in which God's will is accomplished through the vanquishing of the forces of evil by the forces of righteousness. Indeed, by using the adjectives "degenerate and decadent," Wallace invokes not just the fall of the Roman Empire, but also the divine wrath meted out on Sodom and Gomorrah. By implication, the dominant order of Jim Crow is located on the side of God, ascribing to it not just righteousness but also the power of historical inevitability. Interestingly, in either case—the Carters' song or Wallace's speech—the audience is positioned at the fulcrum of history, at a moment in which their southern landscape is charged with prophetic possibilities. Furthermore, in both instances, these voices turn to Apocalypse to articulate something that otherwise defies easy explanation. For the Carters, the chaotic, confusing circumstances of the Great Depression are otherwise incoherent and inarticulable; for Wallace, the unspeakable is the reality that segregation is not a divine sanction but an artifice, created and maintained by human action and thus subject to revision like any other governmental policy.

Apocalypse South investigates these apparently contradictory uses of apocalyptic rhetoric and seeks to access its emancipatory possibilities through readings of selected literary texts that respond to the religious culture of the U.S. South. These writers, like the Carters and George Wallace, engage a recognizable *southern apocalyptic imaginary*—a field of reference, drawn from the cosmology of southern evangelical Protestantism, that maps the apocalyptic possibilities of cataclysm, judgment, deliverance, and even revolution onto the landscape of the region. In this "unseen world of archangels and prophets and folk rising from the dead" (to borrow Randall Kenan's language in A *Visitation of Spirits* [16]), catastrophic consequences are ascribed to violations of the boundaries of the race, class, gender, family, community, region, and nation. At the same time, this apocalyptic imaginary is a reservoir of hope: through it, deliverance from injustices and worldly suffering remains possible within the daily experience of place, despite overwhelming evidence otherwise. *Apocalypse South* proposes that, whether it is used to condemn or to offer hope, Apocalypse is perhaps the only culturally available and acceptable discourse that is adequate to accommodate (if only indirectly) stories and experiences that would otherwise by neglected or even silenced by the ways of speaking that dominate in a given community.

In the apocalyptic imaginary, each of the writers considered here finds a vocabulary of images and narrative structures ideally suited to articulate a variety of southern histories that threaten the stability of the prevailing discourses of southern community. By aligning the apocalyptic visions of William Faulkner's *Light in August,* Richard Wright's *Uncle Tom's Children,* Randall Kenan's A *Visitation of Spirits* and "Let the Dead Bury Their Dead," and Dorothy Allison's *Bastard Out of Carolina, Apocalypse South* introduces the apocalyptic cosmology of southern evangelical Protestantism as a crucial but often misunderstood factor in the discursive production and reproduction of southern spaces and places. Furthermore, *Apocalypse South* suggests that this cosmology, deeply informed by the peculiar histories of the South, exerts an important but unattended influence on the ideologies of American exceptionalism and U.S. millenarian nationalism.

Apocalypse South's most significant scholarly intervention occurs in its introduction of theories of apocalyptic discourse to discussions of the peculiarly eschatological production of southern identities and southern communities. In *Seeing Things Hidden: Apocalypse, Vision and Totality*, Malcolm Bull asks:

> What is apocalyptic? A genre in which the heavenly mysteries are communicated through supernatural revelation? A belief that all history has a single irreversible conclusion? A teleological framework for the understanding of evil? An attempt to usher in a new era by redefining the rules of the redemptive process? A sense that each passing moment stands in some significant relation to a beginning and an end? A tone of disclosure, perhaps distinct from the content of the discourse, revelatory if only in that it reveals itself? (47)

Of course, Bull would not ask such questions if the answer was not implicit: Apocalypse is, can be, and has been all of the above. According to Douglas Robinson, Apocalypse is a "branch of eschatology" (or "doctrines about last things") that seeks "to explore the unveiling of the future in the present, the encroachment of a radically new order into the historical situation that has disintegrated into chaos" (xii).[4] In a very general sense, these concerns are central to much writing about the South. Citing exchanges between Allen Tate and Robert Penn Warren—two towering figures in the southern literary Renascence, both involved in the Agrarian manifesto, *I'll Take My Stand*—Scott Romine writes that "an overdeveloped eschatological sense is one of the more enduring characteristics of the southern literary tradition: the southerness of place, it seems, is always in danger of expiring" (26). The literary tradition that Romine takes on is predicated on a sort of apocalyptic paradox: it is brought to life out of the fear of its own, inevitable disappearance.

Writing eleven years after *I'll Take My Stand*, Wilbur J. Cash describes a very different strand of southern apocalypticism—namely, that evident in the fundamentalist faith of the working and poor whites of the region. His mythic Southerner preaches "a faith to draw men together in hordes,

---

4. Robinson's choice of the word "unveiling" is not a mere coincidence. "The Greek word *apokalypsis* means to unveil, to disclose, to reveal," according to Catherine Keller (xii), and "[p]rebiblically . . . connotes the marital stripping of the veiled virgin" (1).

to terrify them with Apocalyptic rhetoric. . . . A faith, not of liturgy and prayer book, but of primitive frenzy and the blood sacrifice—often of fits and jerks and barks" (55–56). Both Cash and Romine investigate prophetic visions, but the intersections of these visions have not been sufficiently investigated. The "overdeveloped eschatological sense" of southern writers and the apocalyptic and millennial beliefs of southern fundamentalists have been divided along the lines of class and engagement with the world outside the region, with the former positioned as cosmopolitan and aligned with modernism and the latter imagined as provincial, isolated, and disengaged from any broader intellectual movement. However, each of these visions emerges from the confrontation with modernity—either a dread or a dream that something fundamental about community may be irrevocably torn asunder and that something new will replace it. In "No Depression (in Heaven)," one hears a hope for something new; in *I'll Take My Stand* and in Wallace's speech, fear at the collapse of existing order.

Rather than interrogating the broad connections between the various forms of apocalyptic rhetoric, scholars working in southern literary studies have often ignored or reduced apocalyptic visions to several categories that are essentially adjuncts of other discussions. One trend, rooted in a tradition that includes works like Cash's or Lillian Smith's *Killers of the Dream* and even influenced by H. L. Mencken and Richard Wright, positions the evangelicalism and fundamentalism of working and poor whites work as a reactionary force inhibiting social change, thus reducing it to a sacralization of Wallace's message. Other lines of inquiry, including those begun by the New Critics, attend to the particular eschatology of the Southern Renascence noted by Romine. Despite the possibilities of rejuvenation suggested by the name, the figures of the Renascence and their New Critical brethren often mourned the expiring old verities in the face of modernity and industrialization. In their fiction and poetry, that apocalypticism was manifest in representations of the region as peopled with half-mad, grotesque preachers, espousing the faith described by Cash; in their criticism, these writers implicitly juxtaposed that provincial faith to the high church practices of the plantocracy and looked to Christianity as the rich inheritance of Western culture and as a source of symbolic meaning. Another, more recent line of investigation explores the millennial and millenarian belief of African American Christianity, positioning it as a unique countertradition opposed to both the reactionary forces of fundamentalists and the hypocrisy of mainline Protestantism in the South. Regardless of one's approach—that is to say, regardless of whether one seeks a broad understanding across the boundaries of race, class, or denomination, or approaches African American millennialism as a phenomenon distinct and apart from the prophetic vision of white evangelical Protestantism— the implication of eschatology in the production of the region is apparent: the South is always already at a moment of sublime, often cataclysmic transformation.

If we are to understand the eschatological components of regional identity, however, a more thorough investigation of the intersections and commonalities of the prophetic vision of southern evangelical Protestantism, across denominational and racial lines, is urgently needed. Each of the approaches I described above is informed by the particular textures of southern experiences—particularly the region's racial history. Earlier work, like Cash's, that strives for a holistic and comprehensive vision of southern religious practice now seems reductive and essentialist. Southern studies has no analogue to Sacvan Bercovitch's *The American Jeremiad*, a book that investigates the profound influence and myriad manifestations of the prophetic vision of New England Puritanism in U.S. political culture. This absence has had three consequences: first, the particular functions of southern apocalyptic discourse have been unattended; second, an unfortunately reductive racial dichotomy, focused almost exclusively on the racialized rhetoric of southern and civil rights politics, has been imposed on the eschatological visions of southern evangelical Protestantism; and third, Bercovitch's text, which perhaps more rightly belongs to the field of *Puritan* Studies (and perhaps would have been more appropriately titled *The New England Jeremiad*), has become almost the singular voice in scholarly investigations of U.S. nationalism.

Apocalypse South corrects each of these problems, beginning with the first and moving outward. Its methods are historical and rhetorical rather than theological. Throughout the book, I triangulate these literary works between three main critical approaches: the historiography of southern religion; theoretical investigations on the mechanics of apocalyptic belief, rhetoric, and practice; and theorizations of space and place, both generally and more specifically in southern studies.

The foundation of this project can be found in the historical scholarship of southern religion and religious culture, which begins in earnest with Samuel S. Hill's seminal *Southern Churches in Crisis* (1966, updated as *Southern Churches in Crisis Revisited*, 1999). Though Hill's originally formulation of a "transdenominational 'southern church'" embodied by the Southern Baptist Convention dates back to 1966, it has been revisited and revised numerous times (including by Hill himself), and it still maintains a great deal of scholarly traction.⁵ Hill argues that southern Christianity is distinct in its homogeneity and in the dominance of the evangelical tradition. While this brand of evangelicalism shares important tenets of global, historical evangelicalism,⁶ it uniquely privileges individual morality and almost completely rejects the notion of *activism*, or "world changing," that is and has been central to other evangelical movements (including New England Puritans).⁷ In contrast to the progressive social and political actions attributed to evangelicals elsewhere (abolitionism and women's suffrage, most notably, but also public education and public health), southern evangelical Protestantism "stands one of the most conservative varieties of Christianity in modern history," writes Hill (136). Rather than seeking to reform this world to fit the examples of Christian love and devotion, this brand of evangelicalism imagines God as "characteristically moral," furiously angered by "human sinfulness" (77), and intimately involved with earthly affairs, most often in the role of Judge (138). The result, according to Hill, is a "near obsession with heaven and hell." Thus, within the context of the southern evangelical cosmology, one's experience as a Christian is little more than preamble to the ultimate, inevitable, and imminent Day of Judgment—to the moment of deliverance imagined in "No Depression (in Heaven)" and to instance of retribution invoked by Wallace.⁸

5. Certainly, the concept is not without significant problems, in particular, the universalization of a white, masculine experience as identifiably, wholly southern. Indeed, in the preface to the 1999 edition, *Southern Churches in Crisis Revisited*, Hill himself recognized this inadequacy as well as his failure to attend to the important *trans*racial history of southern religious culture. Further revision will be required, however, to address the increasing diversity of religious experiences in the contemporary South: Buddhists, Hindus, Vietnamese Catholics, Korean Baptists. Nonetheless, Hill's analysis of evangelical Christianity as the dominant religious culture of the South continues to prove useful. Keeping in mind the limitations of their totalizing vision of southern religious life, I will draw upon Hill and Charles Reagan Wilson's *Judgment & Grace in Dixie* to identify the core precepts of southern evangelical Christianity.

6. Like all evangelicalism, Hill's southern transdenominational Protestantism is *Bible-centered* and interprets scripture as the inerrant Word of God; preaches "direct and dynamic access to the Lord is open to all"; defines *morality in "individualistic & interpersonal terms"*; and it practices a *loose, informal worship* in which "spontaneity is preferred over prescription" (136).

7. David W. Bebington cites *activism*—the central mission "to create a society that would redeem the rest of the world"—as a crucial component of evangelical theology (Boles 228).

8. This emphasis has only become more entrenched as the once-decentralized, anti-creedal groups like the Southern Baptist Convention have become more centralized and adopted doctrinal creeds. In particular, literalist interpretations of Scripture have given

More recent historical scholarship on southern religion tempers Hill's urgent, even prophetic call for theological reform with materialist analysis and seeks to explain how this faith evolved into the particular reactionary form evident in George Wallace's rhetoric. In the antebellum South, Beth Barton Schweiger argues, the distinction between the northern and southern evangelical traditions was a matter of "[p]olitical economy, not theology" (33). In order to grow their congregations, southern evangelical churches abandoned the socially progressive aims of their northern cobelievers, as well as the radically biracial and egalitarian practices of early revivalism. As the likelihood of secession increased, the racially progressive politics of southern evangelicalism fell to the wayside, and white southern evangelicals emerged from the denominational split as radically anti-modern. At the point of exchange between the discourses of secessionism and religion, a new formulation of regional identity emerged, which envisioned white southern true-believers as uniquely chosen to protect their threatened communities from outside radical upheaval and to protect their families from the threatening depravity and decadence enumerated by Wallace.

Though the scholarship of Hill and his colleagues was energized by an urgent desire to understand and even counteract the sacralization of segregation, their work stumbles when it comes to an understanding of the African American religion. Their models adhere too rigidly to the institutional divisions of southern Christianity into the "black church" and

---

rise to the doctrine of premillennial dispensationalism and the belief in the Rapture, which Charles Strozier deems "probably the single most significant theological innovation in contemporary fundamentalism" (120). *Premillennialism* refers to the belief that "Jesus Christ's bodily [will] return *before* His thousand-year reign, commonly called the Millennium" (Boyer 2); according to the theory of premillennial dispensationalism, "God is revealed to humans through a series of dispensations, or stages, each with its own narrative sequence that ends in violent disruptions in the transition to the next dispensation (the expulsion from the garden, the flood, and so on)" (Strozier 9). Dispensational theorists and theologians "inevitably" position their current moment at the end of the last dispensation: at any moment, the violent conflict that can end the world will begin. Before the conflict occurs, however, the faithful will bodily ascend to heaven in the event popularly known as *the Rapture*. Despite the radical literalism of dispensational theory, "the literal form of the millennium is nowhere explicitly described in the Bible," as Strozier notes (75). Likewise, the Rapture emerged as a theological construct only through a unique interpretation of I Thessalonians 4:17 and a handful of other passages by the nineteenth-century theologian John Nelson Darby. However, it has become a central doctrine of many southern evangelical groups, including the Southern Baptist Convention. The Rapture has entered the popular—and literary—imagination through the wildly popular series of *Left Behind* novels by Tim LaHaye and Jerry B. Jenkins.

the "southern church" (read: "white church"). Scholars have long noted the important interracial interactions that informed early-nineteenth-century worship practices (most notably, in music); religion in the South is nonetheless most often discussed as following two distinct, race-based tracks (with, one can assume, separate and interesting but ultimately less significant tracks for non-Protestant and non-Christian faiths). In some instances, the practices of white evangelicals in the region have simply been presented as representative of a totalizing southern evangelical culture, thereby minimizing or even eliding the critical and consistent role of African American spirituality (among other traditions) as part of the spectrum of religious life in the region. However, to treat African American religious practice as simply another element of southern evangelicalism rather than as a particular tradition reduces its insurgent power as a countertradition that responds to and implicitly critiques the oppressive regimes of white authority. These are all issues to which I will return throughout this project, but for now, I will simply posit that the theology and worship practices of black and white southern evangelicalism are products of the institutions of slavery and Jim Crow as well as the particular interracial dialogues and exchanges that took place both in spite of and because of these regulatory forces. Furthermore, African American religious traditions, while distinct, remain profoundly evangelical in character.[9] While southern evangelical traditions, regardless of race, are charged with apocalyptic energies, African American religious practice emphasizes the imminence of millennial deliverance from suffering in this world in

9. Albert Raboteau succinctly explains the paradoxical relationship of African Americans to evangelicalism: "The opportunity for black religious separatisms was due to the egalitarian character of evangelical Protestantism; its necessity was due, in part, to the racism of white Evangelicals. The egalitarian tendency of evangelical revivals to level the souls of all men before God had been one of the major attractions to black converts in the first place" (93). However, white evangelical "leaders hungry for influence saw no harm in putting their religion in the service of slavery" (Schweiger 54). Nonetheless, the literalist hermeneutic of fundamentalism was certainly appealing to a population in which literacy itself carried such a premium—and was in so many instances prohibited. Moreover, by emphasizing a direct relationship with God, this faith supplied the psychic and spiritual nourishment necessitated by life under plantation slavery and Jim Crow segregation. "Oppression may easily force outward acquiescence, but internal dissent is virtually impossible to control," writes Raboteau. "The inner world of slaves was the fundamental battleground and there evangelical Christianity served as an important weapon in the slave's defense of his psychological, emotional, and moral freedom from white domination. In a brutal system, Evangelicalism helped slaves resist brutalization" (100). The psychological and spiritual conflict between resistance and survival fit neatly with the historical and cosmological battle emphasized by evangelical Christianity.

addition to individual salvation. Timothy E. Fullop writes that "American slaves were primarily millennialists of the quietest sort who waited for Christ to intervene in history, release them from slavery, and usher them into Canaan as God had done for the ancient Israelites" (231). Even after Emancipation, the cosmology of African American spirituality remained essentially millennial and continued to be "steeped in the idea" identified by Paul Gilroy in *The Black Atlantic* as "the revolutionary or eschatological apocalypse—the Jubilee" (56).[10] However, I contend, the important efforts to recognize the particular textures of black spirituality have obscured the millennial and millenarian invocations of Apocalypse by white evangelicals (like those who sang along with "No Depression") and have effaced the reactionary applications of Apocalypse to reinforce the boundaries of gender and sexuality within black communities—a point to which Randall Kenan is crucially attuned.

Given the centrality of apocalyptic thought to southern religious cultures, the apocalyptic imaginary is the ideal site to tease out specific points of difference and convergence between white and black evangelicalism in the South. In order to negotiate the division within the relevant historical work, I have drawn upon the critical theorizations of apocalyptic discourse and thought—something investigations of religion in southern studies have rarely done. The historian Donald G. Mathews has proven to be an important exception. In his more recent work, Mathews engages René Girard's models of the scapegoat and of sacrifice, among other theoretical work, to investigate the theological implications of the ritual violence of lynching. *Apocalypse South* pushes this line of inquiry further and introduces the work of a variety of theorists of apocalyptic discourse and narrative: Girard, Bercovitch, Gilroy, and Frank Kermode, among others.

Most central to my understanding of Apocalypse, however, is the work of Malcolm Bull, who reminds us that Apocalypse can be used both *to conceal* and *to reveal*. Bull meticulously works through the internal logic of

10. In *The Black Atlantic*, Gilroy argues that slave religion offers a criticism of modernity and prevailing narratives of historical progress. Similarly, in *Long Black Song*, Houston A. Baker, Jr., juxtaposes African American religion with millenarian U.S. nationalism: "While white Americans expounded doctrines of progress . . . black Americans looked to an absolute, linear (chronometrical) time moving from the creation to the judgment day, which, they felt, would be the day of their liberation" (46). While their analyses inform my work, it is my contention that this sense of time and history is shared by evangelicals, regardless of race. Indeed, while one would be hard-pressed to fit the "world of toil and trouble" represented in "No Depression (in Heaven)" into a singular, racialized category with millenarian narratives of American exceptionalism, its eschatological vision shares much with those described by Baker and Gilroy.

apocalyptic discourse and identifies it as a manifestation of an ineluctably bivalent epistemology. He contends that nearly every cosmology, regardless of chronological or geographic location, demands at least some basic degree of basic bivalence: male and female, light and darkness, life and death, good and evil, day and night, earthly and otherworldly. Each of these cultures inevitably faces challenges to that bivalence, and so they must develop mechanisms "to regulate the relation between" what he terms *difference* and *undifferentiation*—that is to say, between that which can be obviously located in a binary scheme and that which is ambiguous or inspires ambivalence. In Bull's reading of Hebraic apocalyptic texts, bivalence is a consequence of a fractured existence and of incomplete knowledge; prophetic visions provide insight into the unity of existence and foresee the final moment—Apocalypse—in which bivalence finally gives way to that original unity. In Bull's model, through apocalyptic discourse, an uncertain presence can be "deferred to the future from where it will be reincorporated into the present" (*Seeing Things Hidden* 77). Considered in the context of this interpretation, "No Depression (in Heaven)" mitigates the existential confusion provoked by the suffering of the Great Depression, locating otherwise meaningless suffering as a necessary step in this prophetic narrative; George Wallace's speech effaces the permeability of racial boundaries by casting segregation as an historical inevitability and a function of an orderly universe.

Bull's model of Apocalypse—that it can be used to defer or disavow in order to maintain the illusion of an absolutely binary order—offers great insight into the role religion plays in the production of southern spaces and places, particularly the never-ending discursive work necessary to assert and reassert the division between black and white. This model adequately explains the utility of Apocalypse for Wallace's inaugural address, and prophecies of hope and deliverance fit it just as well. After all, what troubles the bivalent division of the world into good and evil more than traumatic experiences like suffering and oppression? Through Apocalypse, however, such experiences can be addressed, if only indirectly and provisionally. That indirectness of reference can be either problematic or emancipatory: apocalyptic rhetoric can be deployed to displace uncertain presences and, thus, to preserve a dominant discourse, as Wallace does. In these cases, evidence that a binary cosmology is inadequate—that it cannot accommodate a particular presence or experience—is deferred or disavowed. However, in other instances, indirect reference can be preferable to the absence of reference. The otherworldly, allegorical narrative of Apocalypse is open to possibilities beyond the quotidian, and it provides an opportunity to provisionally articulate certain experiences—including suffering, racial hybridity, and transgressions to fixed notions of gender. Apocalyptic discourse thus has the potential to both conceal and to reveal—to defer but also to revisit and reinterpret those things that defy conventional ways of speaking. Crucially, this model provides a path beyond the impasse built up by the commonplace, often racialized, distinction between the prophetic voices of condemnation and millennial deliverance.

Bull's inquiry is focused on the logics of apocalyptic discourse. To understand the role Apocalypse plays in the production of regional identity, *Apocalypse South* applies the chronological narrative spatially—that is to say, it examines how eschatology is mapped onto spaces and places and how historical vision informs cultural practice. In this effort, I have drawn upon a variety of theorists of place and space, as well as scholars who more specifically work on the production of place in the South. Included in the former category are seminal figures like Michel de Certeau, Henri Lefebvre, and Arjun Appadurai. Central to my analysis is Appadurai's notion of the *social imaginary*, "a constructed landscape of collective aspirations" (*Modernity at Large* 31). In particular, I am interested in the prophetic possibilities of those aspirations—in the possibilities they reveal and the anxieties they conceal.

Via its inquiry of the apocalyptic imaginary's role in the production of southern places and spaces, *Apocalypse South* engages the broader project of the New Southern Studies. For earlier generations of scholars, the canon of southern literary culture was configured around an ephemeral "sense of place"—a nostalgic idea used too often to establish a feeling of "stability amid flux," according to Barbara Ladd ("Dismantling the Monolith" 46). However, postcolonial, eco-critical, feminist, and other scholars, often operating under transnational paradigms, have reconceptualized place "as a site of cultural dynamism" and have sought "ways that place can make movement and change possible rather than simply serving as a way of talking about resistance to change" (48). Ladd calls for a new southern studies that will reconfigure place as "a locus for economic, political, discursive, and more broadly cultural transactions, a site of memory and meaning for both the past and the future" (56). If this is to occur, this new southern studies must attend to the diverse experiences of southern religion and to the ways in which faiths shaped and were shaped by the efforts of communities to understand themselves as a stable entities, despite their experience of continual cultural transformation. This project intends to answer that need. It interrogates the progressive past and possibilities of the southern evangelical imaginary, and it excavates experiences and histories that have been displaced by the prevailing southern narratives of region, nation, and religion, all in order both to gain a more complete understanding of the production of region and, hopefully, to access its emancipatory energies.

For some readers, the apocalyptic imagery and rhetoric examined here will be fraught with the familiar echoes of southern Gothicism—a term I do not reject but deliberately (and strategically) avoid. The idea of the "southern Gothic" has been deployed so frequently and so widely to any work of art tinged with the uncanny that, at least for me, it no longer offers any critical utility.[11] Indeed, it is my hope that *Apocalypse South* offers a new conceptual language to address many of the same literary phenomena and a means by which they can be locating within the context of cultural practices and beliefs rather the conventions of a particular genre.

A Note on Structure

The argument of *Apocalypse South* is designed along two axes, one historical and evident in its division into Part I and Part II, and the other, thematic and manifest in the parallel structures of these two halves. The project is chronologically divided in two sections, one of which deals with two works from the 1930s by canonical writers of the Southern Renascence (William Faulkner and Richard Wright), and the other, with two postsouthern writers (Randall Kenan and Dorothy Allison).[12] Part I of *Apocalypse South* is broadly concerned with the apocalyptic implications of the racialized boundaries of southern communities in the first half of the twentieth century; Part II examines the use of apocalyptic discourse in the maintenance of the boundaries of gender and sexuality in works from the latter years of the last century. Parts I and II each contain two chapters and follow parallel structures. Within each Part, the initial chapter (Chapters 1 and 3) examines the apocalyptic imaginary's capacity to conceal the past and to regulate knowledge that would threaten the stabil-

---

11. The generic conventions of Gothic literature identified by Benjamin F. Fisher IV in the New Encyclopedia of Southern Culture certainly apply to all of the works considered in Apocalypse South: the genre "evokes anxieties, fears, terrors, often in tandem with violence, brutality, rampant sexual impulses, and death. All result from persecution, mainly for power, by persons who may be known but untouchable or unknown. In addition, natural, supernatural, or seemingly supernatural forces may cause these negative effects" (145–46).

12. This axis also represents an unplanned geographic distinction: Faulkner and Wright were both from Mississippi, and Kenan and Allison are native Carolinians (North and South, respectively).

ity of the southern communities; each second chapter (Chapters 2 and 4) focuses on the apocalyptic imaginary as an alternative narrative space in which silenced or neglected experiences might be imbued with historical meaning. It should be noted that each of these texts engages Apocalypse in its fullness, and that my analysis will no doubt veer from one element of Apocalypse to the next within these individual chapters. However, this structure simply suggests that certain facets of the apocalyptic imaginary are more dominant in each work than others.

Chapter One, "Southern Jeremiad, American Jeremiad: Region, Nation, and Apocalypse in Faulkner's *Light in August*," examines how apocalyptic imagery and language sacralizes the racial boundaries of community in Faulkner's Yoknapatawpha County. *Light in August* contains several distinct strands of apocalyptic thought and imagery. My reading begins with a consideration of the ways in which apocalyptic thinking informs the shape and substance of the ritual violence of lynchings. Building from that analysis, I contend that the novel stages the convergence of southern evangelical Protestantism and U.S. millenarian nationalism, rather than treating them as related but ultimately distinct phenomena. The disparate strands of apocalypticism and millenarianism come together just as the novel and the community it depicts are both on the verge of complete collapse, suggesting a broader, ecumenical engagement with the Apocalypse of modernism and late modernity. The sum of this multifaceted engagement with apocalypse is a drive to reconsider history—to *re*interpret the signs of the times. In doing so, the novel offers an ironic *prophecy of doom*—a terrifying vision of the cataclysmic consequences of a fundamental misunderstanding of history

Despite the horrific nature of this and other prophecies, apocalyptic visions also provide hope and can catalyze social change. Chapter Two, "'Tearing Down the Temple': Prophetic Time and Richard Wright's Eschatology of Resistance," examines this *revolutionary apocalyptic imaginary*—a prophecy of upheaval, justice, and deliverance that is central to African American religious culture. By casting a Marxist teleology within the typology of Scripture, Wright's short story cycle *Uncle Tom's Children* articulates a call for resistance and revolution that attends to the collective experiences and to the religious traditions of rural African Americans. While much Wright scholarship criticizes his work for its perceived dismissal of black culture, I situate *Uncle Tom's Children* within the conventions of black spirituality, including its prophetic traditions and millennial hopes, as well as the particular eschatology of Seventh-day Adventism, the faith in which his grandmother sought to raise him. I further argue that the cycle disrupts prevailing historical narratives of region and nation: in it, Wright depicts the black suffering that dominant systems of representation disavow and clears out the discursive and narrative space necessary to direct black experiences toward a meaningful telos.

Part II turns from the 1930s to the end of the twentieth century, from the two Mississippians to the work Dorothy Allison and Randall Kenan—two Carolinians, one white, one black, and both queer. If race has been the great contradiction of southern religious life since Faulkner's and Wright's time, gender and sexuality have often dominated the religiously-tinged discussion of community in the last two decades.

Chapter Three, "'Some Say Ain't No Earthly Explanation': Excavating the Apocalyptic Landscape of Randall Kenan's Tims Creek," focuses on the possibility of *revelation* offered by the apocalyptic imaginary. In *A Visitation of Spirits* and the story "Let the Dead Bury Their Dead," Kenan conjures the apocalyptic imaginary from the realm of reference and allusion into stunning tangibility. The demons that walk on his southern landscape function as signs of a lost history that have been displaced or even silenced by the prevailing white narratives of history as well as the patriarchal and heteronormative orders that shape this black community. Kenan does not reject these structures or the southern communities they govern. Rather, his apocalyptic vision, much like Faulkner's, compels us to look back, to reinterpret the past, in order to forestall an otherwise inevitable cataclysm.

Chapter Four, "'An't It Time the Lord Did Something?': Mapping Deliverance and Judgment in *Bastard Out of Carolina*," continues the previous chapter's discussion of marginal spaces in the rural Carolinas. Like the work of Faulkner and Kenan, Allison's novel provokes readers to uncover the past. Like Wright's fiction, *Bastard Out of Carolina* accesses the *emancipatory potential* of the apocalyptic imaginary and deploys its *call for justice and deliverance*. The novel's alienated, adolescent narrator, Ruth Anne "Bone" Boatwright, seeks salvation in gospel music, and she fantasizes about the moment in which a divine justice will be levied against both her abusive stepfather and the social institutions that marginalize her family. While apocalyptic discourse often justifies and even sanctifies the boundaries of class and gender, it also provides a discursive space in which Bone can articulate the traumatic experiences that do not yield to representation through prevailing gendered, heteronormative discourses. By appropriating these apocalyptic spaces, the novel denies the cataclysmic consequences imparted to violations of these boundaries and demands that Bone's experiences be located in the very southern geographies that reject her presence.

The Epilogue, "Apocalypse South, Redux: Searching for Meaning after the Flood," concludes the project with an examination of various invocations of Apocalypse in the aftermath of a relatively recent southern catastrophe, Hurricane Katrina and the flooding of New Orleans. I examine the public comments of various political and religious leaders, the apocalyptic imagery and language in popular media coverage of the flood, and finally, the apocalyptic structure of John Biguenet's play *Rising Water*. I conclude by arguing for the continuing utility of Apocalypse as a discursive and narrative medium, not only for representing the devastation, but also for exploring the genealogy of the event and demanding justice in response to this disaster.

Part I

1

Southern Jeremiad, American Jeremiad

Region, Nation, and Apocalypse in Faulkner's
Light in August

> Are your garments all spotless?
> Are they white as the snow?
> Are you washed in the blood of the lamb?
> Is your soul all spotless?
> Is it clean as the snow?
> Are you washed in the blood of the lamb?
>   . . .
> Have you learnt to love your neighbors?
> Of all colors, creeds and kinds?
> Are you washed in the blood of the lamb?
> I've learnt to love my peoples
> Of all colors, creeds and kinds
> I'm all washed in that blood of that lamb
>   —Woody Guthrie, "Blood of the Lamb"

"DOES A coherent system of religious values and thought inform Faulkner's novels?" Doreen Fowler asks (ix). Given William Faulkner's position as the preeminent chronicler of a culture dominated by evangelical Protestantism, her question is all but unavoidable. The New Critics, always among some of Faulkner's earliest and most ardent proponents, looked toward the Southern forms of community manifest in Yoknapatawpha as well as Faulkner's characteristically modernist use of religious and mythic structures from antiquity as antidotes to the alienating consequences of modernity.[1] Influenced by this line of criticism, studies of religion in *Light*

---

1. In the introduction to *William Faulkner: The Yoknapatawpha Country*, Cleanth Brooks writes that "Faulkner's work . . . embodies a criticism of the prevailing commercial

in August inevitably zeroed in on Joe Christmas as a figuration of another J. C., Jesus Christ. More recent scholarship on this subject, on the other hand, has sought to examine the convergences of religious belief and racial ideologies and between the institutions of faith and the institutions of segregation in Faulkner's South. Michael Cobb asserts that *Light in August* "deploys an irreverent language of religion that is conceptually blasphemous," which "confuse[s], productively, the twinned and mutually dependent categories of time and race" (142). Timothy Caron persuasively argues that *Light in August* "forces readers to reexamine the ways the white South appropriated the Bible to justify its racism" (53). Leigh Ann Duck writes that the novel posits southern religious culture as "a model and a vector for support of a white supremacist status quo"; this culture, she argues, imposes an "imperative of unquestioning submission" that inhibits any "ability to question social and political norms" ("Religion: Desire and Ideology" 270).

These pursuits—all fruitful—expand Fowler's original query; together, they ask whether a coherent system of *religious and racial values and thought* inform Faulkner's novels. The answer, fortunately or unfortunately, remains as elusive as ever. Though race was among the greatest concerns of his greatest works, those texts offer more questions than answers—questions further complicated by the inconsistencies within his public comments on racial politics. If nothing else, the lack of coherent answers reflects the confusing genealogy and implicit contradictions characteristic of the culture that Faulkner's work chronicled. Certainly, the religion of the South reinforced the institutions of Jim Crow in many ways, and the language of religion has been bent to justify that regime, just as it was used to resist and ultimately tear it down. But also, white southern Protestantism was *shaped by* the realities of segregation—by the ever-present threat of upheaval and racial violence, by occasions of suffering and the inevitable guilt for inflicting that suffering, and by the unavoidable existential issues promulgated by the conflation of whiteness and purity, blackness and contamination.

Thus, rather than addressing a singular theological concern, *Light in August* "repeatedly points to the potential for multiplicity in religious faith" and "suggests surprising theological juxtapositions," writes Duck (272–73). While the murder of Joe Christmas certainly recalls the sacrifice of the crucifixion, critical engagement with religion in the novel must expand upon and even move beyond the connection between Christmas and Christ.

---

and urban culture, a criticism made from the standpoint of a provincial and traditional culture" (2).

Of its various convergent and coterminous religious threads, none offers a better foothold for understanding the beliefs of southern community than the apocalyptic imaginary. Within the cosmology of southern evangelical Protestantism, cataclysmic consequences are often ascribed to any violation of the radically bivalent order. As a result of this imposition of an eschatological narrative onto daily life, Apocalypse becomes a lived reality and not simply a theological construct. The white citizens of Yoknapatawpha County collectively employ apocalyptic rhetoric in order to reinforce the unstable racialized boundaries of community, and their apocalyptic cosmology informs the shape and substance of the ritual violence of lynching. In *Light in August*, the southern apocalyptic imaginary is most prominently given voice by the ranting itinerant preacher, Doc Hines; while his blasphemous gospel offers an exaggerated version of the this cosmology, it shares an apocalyptic logic that conditions the white community's response to the presence of his racially ambiguous grandson, Joe Christmas.

However, the novel's engagement with the Apocalypse transcends the mere portrayal of a community's religious culture. In order to understand and expose the contradictions and violent potential implicit within this cosmology, Faulkner stages the confrontation of the southern apocalyptic imaginary with three other eschatological discourses: the millenarianism of New England Puritanism and its adjunct, the nineteenth-century notion of American manifest destiny, which are introduced through the narrative of the Burden family; a twentieth-century millenarian nationalism, articulated by Percy Grimm and informed both by that earlier notion of American nationalism and by southern apocalypticism; and finally, the apocalypticism of high modernism, reflected in the structure of the novel, introduced in the frame of Lena Grove's journey, developed through Joe Christmas's driftings in and out of time, and manifest in Gail Hightower's chronological displacement. These various threads of apocalyptic thought intersect, merge, and dissipate in surprising, often confusing ways throughout the novel, and at the climactic moment of Joe Christmas's death, they finally come together: Hines's exaggerated fundamentalism, the convoluted frontier history of the Burden family, and Percy Grimm's proto-fascist nationalism converge just as both the community of Jefferson and the structure of the novel itself appear on the verge of flying to pieces.

What emerges both individually from each strand of apocalyptic thought as well as from the confrontation of the three, I contend, is a prophecy of an ironic doom. In Faulkner's vision, cataclysm will indeed occur, but not because of some violation to the prevailing social and racial order, as these prophetic voices of Yoknapatawpha foretell. Instead, cataclysm will be brought about by the community's insistence on an absolutely binary social and racial order, even when faced with evidence of the epistemological limitations of their bivalent worldview. The sum of this multifaceted engagement with Apocalypse is a drive to reconsider history—to reinterpret the signs of the times. This jeremiad, both particularly southern and American, imagines the collapse of a society unwilling and unable to accept the revelations offered by the myriad catastrophes of its past, and it suggests that the consequences of this cycle of disasters are not limited to the South.

The chapter that follows examines each of these four strands of apocalyptic thinking. Much of this argument will be spent introducing the southern apocalyptic imaginary as it is voiced by Doc Hines and exploring how the logic of apocalyptic thinking reinforces racial division, informs the ritual violence of lynching, and is invoked to reassert the dominant social order in the face of the transformations of modernity. The chapter will then proceed through the three other strands, asserting that, in Faulkner's telling, each of these ideologies is implicated in each other—that they have emerged alongside each other as different ways to narrate stable collective (local, racial, and national) identities.

"A walking pollution in God's own face": The Apocalyptic Logic of Blood, Contamination, and Purity

Sometimes comic but more often horrific, Doc Hines spews forth a disjointed, fanatical gospel in which the familiar elements of evangelical and fundamentalist Protestantism (the rigid strictures and determinism of Calvinist theology, the emotion and experiential elements of evangelical Protestantism, a literal interpretation of scripture, and belief in an interventionist God) converge with a white supremacist obsession with blood purity. This cosmology imagines daily experience as fraught with the apocalyptic possibilities of vengeance, (racial) chosen-ness, and imminent judgment. In *Light in August*, the apocalyptic imaginary informs the climatic eruption of violence—the castration and murder of Joe Christmas. While Doc Hines does not commit the act, he foments the collective anger that indirectly leads to it; more importantly, he loudly vocalizes the unsettling and often unspoken apocalyptic thinking that is endemic to this southern community and that informs Percy Grimm's pursuit and murder of Christmas. In working through the dialogue between Hines and the community,

Light in August exposes the degree to which the southern apocalyptic imaginary is implicated in and informs the ritual violence of lynching. The religious overtones of Christmas's story have long been noted, and theorizations and narratives of sacrificial violence have often been used to address lynching, both specifically in *Light in August* and also more broadly. While I do not want to dismiss sacrifice (specifically, Christ's sacrifice) as a useful model for understanding the violence in *Light in August*, René Girard's model of *collective persecution* more accurately explains the community's response to Joe Christmas. I contend that this model provides significant insights into the apocalyptic imaginary as a crucial site of inquiry in the effort to better understand the transformative experiences of modernity—including the instability of race, gender, and economy.

It would be inaccurate to characterize Hines's theology as a representative of southern religious culture. He and his wife exist in semi-exile, denied entry to the white community of Mottstown, which views them as "gray in color, a little smaller than most other men and women, as if they belonged to a different race, species" (*Light in August* 341). Hines's family subsists only through the charity of the rural black congregations, to whom he preaches his message of white supremacy. Their location on the margins of Mottstown is indicative of the theological extremity of his message, particularly when it is juxtaposed against the central positions that the mainline Presbyterian church, among other denominations, occupy in the religious life of the novel's southern communities.

And yet, it would be equally wrong to suggest that southern evangelical Protestantism is not implicated in Hines's rantings, just as it is inaccurate to imagine the distinctions between fundamentalist and mainline Protestantism in the U.S. South as impermeable. Samuel S. Hill describes the religious culture of the U.S. South as "popular southern Protestantism," and he argues that this culture shares a "basic set of assumptions about the nature and task of Christianity, which virtually ignores the formal demarcations between the subvarieties of Protestantism" (23). Among these assumptions is "a Calvinist-inspired dim view of human nature," which was filtered through the historical experience of Anglo-Irish immigrants in the southern frontier (Wilson 8). Along the way, the abstracted doctrine of predestination is displaced by the sort of anthropomorphic deity invoked by Hines; this is a "characteristically moral [God] who requires purity and is accordingly outraged over human sinfulness" and is "instinctively thought of, firstly and most representatively, as the Holy Judge" (Hill 77). Likewise, the central position of the "continental" doctrine of election yields a less abstract belief "that the identity of those elected to salvation can be known" (124). The immortal status of an individual's soul should be self-evident, at least, to those who themselves are saved.[2]

For believers these are not simply matters of distant doctrine, but an interpretive system through which they seek to make sense of their experience and upon which they structure their participation in a fallen world. In this context, religion offers a program for daily life, as evinced in *Light in August* by Joe's adoptive father, Simon McEachern. Work and prayer are thus his chief occupations, and he compels Joe to follow suit. Upon adopting the boy, McEachern promises to teach him that "the two abominations are sloth and idle thinking, the two virtues are work and the fear of God" (144). The central place of the Bible in family life is reinforced through Joe's required catechism study and the brutal beatings that follow any failure in this endeavor. McEachern's actions follow the contours of an apocalyptic cosmology, which locates the otherworldly conflict between good and evil in *this* world and which demands that the true believer rigorously and obsessively avoid contact with evil lest he or she suffer moral contamination. According to Faulkner's narrator, "men of [McEachern's] kind usually have just as firmly fixed convictions about the mechanics, the theatring of evil as about those of good" (201). Those convictions are not abstractions; rather, they are mapped onto particular places, which have been designated as evil, and they configure their interactions with other people.[3]

The hardscrabble conditions in which McEachern lives and works clearly influence his faith. Indeed, these are the very circumstances in

---

2. Hill and Wilson have been rightly criticized for eliding any distinction between *white* southern evangelical culture and southern evangelical culture; in the second edition of *Southern Churches in Crisis*, Hill himself criticizes the original edition for failing to attend to the particularities of African American spirituality, to the interracial roots of revivalism and Pentecostalism, and the influence of African American religious tradition on the forms of worship in white evangelical churches (and vice versa). I will deal with African American evangelicalism more specifically in the next chapter, but for now, I will simply say that the moralism, biblical literalism, and denominational permeability described are all also characteristic of African American evangelicalism and Pentecostalism. However, the Calvinist "dim view of humanity" and notion of election are less significant. Instead, black spirituality emphasizes narratives of racial chosen-ness, millennial deliverance, and salvation—what Paul Gilroy has called the "revolutionary eschatology" of African American religion (36).

3. Among these, McEachern includes the diner where Joe meets Bobbie. "Maybe you should never have gone there," he tells Joe. "But you must see such so you will know what to avoid and shun" (175). However, a meal there is necessitated by business in town and the diner's cheap prices. Contact with such places is unavoidable—all the more reason for the paranoid maintenance of the rhetorical distinction between good and evil places.

which popular southern Protestantism flourishes. However, the influences of rural agricultural life do not solely account for the distinctive characteristics of southern religious culture. To understand these, it is first necessary to attend to the significant influence of the ideologies and institutions of Jim Crow. In Lillian Smith's oft-cited assessment, white southern religious culture was founded upon the three pillars of "sin, sex, and segregation," and southern churches implicitly sanctioned the violent oppression of southern blacks (94). However, it is reductive to either posit this theology as simply a response to slavery and segregation or to argue that slavery and segregation were the consequences of popular southern Protestantism. Instead, it is far more productive to examine the influences that the discourses of race and religion exert upon each other. In this context, we see that the shape and form of religious practice and belief—black and white, mainline and evangelical—are deeply affected by the efforts of southern Christians to explain away the inevitable moral contradictions that southern apartheid poses to their beliefs. Likewise, the region's specific textures and institutions of racial difference are as deeply shaped by the worldview offered by the dominant religion.

If Hines's theology (or McEachern's, for that matter) is grotesque and terrifying, it is because he *cannot* be safely exiled to the margins of southern community. He is *not* clearly distinct or distant from its ideological and theological center but rather represents its extreme boundary—its monstrous possibility. His particular "twofisted evangelism" erupts in uninvited, curiously tolerated sermons in which he exhorts African American congregations to display "humility before all skins lighter than theirs" (343). This message is shocking only in the setting in which it is offered. While it might be fanatical to preach this gospel to a black audience, its "unconscious paradox" is the same inexorable contradiction that characterizes the theology of sacralized segregation accepted and even preached by white southern churches (344). In its exaggeration, then, Hines's fanaticism only makes explicit the violent threat that is otherwise implicit in the religious culture of the South, thus giving voice to the most terrifying elements of the apocalyptic imaginary.[4]

Consider, for instance, Hines's remarks to the dietician in the Memphis orphanage:

> I know evil. Aint I made evil to get up and walk God's world? A walking pollution in God's own face I made it. Out of the mouths of little chil-

---

4. W. J. Cash described this terrifying belief as a "faith, not of liturgy and prayer book, but of primitive frenzy and the blood sacrifice—often of fits and jerks and barks" (56).

dren He never concealed it. You have heard them. I never told them to say it, to call him in his rightful nature, by the name of his damnation. I never told them. They knowed. They was told, but it wasn't by me. I just waited, on His own good time, when He would see fitten to reveal it to His living world. And it's come now. This is the sign, wrote again in womansinning and bitchery. (128)

Several crucial elements of apocalyptic thinking emerge just in this paragraph. First among these is the conception of an anthropomorphic, interventionist God: here, God has a *face*. Evil, too, is embodied—as Joe Christmas, in Hines's view—and is an affront to God's presence. Engaging scripture—including Revelation—through a literalist hermeneutic, the fundamentalist cosmology posits *this world* as the battlefield upon which the cosmic conflict between Christ and Satan is carried out by proxies, until they both lead their forces in final battle upon it. According to Charles Reagan Wilson, southern Protestantism is unique in its "overwhelming" belief in "a personal, anthropomorphic God, in Jesus Christ as the Son of God, in Christ's second coming, and in life after death" (13). Belief in an anthropomorphic Satan is likewise prevalent: John Shelton Reed's seminal 1974 study, *The Enduring South*, found that 86 percent of Southerners surveyed believed in "the devil," compared to 52 percent of non-Southerners (Wilson 14). Thus, Hines's contention that he can, in fact, *see* the presence of evil is not an authorial exaggeration. Indeed, it is not even unique within the novel; when McEachern confronts him regarding his "lechery," he sees "not that child's face," the narrator explains, but "the face of Satan, which he knew well" (205). Likewise, when Joe enters a rural black church and assaults members of the congregation, one woman screams, "It's the devil! It's Satan himself!" (322). Joe is not the only figure in the novel on whom ultimate evil is projected. Following his estranged wife's scandalous death in Memphis, the disgraced Hightower is believed to be smiling in a photograph published in the newspaper: in the collective estimation of the town, his "face looked like the face of Satan in the old prints" (69).

The belief in an anthropomorphic God and Satan is telling. Believers do not draw upon evangelical and fundamentalist Protestantism simply for insight into abstract or metaphysical questions. Rather, their belief constitutes a total worldview—an interpretive scheme used to make sense of experiences of *this world* and events that occur in *human time*. The apocalyptic imaginary of southern religious cultures, then, maps an *otherworldly* conflict of good and evil onto the geographies of *this world*. The landscape becomes fraught with threats of sin and damnation as well as the apocalyptic possibilities of judgment, deliverance, and cataclysm. Furthermore, the ability to recognize these threats (that is, to identify and name *evil*) is interpreted as a sign of an individual's holiness (that is, his or her exceptional status among the Elect or Chosen). Thus, in his rant to the nurse, Hines claims that he is capable of reading the *signs* of the conflict as it is played out in this plane; he has simply *waited* on the children, innocents who are uncontaminated by the sin of a fallen world, to recognize the "truth" of Joe's racial status. There are perhaps no more distinct markers of apocalyptic thinking than *waiting* on an inevitable, ultimate resolution and interpreting worldly events as signs of its imminence. At this imagined future moment, the divisions between the narratives of earthly history and sacred time will collapse, ultimate truth will be revealed, and the forces of righteousness will triumph over the armies of evil.

In his assertion of *contamination*—to be repeated years later in his demand that Christmas be lynched—Hines's convoluted ravings move from a generalized apocalyptic fanaticism and into the apocalyptic discourse of sanctified southern segregation,[5] which is manifest most obviously in the text's overwhelming concern with *blood*. In *Light in August* (and in the so-called "one drop" laws that sought to fix racial categories), blood functions as a secondary way of embodying the abstract concept of race (color, obviously, being the first). When Joe is beaten as a young man, his attackers taunt him and claim that, by bloodying him, they seek only to discern his uncertain racial status: "*We'll see if his blood is black*," he hears one say. "*We'll need a little more blood to tell for sure*" (219). Gavin Stevens posits an inexorable conflict between Christmas's distinct racial inheritances and even employs the language of pollution in his assertion of a "stain either on his white blood or his black blood, whichever you will," as the cause of Joe's undoing (448–49). Indeed, Joe himself understands his racial uncertainty in these terms; living in a black community in Detroit, he tries "to expel from himself the white blood and the white thinking and being" (226).

Here, the abstract concept of race is granted tangibility and measurability. Perhaps more importantly, it is inscribed as an essential component of the biological realities of life. Once embodied, the race/blood conflation is subject to the weaknesses of the flesh—disease, infection, contamination,

---

5. Orlando Patterson cites the theologian James Sellars, who "has persuasively argued that Euro-American supremacy and commitment to segregation constituted for the South 'a religion, a theology. It is, in fact, the unrepentant Southern kingdom of God'" (207, citing Sellars, *The South and Christian Ethics*, 118–19).

and pollution. Furthermore, race is spiritually inscribed as the vital substance of moral existence. By imbibing the blood of Jesus (whether transubstantiated or consubstantiated), members of many Christian traditions not only recall his sacrifice but also ingest some of His divinity, ritually purifying themselves; conversely, any physical impurity in blood equates to moral and spiritual contamination. Just as blood is a contaminant, René Girard writes, so too is it a purifier, the only "miraculous substance potent enough" to counteract pollution. However, this potency is accessible only through "the performance of appropriate rites—the blood, in short, of sacrificial victims" (*Violence and the Sacred* 36).

This model has often been used to describe the function of lynching: if "one-drop" laws aim to protect the purity of (white) blood, "the lynching ritual . . . purges the community through sacrificial bloodletting—through which the community isolates or eliminates 'filth' so that its contagion cannot spread," according to Scott Romine (*The Narrative Forms of Southern Community* 191). However, it is crucial here to note that, at least in *Light in August*, black blood alone is not articulated as contaminant. Instead, contamination is the consequence of racial mixing: Stevens does not only suggest that Christmas's black blood pollutes his white blood, but also, or perhaps just as likely, the white blood stains the black. Within the logic of segregation, *pollution* and *contamination* are not synonymous with *blackness*, but with *ambiguity* and *miscegenation*.[6] Crucially, the murder of Joe Christmas is conditioned by the hysterical response and violent rhetoric with which white communities and their leaders responded to alleged acts of miscegenation. One can enumerate dozens of examples of similarly apocalyptic rhetoric used to decry any threat to the stability of racial categories—among them, George Wallace's references to the cyclical falling of empires, discussed in the Introduction. Similarly, when Strom

---

6. That is not to say that the status of pollution is not often ascribed to blackness, as Orlando Patterson and David Brion Davis, among others, have noted. According to Patterson, "the slave and ex-slave had always been the major symbol of sin in Christian theology. . . . Southern Protestants simply maintained and reinvigorated the original Pauline notion of sin as a kind of spiritual slavery from which the Christian had been redeemed" (210). This theological doctrine is compounded by "traditional color symbolism, which identified whiteness with goodness, purity, and beauty, and blackness with ugliness and evil, was fused with 'racial' and religious symbolism" (211). Certainly, this conflation of blackness and evil is evident in the town's collective assumption that Joanna Burden's death is "an anonymous crime committed not by a negro but by Negro" (*Light in August* 289). However, I submit that the maintenance of a stable racial order was the greater concern of southern segregationists in the first half of the twentieth century, and thus, that the maintenance of racial divisions is central to *Light in August*.

Thurmond stated in 1948 that "there's not enough troops in the army to force the southern people to break down segregation and admit the Negro[7] race into our theaters, into our swimming pools, into our homes, and into our churches" (Bass 112), he unmistakably cast the coming conflict over desegregation in cataclysmic terms.[8] The locations he mentioned were not accidental. Theaters and pools are public places, where segregation is mandated by state law and local ordinance. On the other hand, *home* and *church* are intimate, personal spaces, where racial division is a matter of cultural practice. Thurmond's progression implies that a desegregated public sphere will necessarily result in a racially undifferentiated private sphere; his martial imagery ascribes near-cosmic consequences to the conflict, positioning any subsequent confrontations as decisive battles between the armies of righteousness and order and those of evil and chaos. Thurmond's rhetoric is consistent with the exaggerated logic of lynching and miscegenation in the South: the possibilities of intermarriage and/or the violation of white women suddenly are figured as the inevitable consequences of any disruption of the mechanisms of racial difference, and *miscegenation* becomes a metonym for any instance in which the distinctions between black and white become less than absolute.[9] Of course, the immediate threat of transracial sexual activity is simply a product of a paranoid imagination; in *Light in August*, the racial identity of Christmas's father is never more than a matter of Hines's conjecture.

Within the conventional discussions of segregation and racism in the South, those Christians who tolerated or actively engaged in the violent oppression of African Americans are too often located as hypocrites, reactionaries, or as extremists. Understood in this way, their theology is posited as an aberration—the blasphemous appropriation of a true faith that must be or already has been overcome. As Donald G. Mathews has argued, however, this formulation is too easy. It is naïve, he contends, to consider the ideological foundations of segregation as coeval with but distinct from the theology shared by its proponents.[10] Citing the anthropologist Mary Doug-

7. The definitive transcription of this speech offered by Bass reads "Negro," and I defer to his expertise as a matter of consistency. However, whenever I have listened to recordings of the speech—which are now over sixty years old—I am all but certain that he says either "nigra" or "nigger."

8. With regard to fascism, Kermode writes: "The most terrible element in apocalyptic thinking its certainty that there must be universal bloodshed" (107).

9. Of course, this rhetoric also conceals the historical permeability of racial boundaries, including Senator Thurmond's own interracial romance and progeny.

10. Mathews has doggedly pursued this line of inquiry in several essays published since 2000, including "The Southern Rite of Human Sacrifice" in the online *Journal of Southern*

las's definition of *holiness* as "keeping distinct the categories of creation," Mathews asserts that an "evangelicalism ever alert to contamination could nurture segregation, because the holiness of one supported the holiness of the other; both established boundaries and distances that demanded individuals 'conform to the class to which they belong[ed]'" ("Lynching" 163; Douglas 45). This logic, like apocalyptic thinking in general, is predicated upon an absolutely bivalent logic to which any instance of ambiguity is a radical affront.

Ambiguity—or in Malcolm Bull's terms, "undifferentiation"—is "a universal conceptual possibility and differentiation a universal social actuality" (*Seeing Things Hidden* 77). Bull contends that nearly every cosmology, regardless of historical or geographic location, demands at least some basic degree of basic bivalence: male and female, light and darkness, life and death, good and evil, day and night, earthly and otherworldly. Each of these cultures inevitably face challenges to that bivalence, and so they must develop mechanisms "to regulate the relation between" difference and undifferentiation. Bull cites three such discursive mechanisms: the apocalyptic, taboo, and sacrifice, all of which "appear to be concerned with the opposition between undifferentiation and difference, mixture and separation, chaos and cosmos, and all explore the boundary that divides them." In Bull's model, the discourse of sacrifice—including that of the crucifixion—imagines difference as "something established in the distant past through killing or banishing the forces of primordial chaos, and maintained through the symbolic re-enactment of the initial divorce" (78). Taboos, on the other hand, posit that "the undifferentiated is a present and potent danger that must be constantly and rigorously avoided."[11] Purification, whether through ritual expiation or avoidance, is crucial in both models.

Neither sacrifice nor taboo, however, presents a historical model for the ultimate resolution of difference; that is the task of Apocalypse, which in doing so also negotiates between sacrifice and taboo, according to Bull:

> Apocalyptic seems to presuppose that difference is maintained through one or both of the mechanisms of taboo or sacrifice, but suggests that rather than being successfully relegated to the past or excluded from the present, the undifferentiated has been deferred to the future from where it will be reincorporated into the present. (78)

Religion as well as "Lynching Is Part of the Religion of Our People: Faith in the Christian South" in the collection *Religion in the American South*.

11. This is the position voiced by McEachern when he warns Joe to "avoid and shun" the diner (175).

For the writers of the ancient Hebraic apocalyptic texts and, indeed, for many modern theologians, that "reincorporation" of the undifferentiated is total; Apocalypse promises a return to an original unity of existence that preceded Creation. Bull points to the recurrence of hybrid figures in the apocalyptic visions of scripture as evidence: "a lion with eagle's wings, and a leopard with four heads and the four wings of bird in Daniel 7; a beast like a leopard, with the feet of a bear and the mouth of a lion, in Revelation 13, and its companion, a beast like a lamb that speaks like a dragon" (72). These beasts, which combine qualities that should not exist together, are all harbingers of visions and experiences that transcend the bivalent divisions of human forms of knowledge and perception.

In the cosmology voiced by Hines and McEachern, however, bivalence is not unique to this world but rather an ontological characteristic of existence; all things, all individuals, all experiences are either aligned with the forces of God or the forces of Satan and participate, often unknowingly, in the cosmic conflict between the two. Indeed, late in the novel, when she recounts Christmas's birth, Mrs. Hines reports that her husband "looked at the baby and he picked it up and held it up, higher than the lamp, like he was waiting to see if the devil or the Lord would win" (379). Instead of restoring an original or ultimate unity, the Apocalypse imagined by Hines maintains an eternal division. In this cosmology, the state of undifferentiation is brought to a final end in a singular, imminent historical moment in which the Holy Judge will reveal the true nature of all things, including their proper positions within the rigidly bivalent order. Fundamentalist reading practices, which posit the conflict envisioned by St. John in the Book of Revelation as a prophecy of an actual battle at Armageddon, foreclose the possibility of unity. And because the end is foreordained, this cosmology posits ambiguity as an illusion manifest in a fallen world and the appearance of this illusion as a sign of evil and a challenge to purity. In this premillennial eschatology, the presence of hybridity does not presage the end of divisions but rather evinces evil's existence and signals the rising of Satan's armies. Thus (at least in his account to Hightower and Byron Bunch), Hines orders the orphan boy Christmas to "go now and abominate Him in peace until the Day" (385)—the day in which Hines and the white community can answer the divine challenge to expunge the pollution he constitutes. Apocalypse provides a discursive mechanism through which Hines—and others—can avoid confronting the permeability of racial divisions, considering the inadequacies of an absolutely bifurcated system of racial difference, or negotiating the fundamental contradictions within the cultural logic of the South that are exposed by Joe Christmas's ability to move easily across racial boundaries,

This avoidance is neither a small nor an infrequent task. Ambiguity, undifferentiation, and contradiction are endemic to Yoknapatawpha—just as they were in the South of the 1930s. Faulkner and his contemporaries chronicled a region wrestling with the transformative manifestations of modernity, including the emergence of regional industry and the potential collapse of the dominant racial order. According to Orlando Patterson, the collapse of slavery and the failure of Reconstruction thrust the South into a fifty-year period of "acute liminal transitition" from one type of society to the next—a prolonged period of flux that was made all the more chaotic by the instability, uncertainty, and suffering of the Great Depression. As Roger Biles notes, for "southern farmers . . . the Great Depression immediately meant more misery and deprivation" following the collapse of cotton prices in 1920–21, the Great Mississippi Flood of 1927, and the drought of 1930–31 (18). These events—and others—provided impetus and opportunity for the beginnings of the Great Migration, and during the 1920s, fully 14 percent of Mississippi's population of black men between 15 and 34 years old had left the state (Godden 11).[12] Furthermore, wartime experiences in Europe and the availability of industrial jobs in the North encouraged African Americans to exert the rights of citizenship, which had been briefly allowed by Reconstruction but violently curtailed since.

Whatever the anxieties that the increasing mobility of southern blacks might have wrought, the potential for violence was only exacerbated by the shifted economic circumstances of whites during the same period—depicted most obviously in *Light in August* in the industrialization of the region via the timber mills. In the mills of the early twentieth-century South, the hierarchical structure resembled less the autonomy of a small farm than the authoritarian regulation of plantation labor. Here, poor whites were subjected to the rule of the work whistle and the foremen, just as slaves had been subject to the whims and orders of the overseer. In this environment, the mill worker's sense of his own whiteness was suddenly destabilized by a schedule that Lucas Burch (living under the pseudonym "Joe Brown") describes as "Starting in at daylight and slaving all day like a durn nigger with a hour off at noon to eat cold muck out of a tin bucket . . . " (44). As a consequence, the poor white laborers in *Light in August* are compelled to forcefully reassert their racial identity, as

---

12. In 1910, 89 percent of the African American population lived in the South, but by 1930, that number had dropped to 79 percent (Ladd, *Nationalism and the Color Line* 165).

evinced by the response of Brown/Burch's coworker, Mooney: "But a nigger wouldn't last till the noon whistle, working on this job like some white folks work on it." Mooney's violent reaction to Brown/Burch's subsequent description of him as a "slaving bastard" (45) underlies the serious implications of this insult. Once the basic economic structures of white superiority seemed terribly vulnerable to modernity and modernization, so too did the ideologies of racial difference upon which white subjectivity is predicated. As Eric Sundquist writes, the paradoxical question posed by "the enslaving myth of racial hysteria in the twentieth century" is "not how can a black man be a white man, but how can a white man be a black man?" (*The House Divided* 71). While the conditions of the mill might prompt this question, it need not be asked during a lynching; the delineations are made clear.

Race is hardly the only mechanism of difference destabilized in Faulkner's South. The southern discourse of gender, much like the region's discourse of race, demands absolute difference, despite great evidence of its fluidity and instability. And as is the case with Hines's ravings about Joe's racial identity, transgression of the prevailing formulation of gender is often equated with contamination, impurity, and filth by various characters in *Light in August*. The centrality of these concerns is evinced by the framing of Christmas's narrative within that of Lena Grove. In Ladd's estimation, Lena's appearance in Yoknapatawpha realizes "one of the most terrifying possibilities imaginable by a culture preoccupied with racial purity as was the white South in the 1920s" (*Nationalism and the Color Line* 167).[13] The farmer Armstid divines her circumstances within seconds, knowing "that she wears no wedding ring" without ever looking "full at her" (12), and he correctly anticipates his wife's disapproval of her presence in their home. Though they both show her a degree of kindness and perhaps pity, they quickly and resolutely assign to her a negative value on the spectrum of holiness and purity. Mrs. Armstid is careful to limit their contact, as if Lena requires quarantine, and they soon send her on her way. Their response

---

13. The paradigm of the "cult of white womanhood" provides the predominant means of discussing the racial and gender hierarchies in the South. Simply, white southerners, particularly among the upper classes and the plantocracy, fetishized white women as the embodiment and receptacle of purity; within this framework, the mere possibility of a violation of the restrictive standards of feminine virtue equates to contamination and impurity. Among the best of many thorough examinations of white womanhood in the South are Anne Goodwyn Jones's *Tomorrow's Another Day: The Woman Writer in the South, 1859–1936* and Elizabeth Fox-Genovese's *Within the Plantation Household: Black and White Women of the Old South*.

to Lena hints at the apocalyptic consequences ascribed to violations of bivalent gender norms. Within this framework, the mere possibility of a violation of the restrictive standards of feminine virtue equates to contamination and impurity.

Indeed, women throughout are damned by the community for their transgressive behavior.[14] Crucially, those condemnations are articulated in apocalyptic terms and invoke a specific scriptural analogue: Jezebel.[15] Doc Hines refers to the dietician as "Jezebel" three times—the first time, to her face, and subsequently when recounting Joe's childhood to Byron and Hightower (132, 384–85); McEachern hurls the epithet at Bobbie ("Away, Jezebel!") when he confronts Joe over his "lechery" (204). For both men, any sexually active woman realizes the archetype of the wicked woman embodied by the Old Testament Jezebel. While this earlier figure is most often cited as the source of the familiar epithet, the apocalyptic implications of the Jezebel figure are most evident in Revelation—specifically, in Christ's Message of Thyatira.[16] This Jezebel is a false prophetess who seduces members of the Church and encourages them to "commit fornication, and to eat things sacrificed unto idols" (Revelation 2:20). Like the Old Testament figure she recalls, the Jezebel of Revelation is subject to divine wrath: Christ promises to punish her (even to kill her children) as well as "them that commit adultery with her, except that they repent" (2:22). Perhaps surprisingly, it is this figure, not the more familiar Old Testament queen, who is explicitly accused of the sexual licentiousness and deviance that accompanies their name.[17] Instead, sexual infidelity and wickedness are metonyms for infidelity toward God and idolatry; the crime

---

14. This ideology plays a significant role in Hightower's position as a pariah in Jefferson, for while his bizarre theology troubles the congregation, the community effectively exiles him as a consequence of the impurity ascribed to his wife. Her scandalous demise literally and figuratively enacts the narrative of a "fallen woman": she plunges to her death from a Memphis hotel room she is sharing with her lover, who is found drunk by the police.

15. The appellation, used to describe a wicked woman, would not be unfamiliar to Faulkner's audience. Just six years later, Bette Davis portrayed a scheming southern belle in William Wyler's *Jezebel*.

16. That is not to say that the Old Testament figure is not relevant here. The Phoenician-born queen of Israel turns her husband Ahab and his people from worship of YHWH, the God of Israelites, and toward the Ba'al cult of her people, and her subsequent conflict with the prophet Elijah is detailed in I and II Kings. Elijah correctly prophesies her end: the "cursed woman" is thrown from a window (like Hightower's wife) and then consumed by dogs (II Kings 9:34). Thus, her narrative concludes with the realization of prophecy and the rendering of God's judgment—critical elements of apocalyptic discourse.

17. Though, as Janet Howe Gaines notes, the Old Testament Jezebel is referred to as a "harlot" in II Kings, no act of marital infidelity or sexual deviance is attributed to her (xv).

of seduction equates to encouraging apostasy and undermining the patriarchal authority that was central to the Israelites (and which is central to the theology of Hines and McEachern). From the historical figure in the Old Testament and the New Testament figure who explicitly invokes her, an archetype of a wicked woman emerges—one who poses threats of moral contamination and undifferentiation by subverting the bivalent distinctions of gender. Crucially for an understanding of Hines's and McEachern's allusions, the threat posed by both women is resolved through an apocalyptic operation: the prophesy (or the realization of the prophesy) of judgment rendered upon them by God effectively counteracts their subversive presence and restores the ontological status of the gendered social order that they challenge. By invoking the Jezebel figure, then, McEachern and Hines each apply an apocalyptic narrative to reinforce prevailing gender norms in a moment in which those norms appear unstable.

The Apocalyptic Ritual of Lynching

While rhetoric provides a powerful tool for the maintenance of difference in *Light in August*, it is through the apocalyptic ritual violence of lynching that difference is ultimately regulated. Indeed, lynching maintains the absolutely bivalent differentiation of white and black, despite the contradiction posed by the reality of hybridity and undifferentiation. Most immediately, the ritual violently and murderously expunges the threat to the bifurcated cosmology. Furthermore, it allows the members of the lynch mob to ritually perform their own holiness. The mob, as Doc Hines does, claims both to be acting as the agent of God's will and to possess the ability to recognize eternal and absolute difference in what appears to be ambiguity.[18] In all of this, the mob nearly exactly follows the script of lynchings articulated by Mathews. "Religion permeated communal lynching because the act occurred within the context of a sacred order designed to sustain holiness," writes Mathews ("The Southern Rite of Human Sacrifice"). "Holiness demands purity and purity was sustained in the segregated South by avoidance, margins, distances, aloofness, strict classification and racial contempt"—that is, through the maintenance of taboo. Lynchings were not only ritual responses to instances of undifferentiation—to alleged, individual violations of the codes that determined the proper interactions

---

18. "It's the Lord God's abomination, and I am the instrument of His will," he tells his wife in her account of Christmas's birth (380).

between races; they also responded to macro-level threats to the broader stability of communities that were governed by absolute differences in race and gender. But while the articulation of lynching as human sacrifice works as a rhetorical assault upon lynch law, it would not accurately describe the lynchers' vision of their actions. Instead, the theological authorization of lynching is predicated upon the event as a singular Apocalypse—a retributive and cleansing expiation of a threat to community and an agent of evil that simply enacts a divine judgment that has always-already been made.

Scholars disagree on whether Christmas's death should be read as a lynching, as the episode lacks many of the specular qualities associated with the act. Cleanth Brooks argued that the murder and mutilation of Joe Christmas are *not* communal events but instead are enacted solely by Percy Grimm, who claims to prevent any attempt by would-be lynchers to bypass the official mechanisms of state *and* federal juridical authority (51). Only a handful of people—a delirious Hightower and two deputies—witness the act, and none participate. Nonetheless, an understanding of the religious implications of lynching offers much insight into *Light in August*. Certainly, the specter of lynching is introduced through the town's initial impulse toward mob violence and Doc Hines's attempts to incite the mob toward a lynching. And despite Brooks's observation, Grimm's castration of Christmas unmistakably enacts the critical elements of the lynching ritual. When he announces, "Now you'll let white women alone, even in Hell" (464), he deploys Apocalypse in the manner of the lynching ritual: he defers resolving the existential contradiction posed by Christmas's racial ambiguity and instead commits it to the moment of God's ultimate judgment.

Studies of lynchings, including literary lynchings like that depicted in *Light in August*, often incorporate models of sacrifice and sacrificial violence, and indeed, these models seem to fit the exigencies of the lynching ritual, generally, and Christmas's death, specifically. Orlando Patterson writes that "sacrifice enacts and symbolically recreates a disrupted or threatened social world, and it resolves through the shedding of blood, a specific crisis of transition" (175). In *Violence and the Sacred*, Girard posits sacrifice as a ritualistic displacement of the violence within a community onto a victim chosen, most often from outside the community, to embody the threat. By deferring its internal conflict and/or repressing the knowledge of its instability, the community maintains itself as a stable, coherent whole. The white community of Jefferson indeed seems to enact this very script as they loiter with nervous energy while the Burden mansion burns. The narrator steps back from their thirst for vengeance and tells us that it exists because it makes "nice believing":

Better than the shelves and the counters filled with long familiar objects bought, not because the owner desired them or admired them, could take any pleasure in the owning of them, but in order to cajole or trick other men into buying them at a profit; and who must now contemplate both the objects which had not yet sold and the men who could buy them but had not yet done so, with anger and maybe outrage and maybe despair too. (289)

This is "a town whose normal systems of exchange have broken down and whose citizens are virtually at each other's throats," Romine writes. "Yet out of this community seething with violence, the rape narrative produces not only a consensus, but a single body" (*The Narrative Forms of Southern Community* 171). Though the discourse of sacrifice is central to *Light in August*,[19] I want to pursue the issue of racial violence through the lens of Apocalypse in order to move beyond now-familiar insights and to develop a richer understanding of a culture that fostered the sort of ritual violence represented in the novel. If we consider Joe's murder as *only* the displacement of internal violent tensions, we reduce the consequences of lynching to the death of a single sacrificial victim and fail to recognize the intended terrorist effect—namely, to threaten any African American who might, through his or her actions, destabilize the bivalent racial order. The sacrificial victim, according to Girard, is typically an outsider about whom little is known. Consequently, the community can easily reconfigure him/her as the emblem and cause of its internal disorder. While whites certainly projected their own fears and anxieties onto African Americans, the victim functions (for the mob) as a representative of the black community, and the spectacle of the lynching works to remind African Americans of the horrific consequences of any violation of the prevailing racial codes. The sacrificial model seems to work in the specific case of Christmas *because* he is an outsider, utterly disconnected from any community, white or black. However, this model fails to recognize that through the lynching he is reconfigured as *Negro*—representative of the very group the would-be lynch mob intends to threaten.[20]

19. Sacrifice is first introduced through Christmas's sacrifice of the sheep. Horrified by the abject realities of menstruation—the notion that the object of his desire might be "doomed to be at stated and inescapable intervals victims of periodic filth" (185), the adolescent Joe shoots the animal and plunges his hands into its blood as it dies, hoping that through this ritual, he might protect himself from the "filth," and from the myriad threat of contamination it poses.

20. While my concern is largely for the religious implications of lynching, I do not

Through two subsequent but less frequently cited models, *collective persecution* and the *scapegoat*, Girard further develops the imagined threat ascribed to the sacrificial victim. Collective persecution emerges on a systematic scale alongside "an extreme loss of social order evidenced by the disappearance of the rules and 'differences' that define cultural divisions," he writes (*The Scapegoat* 12). While diversity certainly exists in stable societies, the differences between categories are often rigidly maintained. The processes of that maintenance are concealed by the institutions of culture and mechanisms of exchange, and thus a binary system of difference is made to seem natural or ontological (13). Crisis, however, exposes the permeability of the categories of difference, which is more successfully repressed during periods of stability. This revelation of instability initiates within the community a sense of cultural collapse or, in Girard's terms, "eclipse"—as if something entirely new is replacing the extant order. "The terror inspired in people by the eclipse of culture and the universal confusion of popular uprising are signs of a community that is literally undifferentiated, deprived of all that distinguishes one person from another in time and space," writes Girard (16).[21] While he does not specifically address the apocalyptic implications of "eclipse," the prophetic visions of collapse and cataclysm and the terror inspired by the dissolution of the firm boundaries of difference are both consistent with Bull's models of apocalyptic discourse.

Terrorized by the apocalyptic possibilities, the community attempts to restore what it imagined to be the prior equilibrium, including the cultural systems that regulate difference. However, the causes of the instability are beyond their reach or their comprehension. Among the possible causes of eclipse, Girard includes natural phenomena such as a flood, disease, and

---

mean to suggest a religious belief in the racial division was the sole factor motivating lynchings in the South. Indeed, as Orlando Patterson notes, lynching law took effect in an economic climate in which African American workers posed a new competitive threat to poor whites (181). This rivalry proved advantageous for the plantocracy (as well as mill owners), which sought to discourage the possibility of cooperation between white and black workers. Patterson and Robyn Wiegman, among others, have offered thorough and compelling considerations of the economic forces that influenced lynching. My argument, however, will continue to focus on how religious belief was used to endorse the racial violence that resulted from these economic anxieties and how both these anxieties and incidences of violence influenced the religious culture of the region.

21. In Patterson's model, such moments of transition overwhelm "each and every individual whose life is at risk; . . . the entire community, whose whole way of life is in peril; and . . . time and history itself, which has been halted in the chaos of meaning as people try to come to terms with what has happened to them, to their community, to their culture, and to their history" (185).

famine, as well as the often unfathomably complicated phenomena of economic collapse. While such social turmoil might be ignited by such events, it is made possible by a fundamental instability or contradiction within the culture. In the case of Faulkner's Mississippi, the inherent permeability of racial divisions are made all the more apparent by (among other things) the industrialization of the South and the social flux that follows. Rather than confront the reality of its own instability, the community "looks for an accessible cause that will appease its appetite for violence"—that is to say, an individual or category of people—*scapegoats*—upon whom it might localize the instability and cite as the cause of a potential cataclysm (Girard 16). "Those who make up the crowd are always potential persecutors," writes Girard, "for they dream of purging the community of the impure elements that corrupt it, the traitors who undermine it" (17). And, crucially for this discussion, the scapegoat is accused of the most heinous crimes—crimes that cite the alleged perpetrator as a cause of communal pollution and contamination, including rape, incest, and bestiality, as well as great violations of specifically religious taboos, such as "the profanation of the host" (15).

Accusations of rape and contamination of the sacred emblems of white Southern Christianity—the white female body—are central to the ritual of lynching. Abdul R. JanMohammed describes "rape" as metonymically linked to any violation of racial taboos in the Jim Crow South (49). Certainly, the exercise of fundamental citizenship rights would constitute such a violation, removing citizenship as a basic institutional mechanism of difference.[22] However, the rhetorical use of rape in this manner is not

22. The creation of this idealized, fetishized figuration of white femininity is contingent upon fantasies of black masculinity. White southerners projected the fundamental instability of their construct (and displaced the repressed histories of transracial sexual contact) onto an imagined epidemic of rape of white women by black men. Black men, then, were located as the preeminent threat to social fabric of the white community. However, this operation contains an unavoidable paradox: while both white supremacy and the fetishization of feminine virtue are implicated in the radical bivalence of southern religious culture, they are in some ways competing logics. The ritual mutilation and castration often incorporated into lynching provides a mechanism for negotiating the contradictions between these coeval hierarchies, Robyn Wiegman contends. Slavery and Jim Crow segregation conspired to refuse black males the ability to perform many of the basic functions of manhood. Reduced to property themselves, slaves obviously had no legal rights of ownership; the white possession and rape of black women and the denial of the validity of conjugal unions under slavery prohibited them from assuming the most basic familial roles. Thus, male slaves posed no threat to the gender hierarchy. Under Reconstruction, however, African American men asserted themselves in traditionally masculine roles, claiming the rights of citizenship, installing themselves as heads of households, and, consequently, in-

unique to the South: as I stated earlier, rape is among the crimes stereotypically attributed to the scapegoat by a community during moments of social instability. Crucially, so are the profanation of sacred places and the contamination (possibly even the poisoning) of the community. All three of these—rape, profanation of the holy, and communal pollution—converge in the twinned figurations of the black rapist and the idealized white woman. Any distinctions between moral, physical, and racial purities are elided. Consequently, a violation of the bivalent racial code becomes embodied as rape, and that violation is in turn abstracted as a profanation of the Holy of Holies.

In the moment of eclipse depicted in *Light in August*, Joe Christmas's existence poses an unavoidable threat to the dominant systems of race and gender, and thus, to the collective ability of the white community to articulate itself as a coherent entity. He has lived as a white man, and he has lived with a white woman. In the novel's climactic moments, all of Yoknapatawpha appears on to be on the brink of a cataclysmic violence and perhaps even a total collapse. It is only by enacting the lynching ritual—by collectively narrating the story of Joe Christmas and Joanna Burden as a rape of a white woman and subsequently demanding the death of the black rapist—that the white community maintains a sense of cohesion and of its difference from its black counterparts. As Romine has noted, much of the novel is narrated by "something like the community's continuous mind," rather than by a single individual (159). By rejecting "the discrete cognitive boundaries between private and public space" and establishing that, while "community is *different* from, it is not *separate* from the individuals who comprise it" (160), Faulkner gives voice to both to a culturally-held and maintained cosmological narrative, as well as to the collective effort to regulate the mechanisms of difference. It is this voice that, after the burning of the Burden place, expresses a belief that the murder of Joanna Burden "was an anonymous crime committed not by a negro but by Negro" (*Light in August* 289). This collective voice also articulates both the awful desire "that she had been ravished too: at least once before her throat was cut and at least once afterward," as well as the bloodlust that precipitates the search "for someone to crucify" (289).

---

serting themselves into existing gender norms. The myth of the black beast rapist emerges in response to the sudden assertion of a black masculinity that was, in many ways, very conservative. Ritual castration, Wiegman writes, "aggressively denies the patriarchal sign and symbol of the masculine, interrupting the privilege of the phallus and thereby reclaiming, through the perversity of dismemberment, the black male's (masculine) potentiality for citizenship" (83).

Just as the dietician claims to have "known it all the time that he's part nigger" (129), the collective voice retrospectively denies the threat to the institutions of segregation Christmas's passing might pose: " . . . they told it again: 'He dont look any more like a nigger than I do. But it must have been the nigger blood in him'" (349). Likewise, when he is caught, the community is more offended by the nonchalance with which he responds than his actual crime:

> He never acted either like a nigger or a white man. . . . That was what made the folks so mad. For him to be a murderer and all dressed up and walking the town like he dared them to touch him, when he ought to have been skulking and hiding in the woods, muddy and dirty and running. It was like he never even knew he was a murderer, let alone a nigger too. (350)

The verb "act" suggests that the collective voice in some way recognizes the performative nature of race; "nigger" (including its subset, "nigger murderer") and "white man" are roles to be played out within the narrative of southern community. The performativity of race and the threatening ambiguity it presents are deferred, however, when they are embedding within the otherworldly drama of cosmology. Within this context, the shape, arc, and conclusion of history are preordained, and its players are only to fill out their designated roles, all of which lead toward a final apocalyptic act. By refusing his role, Christmas appears to disrupt the narrative—to demonstrate a flaw in its ability to generate totalizing meaning. The true believers cannot assimilate the possibility of a flaw in the script that, by definition, is absolutely perfect and complete. Since the endemic bivalence of that logic can brook neither nonsense nor contradiction, the town is assured that Christmas can—and must already—fit within the binary logic. The entire procession of events that leads to Christmas's death, from the communal attempt to capture him to his murder at Grimm's hands, forces him into a fixed racial category. He is, in Michael Cobbs's words, "lynched into a racial logic of intelligibility" (167). While Grimm acts alone, the white community is certainly complicit in his actions. Its members may reluctantly pass over the ritual sacrifice of a lynching and defer to the sheriff, but they do not relinquish their collective authority over Christmas: he "belongs" to Jefferson, as a man in Mottstown tells Mrs. Hines (347). A trial is scheduled, but its outcome is foreknown. At best, it will simply parody African American claims to the rights and privileges of citizenship, and at worst, it will reinforce the position of white southerners as the ultimate judges of the limitations upon black mobility.

Just as Joe Christmas is "lynched into . . . intelligibility" by his pursuers and murderer, so too does the community seek to finally locate Joanna Burden within the prevailing logics of race and gender. By circumscribing Christmas as *Negro rapist* and Joanna as *white southern woman*, the community effectively negates the threat they—individually and together as lovers—pose to the racialized and gendered order upon which the coherent, collective identity of the community is predicated. Prior to her death, Joanna is "a foreigner, an outlander" in her own home (289). The white residents of Jefferson stay away from the Burden place and deem Joanna an outsider rather than confront the possibility of ambiguity posed by the Burden family's abolitionist legacy, her own interaction with the black community, and her status as an unmarried, middle-aged woman. The collective voice does not seek to position her as a Jezebel figure; indeed, the novel offers no evidence that, prior to her death, she is sexed at all within the town's imagination.[23] However, once the fire at her home consumes her body, she is abstracted as *white woman*, just as her murderer becomes not "a negro but . . . Negro." With the physical evidence of her existence gone, the community is free to write the meaning of that existence and to claim ownership over both Joe and Joanna. Thus, in castrating Christmas, Percy Grimm enacts an overdetermined, apocalyptic racial script that is predicated on the rhetoric of civic order, which is so frequently justified by the sanctification of white womanhood that any distinction between the secular and the sacred is removed. When Grimm forces Joanna Burden and Christmas into this simplified narrative, he reduces the complicated reality of their relationship to the simple binaries of white woman and Negro murderer and expunges the threat their union poses both to the dominant racial and gender hierarchies and to the bivalent, apocalyptic cosmology in which they are embedded.

"Lincoln and the negro and Moses and the children of Israel": American Millenarianism and the Burden Narrative

While the southern apocalyptic imaginary offers an obvious and obviously horrifying eschatological vision, Faulkner steps away from it midway

---

23. This is not the case for Joe, however, and he believes that she is "corrupting him" (260).

through the novel to address what seems to be a distinct and separate teleology. In a conversation that critics have often neglected, Joanna recounts to Joe the family's pattern of migration from colonial New England to the early Midwestern frontier, into the expansion into the old West, and back into the South during Reconstruction. Immediately, the truncation of "Burrington" to "Burden" evokes the weight of history borne by its inheritors. Indeed, their familial history realizes a plan envisioned by Puritan millennialism and adapted into nationalist, secular mythology of unending, unlimited progress. In this vision, redemption is explicitly national and democratic, and it necessitates the expansion of democratic structures and national power westward and, via Reconstruction, into the U.S. South. However, the Burdens' geographic mobility does not grant them privileged position. Despite the breadth of their American experience, the people of Yoknapatawpha situate them as outsiders who threaten the stability of the extant social and racial order. "They hated us here," Joanna tells Joe. "We were Yankees. Foreigners. Worse than foreigners: enemies. Carpet baggers. . . . Stirring up the negroes to murder and rape, they called it. Threatening white supremacy" (251).

In addition to troubling the boundaries of race within Yoknapatawpha, the Burden narrative suggests the permeability of national borders. Living in Spanish-controlled California, Joanna's great-grandfather Calvin Burden learns to read the Bible from Roman Catholic missionaries—in Latin. Consequently, the mission he assigns to the next several generations of his family is dependent on a reading of God's Word filtered through a language viewed by Protestants as that of foreigners and heathens. Almost from the beginning, then, the archetypal American experience of the Burden clan is one of dynamic intercultural exchange. However, that exchange is displaced by a performance of racial and national identity that promises to redeem the contamination posed by the nation's decadent, slaveholding European origins.[24] Traveling westward, Calvin Burden marries a woman "of Huguenot stock"—a branch of Calvinism, but Continental nonetheless—and denounces Catholicism as "the church of frogeating slaveholders" (241). Years later, Calvin's son, Nathaniel, returns from the frontier of Mexico with a wife, whose resemblance to his French-blooded mother deeply troubles his father: "Another damn black Burden," Calvin Burden says. "Folks will think I bred to a damn slaver" (247).

24. Ladd contends that, in this historical vision, the Burdens and other Anglo-Americans have been "'colonized by a European slaveholding economy and by Catholicism" as a consequence of this contact (160).

What is most crucial here is Calvin Burden's appellation of "slaver" rather than "slave." Miscegenation is not his concern. Equating "hell and slaveholders" (243), the "blackness" he sees is not indicative of race, but rather, is a sign of a moral contamination. "Slavers," in Grandfather Calvin's view, are "lowbuilt black folks: lowbuilt because of the weight of the wrath of God, black because of the sin of human bondage staining their blood and flesh." Unlike Gavin Stevens's or Doc Hines's formulations of blood, which each posit the mixture of race as a stain upon blood purity, Calvin Burden imagines the stain as a consequence of contact with sin and with the wicked Old World culture that established New World slavery. In his view, "the French, the Spanish, the Rebel, and the Negro . . . belong to the same party," Ladd notes (*Nationalism and the Color Line* 162). Unlike Hines, he views miscegenation in millenarian rather than apocalyptic terms: the original sin of slavery has left the nation contaminated, but it will ultimately be expiated. By ending slavery, the Union—the military embodiment of his Puritan ideal—"freed them" all from the moral stain of slavery: "They'll bleach out now. In a hundred years they will be white folks again. Then maybe we'll let them come back into America" (247–48). This religious vision articulates a confusing version of the theology of abolitionism and its forebear, the Puritanism of New England, which conceived their errand as the millennial (and later, millenarian) redemption of humanity. His speech at Joanna's parents' wedding explicitly employs the language of millenarian deliverance. He positions "Lincoln and the negro and Moses and the children of Israel" as analogous and describes the Red Sea as "just the blood that had to be spilled in order that the black race might cross into the Promised Land" (252). He envisions a history in which racial reconciliation is complete and literal and in which emancipation bleaches away any evidence of blackness. Blacks may inherit the mantle of chosen-ness but only by following their white Moses into the Promised Land of democracy.

Despite their experiences across the continent, the Burdens hold fast to the theology of New England, and this wedding-day address enacts the familiar script described by Sacvan Bercovitch in *The American Jeremiad*. At the core of Calvin Burden's cosmology is the seemingly contradictory belief that "God's punishments were *corrective*, not destructive" (Bercovitch 8). The wedding feast might strike the reader as such an inappropriate time for this sort of exhortation, and consequently, the reader is apt to liken the eldest Burden to the fanatical Hines. However, in the context of New England Puritanism, the performance of the jeremiad is celebratory. God's vengeance is "a sign of love, a father's rod used to improve the errant child," writes Bercovitch. "The Puritans did not seek out affliction, but where they found it they recorded it zealously, and almost as gratefully, as they recorded instances of God's mercies toward them." In this context, Calvin Burden's speech suddenly seems less inappropriate: by blessing the mission undertaken by the Burden family and prophesying its ultimate triumph at the moment in which its next generation is celebrated, the speech fits the generic conventions of the wedding toast just as well as those of the New England jeremiad.

However, in the moment of this speech, that triumph had not yet arrived—even in Calvin Burden's view. For Burden, both former slaves and slavers would have to "bleach out" in the desert before they are "let back in" the Promised Land of America. This historical vision fails to account for the fact that, though their rights have been radically circumscribed, blacks *already* lived in the United States. Furthermore, the regimes of white authority were "let back in" far sooner than Calvin Burden might have predicted, despite their temporary removal from power during Reconstruction. Decades later, when Joanna recounts the story, the institutions of racial difference have not been overcome. Consequently, it is Joanna and Joe, not the Confederates and their descendants, who are exiled to the margins of community and denied the rights of citizenship. Their exile is a stark contrast to the discursive and imaginary exile of Calvin Burden's speech, and its consequences are violent, if not cataclysmic. Joanna's father Nathaniel edges toward this recognition: he rejects his father's (Calvin's) millenarian vision in favor of a convoluted articulation of the nation's racial history in the apocalyptic terms of doom. In his view, the black community remains God's chosen people but only because its members were chosen to suffer the consequences of the white race's sins (253). African Americans, then, are cursed—*chosen* to suffer—while whites are *doomed* to eternally pay for their sins. Her father's racial vision is irrevocably bifurcated: the races each occupy eternally separate roles within the unfolding drama of sacred history, and the white role is, at best, benevolently patriarchal. Nathaniel Burden continues to ascribe suffering as a sign of election and chosen-ness. However, he necessarily strays from the conventions of the jeremiad. Faced with the suffering of African Americans, he cannot claim this status for himself. The only alternative in this bifurcated cosmology is doom.

Despite its inability to transcend the limitations of bivalence, Nathaniel Burden's vision of doom comes closer to the reality of race in Faulkner's fictional world and to the American experience as it is lived out in the Burden family history: the grandfather Calvin Burden kills a man in St. Louis "in an argument over slavery" (242); when his son Nathaniel (Joanna's father) sends word from Colorado, the messenger has lost an arm as veteran of a "partisan guerrilla horse in the Kansas fighting" (244), a reference to John Brown's radical abolitionism; this one-armed messenger reports that Nathaniel has killed a Mexican alleged to have stolen his horse;[25] and finally, once the family arrives in Yoknapatawpha during Reconstruction, Joanna's brother Calvin is killed by General Sartoris, "over a question of negro voting" (248). The landscape of the southern and western frontier is littered with bodies, Anglo- and African American, mestizo, and (as Faulkner further explores in Go Down, Moses) Native American, which illustrate the inevitability of racial conflict. Ultimately, this overwhelming specter of racial doom situates Light in August within the tradition of the American jeremiad—alongside the works of Herman Melville, another author who recognized the implicit contradiction the institutions of racial difference posed to the millenarian nationalism of the United States and who used an aesthetic of doom to challenge its notions of historical mission and progress. Of the various millennial and millenarian visions in Light in August—all intersecting, contradictory, and coeval—none seem to offer the possibility of deliverance. The narrative of doom finally consumes both Joanna Burden and Joe Christmas. Joanna cannot escape the dream of a cross-shaped black shadow, looming over successive generations of white children (253). Confounded by the impossibility of that burden, she seeks to seal her damnation by finally violating the ultimate division of race and engaging in a sexual and romantic relationship with a black man. However, this requires Christmas to forego his racial ambiguity, accept a stable racial identity, and thus surrender to the fate to which his grandfather doomed him as a child and which he has resisted since. Despite his rejection of a stable, bourgeois black identity, that fate seems unavoidable. The final image of Joe and Joanna together is one of conflict, each facing the other with a weapon in hand. This, it seems, is the terrible and violent culmination toward that they believe their transgressive relationship—indeed, their transgressive lives—has been inevitably and unavoidably leading.

Percy Grimm:
Nationalizing the Southern Apocalyptic Imaginary

Heretofore, I have located the act of lynching specifically in the U.S. South; I have presented it as a product of the intertwined development of

---

25. The messenger's rendering of the Mexican as a racial and national Other presages the purported national and ethnic identity of Joe Christmas's father.

the regionally specific institutions of racial apartheid and evangelical Protestantism, all in an economic context that was likewise regionally distinct, and I have defined it as a ritual displacement and denial of the unavoidable contradictions of the absolutely bifurcated structures of gender and race. In its ritual maintenance of the institutions of difference, lynching was fundamentally *not* about the reification of regional difference; mobs did not assert a claim to a southern identity but rather to a *white identity* that was inexorably connected to notions of democratic citizenship. As a representation of southern racial violence, *Light in August* is compelling because it refuses to narrowly localize the threat of racial cataclysm—or of Joe Christmas's racial ambiguity—in the South. Instead, the novel demands that the reader confront the possibility that the southern apocalyptic imaginary (i.e., the jeremiad offered by Doc Hines) and U.S. millenarian nationalism (the jeremiad articulated by the Burdens) exist in dialogue with each other. In the final act appearance of Percy Grimm, the lyncher in national military uniform, these ideologies finally converge in an eruption of protofascist violence.[26]

As acts of sacrifice and martyrdom, lynchings may have contributed to the reification of the cohesive and coherent boundaries that separated white and black communities into localized units. However, their role in defining a cohesive regional identity existed largely in the minds of outsiders, horrified by the reports of racial violence "down there."[27] While the ritual mutilation of black bodies can be located, generally, in the South and the western frontier, lynchings produced and enacted a claim to a white identity conceived to be as much American as southern. The response of African Americans was likewise conditioned by their own claims to the rights and identity of American citizenship.[28] Rather than

26. Of Grimm and *Light in August*, Faulkner famously said, "I wrote that book in 1932 before I'd ever heard of Hitler's Storm Troopers, [but] what he was was a Nazi Storm Trooper" (*Faulkner in the University* 41).

27. Leigh Anne Duck suggests that nation and region are produced through "projective fantasies," in which U.S. histories of racism, conservatism, and violence are repressed and projected onto an "anomalous South" (*The Nation's Region* 3). As I will discuss in the next chapter, one need only look at Wright's *Black Boy*, *Native Son*, or *Lawd Today!* to see how ritual violence in the South in fact *destabilized* the boundaries of region and provoked the beginnings of the Great Migration. Likewise, these novels also provide a sense of the racial injustice throughout the country, which was obscured by the national focus on the South.

28. In Robyn Wiegman's astute analysis, the lynching ritual is "a denial of the black male's newly articulated right to citizenship and, with it, the various privileges of patriarchal power that have historically accompanied such significations within the public sphere" (83).

imagining their southern communities in opposition to the larger community of nation, as their forebears had during the Civil War or the Reconstruction period that followed, these white southerners simply reinscribed their racist policies as *American*. Ultimately, lynchings were bound up in the discourses of nation as well as the regionally-specific discourses of race, gender, and religion that previous examinations have considered.

Like Hines, Grimm is both comic and terrifying—offering the monstrous possibility of southern apocalyptic ideologies of race writ into a sense of American millenarian national mission. In his "sublime and implicit faith in physical courage and blind obedience, and a belief that the white race is superior to any and all other races and that the American is superior to all other white races and that the American uniform is superior to all men" (451), Grimm seems ridiculous upon his first appearance. Likewise, the manner of his final pursuit of Christmas—pedaling furiously through town on a borrowed bicycle—undercuts both his claim to martial authority and the familiar conventions of a climactic chase. However, the community's readiness to accept his uniformed authority, despite his absurdity, is deeply troubling.

A nascent, cynical version of Grimm's nationalism can be found in Jason Compson's wide-ranging, ill-defined anti-Semitism in *The Sound and the Fury*,[29] which reverberates with the nativist blood obsession that swept the U.S. in the late 1920s and early '30s (and which ultimately informed the Ku Klux Klan's rise from a terrorist response to Reconstruction to a national political force). Like Jason, whose concern with the contemporary global economy juxtaposes his brother Quentin's obsession with the institutions of the Old South, Grimm is a product of the complex exchange between regional and national identity.[30] While he may seek to forestall the extralegal activities of a Mississippi lynch mob, he does not reject them entirely; rather, he simply performs them in uniform, enacting a script conditioned by the southern discourses of race and religion while claiming the mantle of national order. Likewise, he does not dismiss the regional civil

---

29. One thinks of Jason's exchange with a shopkeeper, in which "Jews" are contrasted to "Americans": "I have nothing against jews as an individual. . . . It's just the race. You'll admit that they produce nothing. They follow the pioneers into a new country and sell them clothes" (237). Later, anxiously watching fluctuations in the stock market, Jason blames "those New York jews" for his financial failings: "Well, I reckon those eastern jews have got to live too. But I'll damned if it hasn't come to a pretty pass when any damn foreigner that cant make a living in the country where God put him, can come to this one and take money right out of an American's pockets" (237).

30. According to Atkinson, "Grimm's ideology of nationalism and racial purity . . . expands the novel's provincial setting to encompass issues of national and international import" (153–54).

religion of previous generations; instead, he elides any contradiction that might be posed by the South's reentry into national political life—between the southern and national identities worn by a dying generation shaped by the Confederate experience and their grandchildren who fought in Europe under the banner of the United States. When a veteran dismisses Grimm's attempts to organize the local American Legion into a militia and contends that Christmas "is Jefferson's trouble, not Washington's," the old lines are clearly drawn (454). Grimm's response—a rhetorical question about the need to protect "America and Americans"—redraws them, with Jefferson inscribed as wholly American rather than particularly regional or local. Percy Grimm thus embodies an American millenarian nationalism as it is enacted in the U.S. South, and by assuming the role of both an agent of national order and of divine judgment, he reconfigures the previously regional discourses of race, gender, and community as the pure expressions of sanctified American identity.

Faulkner layers these seemingly disparate narratives of nation, region, millennium, and Apocalypse upon his southern landscape, but none of these threads adequately resolves the possibility of racial undifferentiation. Likewise, none offers redemption for the white community of Jefferson, which is at least complicit in Christmas's murder. Barbara Ladd writes that Faulkner and other southern writers, "aware of the implications of defeat in a nationalistic culture, which sees itself as redemptive, as the vanguard of progress, have constructed the South as dangerous territory—a kind of national 'id' . . . " (*Nationalism and the Color Line* xii). In other words, the history of the South disrupts millenarian narratives of American exceptionalism and national mission. Leigh Anne Duck astutely argues that such representations allowed American audiences and readers to project the nation's "imagined grotesques in a restricted space" (*The Nation's Region* 96), thereby obfuscating their own complicity with an unjust social order and reinforcing the prevailing discourse of millenarian nationalism. *Light in August*, however, denies the reader any such opportunity: Grimm's uniform and the continent-crossing chronology of the Burden clan implicate both the geographies of the U.S. and the familiar narratives of U.S. history in the possibility of racial cataclysm.

Modernism, the Cataclysm of Meaning, and the Possibility of Revelation

If, as in Barbara Ladd's assessment, southern literary landscapes are "dangerous territor[ies]" that challenge the millenarian strands of U.S. culture and historiography, it is at least in part because the violent oppression of African Americans under Jim Crow defies any easy narrative coherence, including those that lynchings aimed to reinforce. Faulkner's engagement with the apocalyptic imaginary transcends simple representation of the experiences that disrupt these narratives; instead, the disruption of these different eschatologies is suggested by the novel's very structure. Any attempt to unpack the convergences of the southern apocalyptic imaginary with U.S. millenarian nationalism in *Light in August* is inevitably compounded by the novel's formal engagement with the apocalyptic concerns of modernism.[31] In his analysis of *The Sound and the Fury*, Jean-Paul Sartre describes a style haunted by the past; he imagines Faulkner's vision of the world as the perspective "of a man sitting in an open car and looking backwards." Images fly past, "and only afterwards, when he has a little perspective, do they become trees and men and cars" (266). The present is "full of gaps, and, through these gaps, things of the past, fixed, motionless and silent as judges or glances, come to invade it" (267). This "invasion" of the present by the past is manifest in *Light in August,* as in other Faulkner works, through ceaseless temporal disruptions. Among these are the novel's various leaps between seemingly disconnected narrative threads, flashbacks, repetitions of various images and tropes, and a series of doublings (Hightower and Hines, Hines and McEachern, Byron Bunch and Lucas Burch/Joe Brown, Lucas Burch/Joe Brown and Joe Christmas, Christmas and Lena's child). These often disparate elements converge, collide, and slide against each other in ways that defy systematic categorization. Rather than attempting to align these recurrences in any stable configuration, it is more useful to consider how these uncertain, unstable juxtapositions (re)produce the chaos the novel seeks to represent in Jefferson. While the novel's most immediate critique of the ideologies of southern segregation and millenarian nationalism emerges from its representation of the apocalyptic rhetoric and ritual violence necessary to maintain their stability, its critical stance on this culture is also manifest formally: *Light in August* refuses the linear progression upon which these ideologies are contingent, instead disrupting the normal flow of time and prohibiting the progression toward an ultimate telos by deploying a series of relentless repetitions. The

31. Among these is a concern with the apocalyptic consequences of a waning of meaning. Modernism often vacillates between mourning the ability to represent modern reality and the heroically searching for new, experimental modes of representation. One thinks of T. S. Eliot's "The Hollow Men": "There are no eyes here / In this valley of dying stars. . . . In this last of meeting places / We grope together / And avoid speech" (*Poems* 57). Indicative of the artistic response is W. B. Yeats's famed poetic System, which Kermode describes as "an attempt in the Last Days to provide a language of renovation" (108).

Apocalypse toward which the novel builds is not the triumphant culmination of history, but rather an identifiably modernist conception of a world finally and tragically exhausted by its ceaseless motion, in which revelation might not be possible.

Lena Grove's wanderings across Faulkner's southern landscape initiate the disrupted teleology that is central to *Light in August*. On the cusp of giving birth, Lena is, as many scholars have noted, a figuration of fertility amid the sun-bleached desolation of late summer (Brooks 67). However, this is hardly indicative of the Armstids' view of her. Unwed, pregnant, and dislodged from family and community, Lena epitomizes the threats to community posed by modernity and mobility. The same contradictions are evident in the narrator's description of the Alabama mill town she has left behind: the mill, so central to that community that it is incorporated into its name—Doane's Mill—provides work, but it threatens to destroy the landscape. Once that occurs, the narrator tells us, "some of the machinery and most of the men who ran it and existed because of it and for it would be loaded onto freight cars and moved away" (4).

> The remainder of the equipment, the artifice of human progress, would remain, gaunt, staring, motionless wheels rising from mounds of brick rubble and ragged weeds with a quality profoundly astonishing, and gutted boilers lifting their rusting and unsmoking stacks with an air stubborn, baffled and bemused upon a stumppocked scene of profound and peaceful desolation, unplowed, untilled, gutting slowly into red and choked ravines beneath the long quiet rains of autumns and the galloping fury of vernal equinoxes. (4–5)

Here, the apocalyptic cycle of destruction and rebirth is parodied: the natural world is devoured by the industry, while the most ancient artifact of industrialization—the wheel—is left to be overtaken by the weeds. New machinery replaces old but only until it too is worn out. The result is a cycle of unending and utterly predictable motion, of which the narrator speaks with the certainty of foreknowledge. However, the voice is not prophetic, but resigned; the cycle is unavoidable and unstoppable. Likewise, Lena's journey—"a long monotonous succession of peaceful and undeviating changes from day to dark to day again through which she advanced in identical and anonymous and deliberate wagons as though through a succession of creakwheeled and limpeared avatars" (7)—parodies progress, depicting eternal movement that never reaches any destination.[32]

---

32. The motion of the wagon is likened to "something moving forever and without

Gail Hightower evinces another teleological disruption; he refuses both the blind, forward-looking optimism of millenarian nationalism and the apocalyptic vision of Hines. Instead, he loses himself within the stagnant and doomed regional theology of the Lost Cause, which envisioned white southerners as God's Chosen People who have been chastised and ultimately redeemed through their defeat. In Hightower's cosmology, the sacrifice of Christ gives way to the valorization of Confederate soldiers, and the final conflict at Armageddon is replaced by battles from eighty years prior, elevated to cosmic importance. The collective voice of Jefferson tells Byron Bunch that Hightower, as a young minister, spoke "wild[ly] too in the pulpit, using religion as though it were a dream. Not a nightmare, but something which went faster than the words in the Book; a sort of cyclone that did not even need to touch the actual earth . . . " (62). In his inability to "get religion and that galloping cavalry and his dead grandfather shot from the galloping horse untangled from each other," Faulkner's Hightower both realizes Sartre's analysis of the historical vision of *Sound and the Fury* as irreconcilably backward-looking and anticipates Walter Benjamin's allegorical reading of Gustav Klee's painting *Angelus Novus* in the "Theses on the Philosophy of History." The painting depicts the angel of history, standing outside of history and looking back toward the past, writes Benjamin; he wishes to return to the past, to "make whole what has been smashed," but is blown forward by the violent storm of Progress and is forced to witness the ceaseless (and repetitive) piling up of history's debris. Like the angel, Hightower hopes to heal the past by refusing to leave it, turning his back not just to the future but to the present as well. He attempts to release the fury of the storm in his frenzied sermons, which conflate the secular narrative of history with the sacred narrative of religion.

In its narrow, fanatical focus on defeat, Hightower's theology denies the possibility of progress in a manner distinct from the antimodern message preached by many of his clerical contemporaries. In the early twentieth century, southern evangelical churches adopted a fundamentalist theology as a reaction to secular ideologies, scientific advances, and those processes of modernization that destabilized the familiar, prevailing discourses of gender, race, and place. Hightower is no reactionary, however. Rather than actively thwarting political and social change, he simply ignores the pres-

---

progress across an urn" (7); as many have noted, this recalls the famous image of immortality in Keats's "Ode to a Grecian Urn." The motif occurs again in Joe's nightmare of "ranked and moonlight urns," after he learns that his would-be girlfriend is menstruating (189).

ent moment, even to the point that he ignores his own wife's infidelities. As a result, he is removed from his position, shunned by the community, and dislocated in time. Hightower's historical paralysis is considered blasphemous and discomfits the community. However, his theology is troubling only in that it points to the paralyzing possibilities of the community's own ideology. Just as Doc Hines's message exaggerates the racial ideology implicit within the religion of white southerners, Hightower's halted historical vision is simply a more obvious manifestation of the flawed eschatology upon which the community's vision of its own racial chosen-ness is predicated.

Though Hightower's sermons are perceived as nonsensical and even heretical, his cyclonic frenzy only makes obvious the violent energies and cataclysmic possibilities the southern community attempts to contain within its foundational, cosmological narrative of racial difference. He is hardly the only character overwhelmed by an "invasion" of the past. John T. Irwin notes that repetition in Faulkner's work is indicative of a sense of familial "fate or doom" (60)—"a feeling that an ancestor's actions can determine the actions of his descendants for generations to come by compelling them periodically to repeat his deeds" (61). In particular, this is manifest through the multigenerational relationships of grandparents and grandchildren; as Irwin notes, "Hightower, Joanna Burden, and Joe Christmas . . . have had their destinies determined by the lives of their grandfathers." Formulated in this manner, the cycle of familial *doom* forecloses the possibility of progress as well as free will. Indeed, this force—imagined variously as *doom*, *fate*, and the anthropomorphic Player—is Joe Christmas's ultimate adversary. He attempts to resist this overwhelming specter through the reiteration of his racial ambiguity. At every step, he seeks to disrupt the collective gaze of community that would locate him within its bivalent logic. This pathological need to be unknowable seems borne of his life in the orphanage. There, his attainment of sentience and individuation is determined by his grandfather's gaze: "*That is why I am different from the others: because he is watching me all the time*" (138). That experience initiates Christmas's desire to escape the fate that racial inscription would proscribe as well as his belief in the inevitability of that fate—that is, the overwhelming sense that "*Something is going to happen to me*" (104). "[H]e believed with calm paradox," writes Faulkner, "that he was the volitionless servant of the fatality in which he believed that he did not believe" (280).

While the initial images of the novel evoke stagnation, the repetitions within it generate a frenzied momentum that threaten to spin out of control and plunge both the book and the community it contains into chaos. Just as the wild shape of Hightower's sermons evinces the possibility of collapse, Faulkner "measure[es] the fragility of the South's social and psychological order" through a narrative structure that seems to be on the brink of "collapse into cascading, uncontrolled rhetoric," writes Sundquist (79).[33] However, the novel remains ultimately coherent—held together by "the issue of blood," in Sundquist's estimation. I wish to reframe this: the novel's formal cohesion is not as much a product of the "spurious connections" of blood as its steadfast refusal to answer the question of Christmas's racial background. Frustratingly, the narrative loops around the solution each time the reader nears it. Ultimately, Joe Christmas is the agent of much of this uncertainty; each time he settles into a situation, whether with the McEacherns, in Detroit, Chicago, or in Jefferson, he feels compelled to loudly, forcefully, and even violently confound the bivalent logic of race. Surprisingly, he claims to be black even though he perceives black people and black life as utterly "impenetrable" (116). Nor does he believe that he is knowable to African Americans: "Dont even know they cant see me," Joe says of a group of black Yoknapatawphans (325). Despite his admitted lack of evidence, he continually asserts a black identity. He does so because it is a resistant, disruptive act. These assertions (first to a white prostitute, next to Bobbie, then to Joanna, and finally to Joe Brown/Lucas Burch) occur following prolonged or intimate interactions with people operating under the assumption that he is *white*. By engaging him as a white man, they locate him with the bivalent racial logic. Joe disrupts that logic but only for a moment; rather than claiming a new, hybrid identity, he simply relocates himself within the bivalent racial order. The revelation is shocking and disturbing, but it ultimately reinforces the prevailing logic of race and positions his particular experiences as aberrant or deviant, rather than evidence of that logic's inherent flaws.

Of his many assertions of blackness, his admission to Joanna is ultimately the most calamitous: in the earliest stages of their romance, Joe's desire for Joanna Burden is conditioned by her own marginalized position. As a foreigner in her own home, she seems to provide sanctuary from racial ideologies. Ultimately, however, as her enraptured screams of "Negro! Negro! Negro!" (259–60) make clear, her desire for him is predicated on—and twisted by—her own exceptional logic of race. She names him, first

---

33. Indeed, Romine describes the novel's structure as a paradoxical equilibrium between "its tremendous centrifugal energy—that is, its numerous *kinds* of shifts that threaten to fracture the novel into a multitude of narrative shards—[and] an equally powerful centripetal force that prevents such a dispersal" (151).

during their lovemaking and again when she encourages him to attend the Negro college. When Joanna initiates the discussion while wearing unfamiliar "steelrimmed spectacles" (275), Joe unavoidably becomes the subject of her gaze, watched and categorized by her just as he had been by Doc Hines at the orphanage decades earlier. Later, she demands that he pray with her—an act that would insert him into the discourse of purity and holiness and, thus, would amount to a surrender to knowability. We might understand Joanna's killing as another attempt to disrupt an effort to locate him racially. However, the power of this assertion is tempered by the overwhelming sense that it has always–already occurred, and that in killing Joanna, he has simply fulfilled the fate to which he has been doomed by his grandfather.[34]

Indeed, Joanna's death initiates the novel's most profound temporal disruptions. Eventually, Joe internalizes the disruption he initiates elsewhere. Unhinged from time and place, Joe finds himself in a waking dream, in which "[t]ime, the spaces of light and dark, had long since lost orderliness" (333), running but not conscious of the running until he is completely lost. He finally awakens and begins to resituate himself in time. First he reestablishes the rhythm of daily life through the consumption of regular meals (333). He then calculates the days of the week, "as though now and at last he had an actual and urgent need to strike off the accomplished days toward some purpose, some definite day or act, without either falling short or overshooting" (335). Soon after Christmas is resituated in time, the reader is no longer privy to his thoughts; the remainder of his story is rendered solely through the collective voice. Exhausted by the energies required to fend off the invasions of the past, he apparently surrenders his voice to the collective and allows it to name him whatever it wants.

By following this structure, *Light in August* refuses to yield the ultimate promise of Apocalypse: revelation. Though Joe surrenders to the collective voice, the novel ultimately dismisses its claim to knowledge and exposes the limitations of its bivalent, apocalyptic epistemology. Thus, the more emphatic a claim to Truth is made in *Light in August*—and perhaps in all of Faulkner's work—the more obscured that insight becomes. By denying the possibility of contradictory knowledge, then, the collective voice forecloses the possibility of revelation. When Hightower asks Byron, "But are you going to undertake to say just how far evil extends into the appearance of evil? Just where between doing and appearing evil stops?" (306),

---

34. In fact, when he enters the rural black church and assaults members of the congregation, he becomes a double for his monstrous grandfather.

he seems to support the authority of the community to identify the nature and presence of evil. Hightower, with some irony, posits evil as a human construct, articulated only in its rejection. This sort of operation recurs throughout the text. Blackness, for instance, functions similarly: even for Joe, who has lived as a black man in black communities, African American experience is impenetrable, unknowable "abyss" (116). Likewise, despite the constant telling and retelling of events, the people of Jefferson know nothing of the true nature of Joe and Joanna's relationship.

The foreclosure of revelation is reinforced in Christmas's perplexing surrender to Grimm. According to Sundquist, "his seemingly insane passivity" reflects an "exhaustion" that is indicative both of Joe's own sense of defeat and of the formal necessities of controlling the "frenetic" narrative (73). While the form of his death further supports the conflation of Christmas with Christ and of lynching with crucifixion, the violent climax does not transform the community. If revelation or revolutionary change is even possible, they are perhaps not likely. One of the deputies present for Joe's death recoils in horror and vomits. We might be tempted to view this revulsion as evidence that at least this one person has realized the sheer horror of what is possible within this toxic environment. However, as Romine rightly notes, the deputy's reaction parallels Joe's reaction to the knowledge of menstruation—a revelation that fails to deepen his understanding of gender and femininity (*Narrative Forms* 190). In both instances, vomiting is indicative of an inability to assimilate knowledge and a subsequent rejection of it. One hopes that the deputy has rejected the bivalent epistemology that cannot accommodate this experience; however, the episode concludes as "the scream of the siren . . . pass[es] out of the realm of hearing" (465)—that is, out of the spectrum of intelligibility.[35] Because the meaning of the event is not immediately accessible, the witnesses (and perhaps the town) are doomed to be haunted by it.[36] They will revisit this unassimilated experience only indirectly, as they "contemplate old disasters and newer hopes" in "the mirroring faces" of their progeny. However, they will not directly confront the possibility of their own racial ambiguity; the fundamental instability of the foundational racialized and gendered ideologies; or the cataclysmic future to which this instability

---

35. Richard C. Moreland makes a similar observation about Jim Bond's "unmediated, unconsoled howl" in *The Sound and the Fury* (*Faulkner and Modernism* 119).

36. Cathy Caruth writes that "trauma is not locatable in the simple violent or original event in an individual's past but rather in the way that its very unassimilated nature—the way it was precisely *not known* in the first instance—returns to haunt the survivor later on" (4).

has doomed them. Progress toward a telos might have temporarily been restored, but nothing prevents the coming of the next figure in the repeating cycle of "numberless avatars" (226), each of whom must be sacrificed in order to push back the traumatic, repressed realization that racial difference is not fixed.

The reader is left with a community doomed to burn out in its own frenzied attempt to control the complexities of modernity and the contradictions it refuses to acknowledge. Meaning itself is exhausted by these ceaseless repetitions. The apocalyptic rhetoric of Doc Hines and the apocalyptic theology of racial difference (through which the community defines itself as pure) give way to the Apocalypse of modernism—to obsessive concerns with the incompleteness of language, with the moral failings of modern industrial society, and with the problems of representing "the immense panorama of futility and anarchy which is contemporary history," in T. S. Eliot's words (177). In many ways, the narrative experimentations of modernist writers sought to realize the promise of Apocalypse; Bull suggests that "[i]n societies where bivalence is assumed to be natural, the undifferentiated is inaccessible to normal patterns of thought, so access can be gained only by means that circumvent the accepted modes of cognition" (83). The modernist effort to find radically new ways of articulating human experience and to approach an originary unity of meaning that would overcome the limitations of language, reaches toward the reincorporation of the undifferentiated, the unintelligible, and the unrecognizable. *Light in August* exposes the limitations endemic to that effort *as narrative*. It offers no antidote for violence and prescribes no practicable, actionable solution.

Instead, it contains the possibility of collapse within the frame of Lena's boundless, unflappable faith and the possibility of new life. The birth of her son initiates another temporal disruption through repetition: Mrs. Hines becomes dislocated from time and conflates Joe's birth and the birth of Lena's child with such certainty that even the new mother is confused about the child's paternity. The novel offers some limited sense of hope, as the birth restores Hightower to the regular flow of time. But if any character experiences a revelation, it is Byron Bunch. He is able to overcome the collective response to Lena as a contaminated figure—a response that he in fact shares earlier. As Richard C. Moreland notes, "Byron is drawn not away from Lena, nor to scapegoat or dominate Lena as a threat to his sense of his own masculinity, but toward Lena, as if to learn how she thinks and acts what so many like himself have thought unthinkable, unbearable, unacceptable" ("Faulkner and Modernism" 28). Lena remains a figure of undifferentiation, unsettling the conventional discourse of judgment. In accepting her, Byron is willing to accept the *possibility* of something that transcends these prevailing narratives. However, what that means remains unresolved. If there is a path toward meaningful historical progress, revelation, or deliverance, *Light in August* does not chart it for us. Instead, the novel simply feints toward its possibility and remains deeply skeptical.

2

"Tearing Down the Temple"

Prophetic Time and Richard Wright's Eschatology of Resistance

> Hound dogs on my trail
> School children sitting in jail
> Black cat cross my path
> I think every day's gonna be my last
> Lord have mercy on this land of mine
> We all gonna get it in due time
> I don't belong here
> I don't belong there
> I've even stopped believing in prayer
> . . .
> Picket lines
> School boycotts
> They try to say it's a communist plot
> All I want is equality
> for my sister my brother my people and me
> Yes you lied to me all these years
> You told me to wash and clean my ears
> And talk real fine just like a lady
> And you'd stop calling me Sister Sadie
> Oh but this whole country is full of lies
> You're all gonna die and die like flies
> I don't trust you any more
> You keep on saying "Go slow!"
> "Go slow!"
>
> —Nina Simone, "Mississippi Goddam!"

THROUGHOUT his life and his works, writes his biographer Michel Fabre, Richard Wright "attempted to reject what the South stood for in his mind but he also kept reaffirming, repeatedly and compulsively, what it had meant for him and how he had been molded by it" (78). If the word "religion" were replaced with "the South" in this sentence, the accuracy of Fabre's original statement would not be diminished; indeed, Fabre's argument would hardly be altered. As I hope I demonstrated in the previous chapter, any inquiry into the history and culture of the U.S. South necessarily includes an examination of its religious cultures. In Wright's work, region and religion are often inextricable. The southern childhood recalled in his 1945 autobiographical narrative *Black Boy* is haunted, not just by the specter of southern racism, but also by the stifling Seventh-day Adventism of his grandmother. Though the black church was the central institution of the community into which he was born, religion proved to be the cause of great strife within Wright's family. He viewed his grandmother's faith as yet another agent of oppression in a horribly oppressive environment—a suffocating force that stifled his intellectual achievement and yet another set of arbitrary social codes that he was expected to perform and ideologies he was expected to passively accept.

Given the directness with which it addresses this topic and its overall centrality in his oeuvre, it is not surprising that examinations of Wright's engagement with religion often begin and end with *Black Boy*. Written at the height of his fame, the book evinces the same internationalism, historical materialism, and social realist aesthetic that characterize his other masterwork, the 1940 novel *Native Son*, and that would later develop into the anticolonialism and existentialism of his later work, including reportage, travel writing, and novels like *Savage Holiday* (1953) and *The Outsider* (1954). Indeed, the notion that Wright's work rejects religion is so commonplace that it continues to play a determinative role in the critical reception of his work. For some critics, Wright's atheism amounts to an unfortunate rejection of his own blackness, while for others, it is a powerful act of resistance against an institution that has been complicit with black oppression.[1] The terms of this debate are reductive: while Wright's atheism is not in dispute, the sum of his work offers neither a dismissal of the black church nor a full-scale assault on religion. Instead, Wright is like countless other African American writers who, in Qiana Whitted's estimate, "attempt to negotiate abstract religious grievances with empowering

---

1. For the former view, see James W. Coleman, *Faithful Vision: Treatments of the Sacred, Spiritual, And Supernatural in Twentieth-century African American Fiction* (Baton Rouge: Louisiana State University Press, 2006). Recent examples of the latter include Michael Lackey's *African American Atheists and Political Liberation: A Study of the Sociocultural Dynamics of Faith* (Gainesville: University Press of Florida, 2007) and Qiana Whitted's "*A God of Justice?": The Problem of Evil in Twentieth-Century Black Literature* (Charlottesville: University of Virginia Press, 2009).

dimensions of its practice in oppressed communities" (26). Like so many other black writers, Richard Wright's engagement with religion is complicated, discontinuous, and fraught with a "deep ambivalence."

That negotiation constitutes important political work, particularly in his earliest works. For at least a moment in his writerly life, Wright found some utility, a rhetorical lineage, and even the possibility of radical change in the language and the narratives of African American religious traditions. In the essay "Blueprint for Negro Writing" and the short story cycle *Uncle Tom's Children*, the African American church clearly retains a vital role in Wright's vision of a meaningful and revolutionary mass black workers' movement. The presentation of religion in the collection is not limited to the depiction of the church or the evaluation of it as a potential vehicle for resistance, however: in African American religion, Wright finds the material necessary to articulate a nascent, revolutionary black theory of history. In "Blueprint," he writes that

> in order to depict Negro life in all of its manifold and intricate relationships, a deep, informed and complex consciousness is necessary, a consciousness which draws for its strength upon the fluid lore of a great people, and moulds [sic] this lore with the concepts that move and direct the forces of history today. (43)

Such a theory is dire necessity, he continues: " . . . any one destitute of a theory about the structure, direction, and meaning of modern society is a lost victim in a world he cannot understand or control" (45).

The question of the *direction* of history is preeminent in *Uncle Tom's Children*, and it is at least in part what prevents the atheist Wright from the unequivocal rejection of religion that critics often ascribe to him. These stories each invoke the prophetic time of African American religious culture. Unlike the notions of historical progress that justified European colonial projects and the millenarian nationalism of U.S. political culture, the particular apocalyptic imaginary of black religion offers the possibility of *rupture*, of a radical break and a totalizing apocalyptic reordering of an oppressive social order. Wright's fascination with eschatological visions is evident in the apocalyptic aesthetic that characterizes much of his writing. In *Black Boy*, Wright describes the frightening cosmology of his grandmother's Seventh-day Adventist faith as

> a gospel clogged with images of vast lakes of eternal fire, or seas vanishing, of valleys of dry bones, of the sun burning to ashes, of the moon

turning to blood, of stars falling to the earth . . . ; a salvation that teemed with fantastic beasts having multiple heads and horns and eyes and feet . . . a cosmic tale that began before time and ended with the clouds of the sky rolling away at the Second Coming of Christ; chronicles that concluded with the Armageddon, dramas thronged with all the billions of human beings who had ever lived or died as God judged the quick and the dead. . . . (102)

This terrifying invocation of the apocalyptic imaginary is by no means unique to *Black Boy*. Indeed, apocalyptic imagery figures prominently in the landscapes of the rural South and the urban North explored in Wright's fictional universe. Like that of his fellow Mississippian William Faulkner, Wright's apocalyptic vision reveals the cataclysmic consequences of race for the region and the nation. Unlike Faulkner, however, Wright has little concern with the souls of white folk or with revealing the long histories they have repressed. Instead, his work explores the suffering of African Americans and looks forward to the possibility of resistance.

Though the southern apocalyptic imaginary clearly informs Wright's artistic vision, his representations of societies on the brink of collapse are rooted in beliefs he frequently and vociferously claimed to disdain. For Wright, any rupture in history would not be brought about by divine intervention, and its form would not be that prophesized by St. John and imagined in spirituals and hymns. Instead, the eschatological vision of both "Blueprint" and *Uncle Tom's Children* is a Marxist one. In our current political discourse, fundamentalist Christianity and communism are positioned at opposite ends of the ideological spectrum. An immediate and obvious connection, however, might be found in the eschatological emphasis of both systems: both communism and fundamentalist Christianity envision an inevitable, potentially violent conflict that will bring an end to the current, deeply flawed social structure in favor of something more just. However, in Wright's view, the apocalyptic hopes of black religion have failed its adherents, and its promise of inevitable divine action has become complicit with the static, ahistorical condition imposed by the institutions of southern oppression.

Only through a Marxism that attended to the particular experiences of rural African American life, Wright believed, could the African American subject be restored to history. *Uncle Tom's Children* was written and published at a crucial period in Wright's career: before the fame garnered by *Native Son*; before his break with the Communist Party USA; before his move to Paris and his engagement with Sartre and existentialism; in a moment of youth that was energized by the ideas exchanged and ideologies explored in CPUSA-sponsored publications like *New Masses* and the *Daily Worker*, to which he contributed, and in the Marxist intellectual circles of the John Reed Club, the Chicago chapter of which he would become head (Fabre 36–37). In this moment, in which his worldview was decidedly materialist, his attention was nonetheless turned toward African American religion. And in *Uncle Tom's Children*, Wright seeks to realize the strategy announced in "Blueprint for Negro Writing" and deploy a mode of black Marxist writing that would awaken the latent revolutionary potential within African American culture. Individually, each of the five stories in the cycle—"Big Boy Leaves Home," "Down by the Riverside," "Long Black Song," "Fire and Cloud," and "Bright and Morning Star"—surge with the emancipatory energies of the apocalyptic imaginary. But when the work is taken together as a singular work, these two eschatologies, heretofore parallel and disparate, finally converge.

This chapter will explore the apocalyptic imaginary as the discursive space suited to the aims of Wright's early writing—that is, to the development of a Marxist message that, by attending to the particular experience of African Americans in the rural South, would revitalize an exhausted revolutionary energy within black culture. In locating this in my broader study of the southern literary and religious culture, I do not intend to minimize either the obvious or the subtle distinctions between the forms of evangelical Protestantism practiced by black and white believers; regardless of race, visions of Apocalypse are critical to the religious culture of the South, and differences between forms of engagement with the apocalyptic imaginary reflect the particular cultures and historical experiences of the communities of believers.

In an effort to interrogate these differences, this chapter will first examine Wright's depictions of what I will call the ahistorical condition of African Americans under Jim Crow, before interrogating the ways in which *Uncle Tom's Children* works to restore the colonized, brutalized black subject into a meaningful teleology. The cycle deploys two specific strategies to do this, both of which engage the prophetic, millennial vision of African American religion in some way: first, its structure casts the black experience in a typology drawn from Scripture; second, this typological structure demands that the collection's characters experience multiple ruptures in time. These localized apocalypses are most often initiated by an eruption of horrific violence (not unlike the lynching of Joe Christmas in

Light in August). But rather than restraining and demoralizing the victim (as each of the white promulgators intends), these beatings, lynchings, and murders offer the possibility of revelation and rebirth.

"We git erlong widout time": The Ahistorical Condition of Jim Crow

Equivocation is not a mode often attached ascribed to Richard Wright. Ideology is often front and center in nearly eight decades of critical response to Wright's work, and in the realm of propaganda and agitprop, little room exists for uncertainty and ambivalence. However, as critics like Timothy Caron, John Lowe, and Qiana Whitted have noted, Wright's corpus is more complex than this. This even holds true for *Uncle Tom's Children*, even though, if this work is considered solely in the context of Wright's biography, it would seem a likely candidate for his most polemical work. At the time of its writing, he was still a committed member of the Communist Party USA and worked as Chicago head of the John Reed Club. With regard to the debates of their historical moment, the stories entertain no uncertainty: African Americans must take decisive action to overcome the rule of Jim Crow and lynch law, and if any justice is to be achieved, they ultimately must join with other poor and oppressed peoples. However, the stories' depictions of black religion and its relationship to resistance are not nearly as unequivocal.

Within Wright scholarship, the middle story, "Long Black Song," often gets short shrift, perhaps because of the author's notorious reputation for problematic representations of women in his writing (and reputation for even more problematic relationships with them in his own life).[2] The protagonist of the story is Sarah, a young black woman stagnating on an isolated farm and in any unhappy marriage; during one of her husband Silas's frequent absences, she is either seduced or raped by a white salesman, who is traveling across the rural landscape to hawk record players. Silas ultimately discovers what seems to be an act of betrayal and believes that it undoes his years of work to be "as good as any white man" (147); abandoning all hope of attaining any autonomy, he forces Sarah and their

2. Most recently, Linda Chavers has offered a fascinating examination of Wright's "implied complicity in women's oppression" in *Black Boy*, in which "he presents a pattern of pseudo-rebellion against restrictive female figures in the lives of his male protagonist"; Fabre thoroughly covers Wright's relationships with various women in *The Unfinished Quest of Richard Wright*.

infant daughter from their home and embarks down a "long river of blood" (153), first whipping the salesman (who returns to finalize the transaction) and, later, shooting other white men who come to arrest and likely lynch him.

The initial impact of the story emerges from its depiction of violence, and the related (and problematic) exploration of the pathologies of black masculine anger and black female victimhood: Silas's efforts to assert a fairly conservative notion of masculine autonomy—that is to say, to be a successful provider and earner, to marry and raise a family—are thwarted by the intrusion of the white salesman upon his real and conjugal property. Like the Eve of Genesis, Sarah's capitulation to temptation (and to the evil embodied in a seemingly pleasant white man) initiates a tragic course of events, which she can only observe. The takeaway: the mythic models of American success, whether the Jeffersonian ideal of the yeoman farmer or subsequent (Horatio) Algerian American dreams of commercial success, are traps for black folk; any apparent triumph is merely a fata morgana, concealing an inevitable assertion of white superiority that will tragically destroy black men and black women. Here, Wright leaves little room for uncertainty.

Ambivalence, however, characterizes many other elements of the story. In particular, the exchanges between Sarah and the salesman evince the complexity and confusion of the black subject's relationship to time and history. The conversation begins when the salesman notices Sarah's infant daughter, Ruth (to whom the narrator curiously applies the pronoun "it") banging a broken "old eight day clock," which Sarah had previously given her as a plaything (126). The salesman is shocked to learn that this is the only clock in the house. "But how do you keep time?" he asks.

"We git erlong widout time."
"But how do you know what time it is when you get up in the morning?"
"We jus git up, thas all."
"But how do you know what time it is when you get up?"
"We git up wid the sun."
"And at night, how do you tell when its night?"
"It gits dark when the sun goes down." (131)

To this point, the exchange has the comic feel of a typical country-mouse, city-mouse story. Both laugh, and Sarah cannot help but think that the salesman in his naïveté and ignorance of the particular rhythms of rural life, is a "Jus lika lil boy." However, greater significance and ambiguity are imparted to the conversation by the final punchline that precedes their laughter, as well as the troubling sexual encounter that follows it. Before the fun ends, Wright carefully shifts the terminology from *keeping* precise time to living in the *absence* of time. "I don't see how in the world anybody can live without time," says the salesman. "We just don't need no time, Mistah," Sarah responds.

Prior to this additional dialogue, the salesman appears foolish—so dependent on modern mechanisms and structures of thought that he can no longer understand what is obvious: the rhythms of time do not originate from any artificial device but are in fact manifest in the natural world. After this final exchange, however, the situation is murkier, and the reader must question the implications of living outside of time. Is this a parable about the fundamental cultural misunderstandings that characterize interactions between white and rural black people—a problem Wright confronted in his role as the designated black voice in a Communist Party infrastructure dominated by white people from the urban North? Or is this episode another manifestation of a theme that recurs throughout Wright's work—namely, the idea that black people "have never been allowed to catch the full spirit of Western civilization" (*Black Boy* 37)? Does this moment suggest that the ideology of white supremacy and the institutions of segregation have so severely restricted any assertion of black agency that the very possibility of rational progress has been foreclosed?[3]

Indeed, prior to this conversation, Sarah's existence is depicted as profoundly ahistorical. The dislocation and stagnation of her current moment are contrasted to the joyous sense of possibility that characterized her romance with Tom, her lover who was deployed to the front in Europe, as well as the earliest days of her marriage to Silas:

> Yes; there had been all her life the long hope of white bright days and the deep desire of dark black nights and then Silas had gone. Bang! Bang! Bang! There had been laughter and eating and singing and the long gladness of green cornfields in summer. There had been cooking

---

3. This interpretation is given credence by Sarah's ignorance of the meaning of word "science," which the salesman tells her he studies (134). While later African American writers might strongly critique or even reject Enlightenment notions of rationality and progress, the young Wright—still embracing Communism, not yet engrossed in the existentialism that characterizes his later work—would be unlikely to fully dismiss the methods of science, empiricism, or Western thought as too complicit in the ideological domination of non-Western peoples to play a role in the fight against oppression.

and sewing and sweeping and the deep dream of sleeping grey skies in winter. Always it had been like that and she had been happy. But no more. The happiness of those days and nights, of those green cornfields and grey skies had started to go from her when Tom had gone to war. His leaving had left an empty black hole in her heart, a black hole that Silas had come in and filled. But not quite. Silas had not quite filled that hole. No; days and nights were not as they were before. (129)

Without hope in the possibility of a new day, the joyous, pastoral rhythms of agrarian life dissolve into a numbing repetition of meaningless events. From this perspective, little alternative is possible. Any movement through time and across physical space are so foreign that they threaten to negate the self; musing on Tom's deployment to Europe, Sarah feels "that merely to go so far away from home was a kind of death in itself" (127).[4]

Sarah's hopeless, existential yearning for something more complicates a common criticism of Wright's work—that his work denies the affirmative, sustaining elements of African American culture and instead only depicts the "cultural barrenness of black life" he laments in *Black Boy* (37). The life Sarah remembers is hardly barren, but her current circumstance might be characterized that way. Here and elsewhere in Wright's fictional universe, the difference between the two states—between the fecundity and pleasure of rural black life and the emptiness Sarah now feels—emerges from shifts in the individual's and the community's relationships to time. If the black culture represented in Wright's corpus is indeed barren, it is only because it is profoundly ahistorical. Throughout his work (and particularly, in *Uncle Tom's Children*), Wright articulates the freedom that he and his characters desire in both spatial and temporal terms. While he recognizes African American religion as a source of spiritual nourishment necessary for survival under the conditions of slavery and Jim Crow, it offers little opportunity for movement or progress in his fiction. In the autobiographical essay "The Ethics of Living Jim Crow," he reports being warned by his family to "never again attempt to exceed my boundaries. When you are working for white folks, they said, you got to 'stay in your place'" (7). He continues this argument in *Black Boy*: "I knew that I lived in a country in

---

4. This sentiment fascinatingly juxtaposes the relatively carefree attitude of the wandering mother Lena Grove in *Light in August*. Lena willingly transgresses upon any social restriction on her mobility, but rather than opening the possibility of deliverance, her travels seem as pointlessly repetitive as Sarah's life on the farm. For Faulkner, movement is made possible when Byron Bunch joins her and helps form a de facto family unit; Sarah, on the other hand, is driven to despair by the emptiness of her domestic stability.

which the aspirations of black people were limited, marked off. Yet I felt that I had to go somewhere and do something to redeem my being alive" (169). The young Wright desires to leave his southern home in favor of a place where personal progress—movement toward a telos—is possible. While the adolescent Wright who emerges in these writings chafes at these restraints, other African Americans often seem complicit in them and, in the case of his grandmother, even reinforce them. His classmates, for instance, are "not conscious of living a special, separate, stunted way of life. . . . Although they lived in an America where in theory there existed equality of opportunity, they knew unerringly what to aspire to and what not to aspire to" (197). The choice of the word "aspire" is critical in the context of this conversation: unlike the more passive *hope*, which implies waiting on something beyond oneself, to *aspire* requires a vision of progress and work over time toward a definite goal. Aspiration is, then, teleological, but in Wright's estimation, progress toward any goal is inevitably "stunted" by the regime of southern apartheid.

This spatial and temporal formulation of freedom is encompassed in Houston A. Baker, Jr.'s term "United States Black Modernism." Under the regimes of white authority, there exists no "*black public-sphere mobility*," writes Baker (83; the italics are his). African Americans have been denied the "*fullness of United States black citizenship rights of locomotion, suffrage, occupational choice and compensation that yield what can only be designated a black-majority, politically participatory, bodily secure GOOD LIFE.*" "Modernism" clearly implies a chronological break with the past, but Baker also defines it in terms of "mobility" and "movement" in space: *United States Black Modernism* is thus a transformative condition in which black people would be able to move *in* space and *through* time *toward* a goal.

The freedom Baker claims here is the same freedom to aspire and achieve that the young Wright finds absent in his community. His posthumously published first novel *Lawd, Today!* layers the collapsing personal life of Jake, a black Chicago postal worker, within both the collapse of the black community to which he belongs as well as the apocalyptic collapse wrought by the Depression in the U.S. and the rise of the Third Reich in Europe. A failed schemer, Jake is incapable of imagining success beyond the terms of immediate physical and material gratification. Likewise, the protagonist of *The Long Dream*, Fishbelly, learns from his father to check any aspirations that he might have of a life beyond the limits of Jim Crow: "Dream only what can happen. . . . If you ever find yourself dreaming something that can't happen, then choke it back, 'cause there's too many dreams of a black man that can't come true" (80).

Prior to the events of "Long Black Song," Silas has not yet learned this lesson; he is driven by the dream of mobility and autonomy—and of achieving them in the manner in which the white farmers around him do. "Ef yuhs gonna git anywheres yuhs gotta do just like they [white people] do," he tells Sarah (140). But, as Baker notes, the institutions and practices of Jim Crow foreclose the possibility of any real mobility. After years in which Silas dutifully "work[ed] hard and saved his money" in order to buy a farm and "grow his own crops like white men" (147), the act of infidelity reveals the inevitability of white authority and exposes the naïveté of his aspiration for autonomous dominion over his own land.

As a black woman, Sarah's position is even more restricted, and her ahistorical condition leads to her undoing. Wright's representation of women is often problematic, and Sarah's sexual encounter with the salesman is no exception. The degree of her complicity in the encounter is troublingly uncertain; one struggles to determine if this is a depiction of the powerlessness of black women (that is, she relents to his advances because she is powerless to do otherwise) or an example of the emasculation of black men (that is, despite his best efforts, Silas can never truly possess the authority of a man, and so betrayal by a woman is all but inevitable). While not discounting either interpretation, I would assert a third possibility: rather than simply offering another parable of the nearly unlimited possibilities for white abuses and black suffering under Jim Crow, this episode reveals the deep connections between desire and history. Operating from this perspective, one views Sarah as neither overwhelmed by the authority of the salesman's whiteness nor repulsed by Silas's powerlessness, but instead, moved by powerful yearning for a restored relationship to history and time.

After all, the white man hardly strikes us as a figuration of authority and power; throughout their encounter, he seems "Jus lika chile" to Sarah (132). Their interaction becomes erotically charged only once the salesman demonstrates the record player with the spiritual "When the Roll Is Called Up Yonder":

There was a sharp, scratching noise; then she moved nervously, her body caught in the ringing coils of music.
When the trumpet of the Lord shall sound . . .
She rose on circling waves of white bright days and dark black nights.
. . . and time shall be no more . . .
Higher and higher she mounted.

> . . . *And the morning breaks* . . .
> Earth fell far behind, forgotten.
> . . . *eternal, bright and fair* . . .
> Echo after echo sounded.
> *When the save of the earth shall gather* . . .
> Her blood surged like the long gladness of summer.
> . . . *over on the other shore* . . .
> Her blood ebbed like the deep dream of sleep in winter.
> *And when the roll is called up yonder* . . .
> She gave up, holding her breath.
> *I'll be there.* . . . (132–33)

Nothing after the song suggests that Sarah sees him differently. It is the song that profoundly affects her, filling her throat with a lump, causing her to tremble. Most critically, though, Wright portrays this arousal in temporal terms: she "feel[s] the rise and falls of days and nights, of summer and winter," for instance. Likewise, when seduction gives way to actual sex, the rhythms of coitus echo the rhythms of time and season:

> A liquid metal covered her and she rode on the curve of white bright days and dark black nights and the surge of the long gladness of summer and the ebb of the deep dream of sleep in winter till a high red wave of hotness drowned her in a deluge of silver and blue that boiled her blood and blistered her flash *bangbangbang*. . . . (137)

Beginning with the song, this encounter with the salesman fleetingly fulfills Sarah's deep existential yearning to exist in time. Crucially, this is not time figured in the way the salesman imagines it—a concept of history that is dependent on clock and in which the value of time is measured by the scientific or industrial progress that has passed. Instead, it is prophetic, apocalyptic time—a sense of history grounded in the particular textures of African American experience, in which the suffering of the current moment ultimately will be redeemed and its meaning will be revealed.

Wright's salesman likely has little conception of the significance of the song he plays; perhaps it is the only "race record" in his collection, and he plays it to appeal to his audience. For Wright, however, the reference is a strategic one: spirituals were among "the channels through which the racial wisdom flowed" ("Blueprint" 40). Like countless other spirituals (and like the Carter Family's "No Depression [in Heaven]") "When the Roll Is Called Up Yonder" provides a spiritual balm, prophesying the ultimate day of deliverance that will redeem the suffering of the current moment. Even under the conditions of bondage, these spirituals allowed African Americans to assume "the role of the chosen people," elected for a special historical role by their earthly suffering and permitted them to "prophesy an apocalyptic end to the world that slaveholders made," according to Baker (*Long Black Song* 53). The revolutionary eschatology of slave religion culminates in the Jubilee, a moment that begins with Christ's joyous return and offers the long-awaited deliverance from the physical bondage of chattel slavery and the spiritual bondage of human sin. As the moment of divine judgment, the Jubilee promises retribution against oppressive regimes of white power—that is, otherworldly justice that transcends the corrupt institutions of human authority. More broadly, as Paul Gilroy persuasively argues, this cosmology amounts to a "critique of modernity" and of its inadequacy to generate totalizing meaning (56). Rationalism and empiricism too easily yield to the prevailing historical order and fail to accommodate the experiences of an oppressed minority; in short, these systems cannot adequately represent the existential pain endured by a group that has been discursively reduced to the status of property. The cosmology of African American religious traditions, however, offers scriptural precedence for bondage and deliverance. This at least offers an alternative historical narrative in which deliverance and justice are not only possible, but imminent.

This notion of sacred, prophetic time is hardly limited to songs. Indeed, the apocalyptic imaginary has proven to be a wellspring for African American writers since the early nineteenth century. In his 1829 *Appeal*, David Walker writes that slaveholding nations

> forget that God rules in the armies of heaven and among the inhabitants of the earth, having his ears continually open to the cries, tears and groans of his oppressed people; and being a just and holy Being will at one day appear fully in behalf of the oppressed, and arrest the progress of the avaricious oppressors; for although the destruction of the oppressors God may not effect by the oppressed, yet the Lord our God will bring other destructions upon them. (3)

The echoes of Walker's prophetic rhetoric are audible in Frederick Douglass's sermon "What to the Slave Is the Fourth of July?" delivered twenty-three years later. "We need the storm, the whirlwind, and the earthquake," he exhorts. "The feeling of the nation must be quickened; the conscience of the nation must be roused; the propriety of the nation must be startled;

the hypocrisy of the nation must be exposed; and its crimes against God and man must be proclaimed and denounced" (344). In *The Afro-American Jeremiad,* David Howard-Pitney introduces this rhetorical model through a reading of Martin Luther King, Jr.'s "I Have a Dream" speech, contextualizing King within this tradition of prophetic millenarianism (3–4). The power of this rhetorical mode to incite strong emotion and debate persists even now, as evinced by the political and media outrage that came once excerpts of sermons by Rev. Jeremiah Wright, once the pastor to the Obama family, were posted to YouTube and broadcast on television during the 2008 U.S. presidential campaign. However, the firestorm Jeremiah Wright's rhetoric caused—and the message of millenarian hope articulated in then-Senator Obama's response—suggests that the complexities and historical underpinnings of this mode remain misunderstood by many of those outside the black community.[5]

For Sarah, however, "When the Roll Is Called Up Yonder" has no explicit political content. For a fleeting instant, the song removes her from the existential malaise that has characterized her life on the farm and reawakens her sexuality; she yearns, wants, and aspires in ways that resist the numbing, suffocating, and dehumanizing effects of Jim Crow. In some ways, this episode in "Long Black Song" functions as the fulcrum upon which *Uncle Tom's Children* pivots. Like the first two stories, it ends tragically and hopelessly: learning of Sarah's liaison with the salesman, Silas embraces the existential meaninglessness of his position and embarks on a murderous rampage, "follow[ing] that old river blood, knowing that it meant nothing" (154); as she watches their house consumed by flames, Sarah is left, "Naw, Gawd!" and knowing that deliverance is not coming (156).

This episode also provides a center around which the cycle coheres—a moment that reveals a key to the larger work's themes. Here, Wright

---

5. David A. Frank offers a thoughtful interpretation of both Obama's and Wright's use of the prophetic voice and African American religious rhetoric in his essay, "The Prophetic Voice and the Face of the Other in Barack Obama's 'A More Perfect Union' Address, March 18, 2008." Frank judges Obama's use of the mode "a masterpiece with small flaws and sequels that do not fully match its excellence," which articulates a nuanced understanding of these misunderstandings and carefully explicates "the hush harbor talk of both blacks and whites" (25). Jeremiah Wright's rhetoric, subordinated to Obama's, is judged problematic in the "melancholic and fatalistic dimension to his thinking about America, which is inconsistent with his theology of hope" (25). However, Frank fails to distinguish between the millenarian modes of prophetic rhetoric and the apocalyptic power of the jeremiad; he discusses the prophetic tradition at length, but does not look toward examples like the "Appeal" or "What to the Slave is the Fourth of July?".

exposes the black subject's alienation from history; the power of the prophetic sense of apocalyptic time to resist that alienation; and its ultimate failure to affect real historical change on its own. For Sarah, the prophetic time of "When the Roll Is Called Up Yonder" may provide an alluring, even nourishing alternative to the existential emptiness of living outside of time, but it does not save her. Looking back from this point, the hopelessness and violence in the prior stories have new coherence; looking forward, the calls to action have greater urgency. The counterhistory offered by black religion, once sufficient to psychologically and culturally resist the brutalizing circumstances of bondage, has failed by Wright's estimation: the "archaic morphology of Christian salvation" only "ameliorate[s] and assuage[s] suffering and denial" ("Blueprint" 39), thereby inhibiting any real threat to the oppressive regime of white authority. The God at whom Sarah screams does not answer and instead allows her to watch as her husband is consumed by his anger.

The cry "Naw, Gawd!" reverberates throughout *Uncle Tom's Children*, as well as much of his other work. In *Black Boy*, in particular, Wright's confrontations with religion range from cynical to frustrating to terrifying. The sum total of this experience, filtered through a Marxist lens, leads him to conclude, "Wherever I found religion in my life I found strife, the attempt of one individual or group to rule another in the name of God. The naked will to power seemed always to walk in the wake of a hymn" (136). Many Wright scholars have contended that his work fails to recognize the possibilities of black religion. Most recently, James W. Coleman has argued that Wright "limit[s] the black cosmos with his own bleak view" (17). Despite occasional reference to scripture, Wright's writings "ignore the Bible's richness and complexity," and offer evidence of "his strong desire to simplify and trivialize, and to distance himself from black people and black culture," according to Coleman (22–23). Coleman's thesis applies a familiar criticism of Wright to this specific topic: by focusing on the dehumanizing consequences of Jim Crow, Coleman argues, his work denies even the possibility of a nourishing African American identity or culture.

This line of criticism reduces Wright's complicated engagement with religion to fit a few, strident statements on the topic. While he may polemically describe the South as a landscape bereft of opportunities for the actualization of the black self and may attack the "cultural barrenness of black life" in his memoir (37), *Black Boy* elsewhere delights in the richness of a childhood spent in that rural space and within that community.[6] Likewise,

---

6. Timothy Caron notes that *Black Boy* "also catalogues many of the joys and strengths

even his rejections of religion are fraught with contradictions, as Whitted has convincingly shown. For instance, Wright writes that his family "was determined to take me by the throat and lift me to a higher plane of living" (*Black Boy* 7), and he explicitly contrasts his grandmother's faith with the "throbbing life of the people in the streets" (102); in doing so, Whitted contends, he establishes that "ecclesiastical space and time seem to exist as a separate planar entity" from the "South's social realities" (65). Even if meant as a dismissal, she continues, this recognition opens up the possibility that religion might respond to African Americans' need for an alternative cultural space "during an era in which *public* space was defined racially and every seat and sidewalk was marked by the profanity of segregation."

And so, while he might rail against the religion of his grandmother, it is inaccurate to describe his engagement with religion as a *rejection* or a *dismissal*. Indeed, in "Blueprint for Negro Writing," he explicitly recognizes that, for slaves, religion constituted "a struggle for human rights," and he includes spirituals as a source of "racial wisdom" (39–40). That essay prompts the Left to look at African American folkways—including religion—not as obstacles inhibiting the mass movement of agricultural workers in the South, but rather, as the means through which such a movement might be realized. *Uncle Tom's Children* follows that blueprint closely, and in "Big Boy Leaves Home" and "Fire and Cloud," it depicts the institution of the black church as a potential vehicle for resistance.

Wright's interest in black religion extends beyond structure to ideology; Sarah's cry of "Naw, Gawd," is answered near the end of "Fire and Cloud," when the protagonist Reverend Dan Taylor triumphantly declares, "Gawd ain no lie! He ain no lie!" (220). This moment in the story proves difficult to square with Wright's atheism or assertions that his work explicitly rejects religion. This apparent contradiction, however, is reflective of the ambiguity with which *Uncle Tom's Children* treats and uses religion. The book, along with the "Blueprint," grapples with the apparent failure of African American messianism and millennialism to give rise to a mass revolutionary movement. Wright recognizes that these traditions generated revolutionary energies for slaves but characterizes them as inadequate in the face of modernity. While Negro folklore and religion "embod[y] the memories and hopes of [a] struggle for freedom. . . . How many John Henrys have lived and died on the lips of these black people?"

---

of . . . black life: the Thomas Wolfe–like lists of beautiful sights, sounds, smells, and sensations of Southern black rural life; the lyrical catalogues of black folk beliefs that he recognized as vital to African-American survival in the South; the indomitable will Wright inherited from his mother . . . " (114).

he asks (41). "How many mythical heroes in embryo have been allowed to perish for lack of husbanding by alert intelligence?" In the works from the period in which "Blueprint" and *Uncle Tom's Children* were written, Wright contends that the black Marxist intellectual could provide that "alert intelligence" and, through properly deployed Marxist analysis, direct these revolutionary energies toward meaningful resistance. *Uncle Tom's Children* seeks to do just this through fiction: to renew black faith for the context of modernity, to reawaken its "racial wisdom" of African Americans to the possibility of resistance, and to locate in the brutalized black bodies the possibility of a regenerated black subject. In that effort, Wright constructs his story cycle around a typology appropriated from Scripture.

Typology and the Apocalyptic Structure of *Uncle Tom's Children*

As John Lowe has pointed out, the typological structure of *Uncle Tom's Children* is fairly systematic (63). The reader is introduced to the timeless, pre-lapsarian paradise of the first section of "Big Boy Leaves Home": the innocence of Big Boy and his friends is violently torn away after they are seen naked by a white woman. The final version of the book concludes violently with "Bright and Morning Star," in which the activist son Johnny-Boy and his mother Sue (the protagonist) are martyred by a white lynch mob. The narrative structures of the stories, as well as the cycle itself, systemically move through a series of scriptural types: "Big Boy" is followed by the flood story in "Down by the Riverside"; "Fire and Cloud" offers the possibilities of spiritual rebirth and messianic deliverance through Rev. Dan Taylor, who is simultaneously a Moses figure (leading God's Chosen People to salvation), the pillar of fire that lit the way for Moses and the Jews, and a figuration of Christ. Twice, characters refer to the betrayal of Judas, whose betrayal of Christ is echoed by the actions of Deacon Smith in "Fire and Cloud" and Booker in "Bright and Morning Star."[7] Several conversions, akin to St. Paul's on the road to Damascus, occur throughout the text, often after characters have suffered or been victimized: the protagonists of each story are all reborn through violence and are, at least to some degree, awakened to the necessity of resistance. In the final story, Sue's martyrdom,

---

7. Perhaps not coincidentally, the *Morning Star* was the name of a steamship that Adventist missionaries used as a mobile base on the Mississippi during their campaigns to reach out to southern blacks during the 1890s and early 1900s (Bull and Lockhart 279).

a crucial element of any crusade, is inspired by her *visions*, which recall both Paul's conversion and the Revelation of St. John (a crucial point to which I will return). Though she approaches the lynch mob on the pretense of tending to her murdered son, Sue transcends the role of Virgin Mother to become both a messenger and an agent of justice.

The initial story (and most frequently anthologized) in the cycle, "Big Boy Leaves Home," functions as a sort of microcosm of the typological structure; it begins in paradise and comes to an end with Big Boy's flight to the Promised Land of the North. His escape is necessitated by the transgression of a racial taboo, when he and his four young friends, all naked from their swim, are spotted by a white woman. Prior to her appearance, the four engage in the play of young boys: they wrestle; they giggle when one offers a silly pun or passes gas; and they make crude jokes at the expense of each other's mothers. In their Edenic surroundings, even the ground seems warm and comfortable: one of the boys remarks that its "Jus lika bed" where he "could stay here forever" (18). Nonetheless, they are aware both of the danger inherent in this place and of the possibilities offered by the world beyond it. Seeing a train barreling northward and out of the reaches of Jim Crow, they begin singing "Dis Train Boun for Glory" (19), a song that conflates the deliverance promised by God in Scripture with that promised by an escape to the North.

In this nearly prelapsarian state, nakedness poses no problem for the boys, and when they reach the swimming hole, they unselfconsciously strip. Once they see the white woman Bertha, however, they "instinctively" cover "their groins" (29), reenacting Adam and Eve's sudden development of modesty. In an instant, their innocence is snuffed out by the reality of the terrifying sexual mores and paranoia wrought by Jim Crow. Their unintentional violation of racial codes leads to a confrontation with the woman's fiancé—a soldier recently returned from the Great War. Big Boy kills him in self-defense, but only after his friends Buck and Lester have been felled by the soldier. The soldier's death precipitates an eruption of white violence against the black community, which culminates in Big Boy's flight to the North and the lynching of his friend Bobo.

Just as the scene at the swimming hole recalls the expulsion from Eden in Genesis, the rendering of Big Boy's escape and the lynching contains horrifying, apocalyptic imagery and, in certain moments, very specifically draws upon the Book of Revelation. For example, Big Boy hides from the mob in an old kiln where he must fight and kill a snake and a dog. The image of a snake evokes the serpent of Genesis most immediately, but the location—a kiln—perhaps invokes the image of the pit or furnace in the ninth chapter of the Book of Revelation. Once the fifth seal is broken, John watches an angel open "the shaft of the bottomless pit, and from the shaft rose smoke like the smoke of a great furnace" (Revelation 9:2). A variety of beasts emerge from the pit, including a creature alternately described as a serpent and a dragon.

Once Big Boy defeats the snake, he faces the dog: "Green eyes glowed and drew nearer as the barking, muffled by the closeness of the hole, beat upon his eardrums" (58). The monstrous dog perhaps does not have a direct analog in Revelation, but it does recall familiar figures from antiquity—the mythic Cerberus—and from African American culture—the demonic dogs sent by overseers, slavecatchers, and posses to track fleeing black men (and most famously invoked in the Robert Johnson song "Hellhound on my Trail"). The connection between this episode and the Book of Revelation becomes only more interesting as it is explored further. The beast from the bottomless pit wreaks havoc, killing two powerful prophets. Afterwards,

> For three and a half days members of the peoples and tribes and languages and nations will gaze at their dead bodies and refuse to let them be placed in a tomb; and the inhabitants of the earth will gloat over them and celebrate and exchange presents, because these people had been a torment to the inhabitants of the earth. (Revelation 11:7–10)

John's vision of people *gloating* and *celebrating* over the corpses certainly would have rung true for anyone who grew up, as Wright did, under the omnipresent specter of lynching. "Big Boy" seems to allude to this passage: the mob sings, "*We'll hang ever nigger t our apple tree . . .*" (55). "LES GIT SOURVINEERS," one members yells, clearly invoking the act of mutilation that was part of the lynching ritual, but also echoing the Scriptural exchange of gifts (56); they playfully argue over who gets to place the noose around his neck and about the proper amount of gasoline needed to douse him.

Big Boy's observation of Bobo's lynching is dramatically and terribly incomplete. He never sees Bobo's body, and through the smoke, he can only partially see the mob. He—and thus, the reader—is removed somewhat but is still witness to the scene:

> He smelt the scent of tar, faint at first, then stronger. The wind brought it full into his face, then blew it away. His eyes burned and he rubbed them with his knuckles. He sneezed. . . . Big Boy slid back into the hole,

> his face buried in clay. He had no feelings now, no fears. He was numb, empty, as though all blood had been drawn from him. (57)

In the wake of this terrible moment, Big Boy no longer fears for his own safety. Instead, he is left dulled by an almost nihilistic inability to react or to make sense of what has transpired. And, indeed, this is the true terroristic function of lynching: not to punish a particular offender, but to terrorize all black people until they accept the subhuman condition required by the white regime of authority.

Big Boy retreats from the scene in order to protect himself from the psychic pain such identification would necessitate. In repressing this pain, however, the threat posed by the lynching to the community—not to the victim—is realized. What Big Boy experiences as numbness amounts to the destruction of any ability to articulate the meaning of the experience and, by extension, the destruction of his ability to articulate his own sense of self. It is as if something intrinsically human—fear, horror, or just anger—has been expunged from his psyche. The lynching ritual renders the African American subject abstract and unparticular; for the mob, the victim becomes a figuration of evil, transforming him into "something that represented the complete negation of humanity, . . . an alien presence, sentient, but as completely unlike white people as a fiend, . . . a 'counter-human' who could be addressed by name and yet destroyed as one would destroy all the evil that white men had ever encountered," writes Abdul JanMohammed (166). Thus, by numbing the very human response of horror, the lynching reforms Big Boy as a subject of white power, whose existence is constrained by the possibility, if not the inevitability, that his or her life will end similarly—violently and at the hand of a white person. At that moment "death has percolated into the innermost reaches of subjectivity," according to JanMohammed (2). This is a profound teleological disruption: this cataclysm offers neither deliverance nor justice. It is simply an End.

In the previous chapter, I examined how lynchings inform and are informed by the cosmology of white southern evangelical and fundamentalist Protestantism; this relationship was a paramount concern for anti-lynching activists and writers, who sought to point out the horrific hypocrisy of ostensibly Christian people committing such brutal rituals. In *Rope and Faggot*, Walter White writes that "[n]o person who is familiar with the Bible-beating, acrobatic, fanatical preachers of hell-fire in the South, and who has seen the orgies of emotion created by them, can doubt for a moment that dangerous passions are released which contribute to the emotional instability and play a part in lynching" (43). White's thesis seems to be manifest in Faulkner's horrific figuration of southern racial violence, Doc Hines. However, the critique of racial violence offered by *Light in August* is limited in an important way, as the consequences of racial violence are almost entirely restricted to the *white* community of Jefferson. The novel's ultimate concern is *their* damnation, the indelible moral stain that is the consequence of their complicity in Christmas's crimes and his death.

The representations of white violence against African Americans in *Uncle Tom's Children* do far more than damn their perpetrators: they offer the possibility of making sense of black suffering, at least provisionally, by locating these horrific experiences into a coherent historical narrative. B. Eugene McCarthy contends that *Uncle Tom's Children* is a historical document, but not in the sense of reportage or even fictionalization of historical events. Instead, Wright creates "models of past structures" that have gone unexamined and unmentioned in the historical accounts of the dominant culture (732). Conventional histories would be insufficient to accommodate the first-hand observation of friend's mutilation and death at the hands of a lynch mob; Mann's experience in "Down by the Riverside," in which he survives a catastrophic flood, only to be conscripted and ultimately gunned down by the state National Guard; or Sarah's story, in which she bears witness to her husband's death in a murderous rampage. However, these were the realities of life under Jim Crow. As awful as these scenes might be, they are given meaning in the context of the cycle. Again, "Big Boy Leaves Home" proves to be a microcosm for this structure. Indeed, the very title suggests the possibility of gaining the mobility denied by Jim Crow. Though no one could call this a happy ending, Big Boy does in fact escape northward and, thus, realizes the hope that African Americans had long embedded in the song "This Train (Is Bound for Glory)," sung innocently by Big Boy and his friends in the story's opening.

It is thus through a typological structure, moving from the expulsion from Paradise to the flight to deliverance, that "Big Boy Leaves Home" rescues the black subject from the existential dead-end that lynching would otherwise impose. This rhetorical move is hardly unique to *Uncle Tom's Children*. It is accurate, very generally, to posit African American religion as inherently typological—that is to say, that its cosmology looks toward antecedents in scripture to coherently narrativize the recent past and present. According to James H. Cone, when slaves told the story of Moses and the deliverance of Israel, they "sang of a God who was involved in history—*their* history—making right what whites had made wrong. Just as God delivered the Children of Israel from Egyptian slavery, drowning Pharaoh and his army in the Red Sea, he will also deliver black people from American slavery" (24). In other words, invocations of the flight of the Hebrews and prophesies of the Jubilee inserted the slave experience into a teleology otherwise denied it and reconfigured slaves' suffering and oppression as necessary steps in a progression toward ultimate deliverance. Cone continues: "Through the blood of slavery, [slaves] transcended the limitations of space and time. Jesus' time became their time, and they encountered a new historical existence" (54). Cone limits his analysis to the traditions of slave spirituals, but this theology clearly informs the religious traditions of African Americans well after Emancipation—and to black understanding of events that fit more conventional notions of "historical." As Albert J. Raboteau notes, "Freedmen . . . referred to Lincoln, Grant, and other Union figures as deliverers and saviors like Moses and Jesus" (102).[8]

While evident in African American religious culture, typological thinking is hardly exclusive to it. In *The Great Code*, Northrop Frye contends that the "general principle of interpretation is traditionally given as 'In the Old Testament the New Testament is concealed; in the New Testament the Old Testament is revealed'" (79); thus, the Old Testament provides a *type*, or initial model, and the New Testament provides an *antitype*, or "realized form," that fulfills the initial model. He continues, in a passage worth quoting at some length:

> Typology is a figure of speech that moves in time: the type exists in the past and the antitype in the present, or the type exists in the present and the antitype in the future. What typology really is as a mode of thought, what it both assumes and leads to, is a theory of history, or more accurately of historical process: an assumption that there is some meaning and point to history, and that sooner or later some event or events will occur which will indicate what that meaning or point is, and so become an antitype of what has happened previously. Our modern confidence in historical process, our belief that despite apparent confusion, even chaos, in human events, nevertheless those events are going somewhere and indicating something, is probably a legacy of Biblical typology: at least I can think of no other source for its tradition.

8. While, in Raboteau's estimation, the conflation of Lincoln and Moses "seems to have been an analogy and not a literal or symbolic identification" (102), the conflation of Moses and Lincoln is also a central precept of the prophetic vision articulated by Calvin Burden in *Light in August*.

Certainly, the sheer scope of Frye's attempt to systematize myth and the Bible's foundational role in Western literature leaves his work open to criticism. However, his analysis—particularly the notion that typology is a "theory of history"—illuminates the sort of apocalyptic thought with which this project is ultimately concerned. In particular, Frye contrasts *typology* with *causality*. Typological thinking, he asserts, looks for prior models to be enacted and perfected in the future, while causal thinking seeks to explain "a mass of phenomena" by systematically reaching back into the past for "prior causes" that reveal "the real meaning of the existence of the effects" (81).

Throughout *Uncle Tom's Children*, characters vacillate between typological and causal thinking. Hiding in the kiln prior to Bobo's death, Big Boy attempts to work out what has led him into this circumstance, entertaining through a number of potential cause-and-effect scenarios. He wonders whether God is punishing him for speaking ill of his friend Buck's mother; he regrets skipping class rather than doing "like Ma told im t do," but then absolves himself of responsibility and blames the school itself (49): "He wouldnt be in all this trouble now ef it wuznt for the Gawddam school!," he tells himself (49–50). He next assigns blame to the inscrutably evil white population of his town: "Gawddam them white folks! Thas all they wuz good fer, t run a nigger lika rabbit!" (51).

The appearance of the lynch mob ends in any effort to make sense of this experience. No model of causality is sufficient to account for this episode, it seems. However, the cycle provides an alternative interpretive mode in its typological structure. In Frye's formulation and in Wright's application, typological thinking can provide coherence and even meaning to events when the empirical logic of causality cannot. In this theory of history, one needs no evidence to believe that, even in the face of such evil, history is moving in an ordered manner in which the meaning of types are revealed by the manifestation of their antitypes (Frye 81).

In its forward gaze, then, apocalyptic thought can be generally described as typological. Apocalypse serves as the antitype of creation, answering the ontological differentiation (figuring as the fracturing of existence's perfection via the Fall of Man) with a restoration of divine unity. Typology is thus a form of teleology, in which history is propelled forward through type and antitype. Within the literalist hermeneutic of southern evangelical and fundamentalist Protestantism, this cosmology envisions an anthropomorphic, often angry God as the force directing history in a systematic, ordered progression toward an ultimate telos. When Faulkner's Doc Hines calls the dietician at the orphanage "the Whore of Babylon" and when

McEachern refers to the prostitute Bobbie as "Jezebel," they are not simply levying insults, but rather, deploying scriptural typology as their primary interpretive system, looking backward to previous types to explain the uncertain presences.

In these instances, typologies prove not just to be effective interpretive mechanisms, but powerful rhetorical tools. Wright cannot be placed among the faithful, but certainly he found utility in deploying these typological structures in an effort to introduce a Marxist teleology. Even in this, though, he might not have been an originator. During their initial encounters with communist ideology during the Depression—and before Wright published *Uncle Tom's Children*—many rural black southerners relied upon a "collective memory," according to Robin D. G. Kelley, evaluating its historical vision through the lens offered by black folkways and experience. Already, African Americans had adapted their narratives of deliverance to the realities of the post-Reconstruction South. "Hidden away in Southern black communities was a folk belief that the Yankees would return to wage another civil war in the South and complete the Reconstruction," writes Kelley (99). The Marxist narrative of class resistance and revolution was just as easily incorporated into these stories, and rural African Americans repositioned northern Communists and even the U.S.S.R. in the place of the Union Army. Significantly, the aging organizers Kelley interviewed and the archival texts he reviewed all articulate this vision in typological terms. "For many black radicals," Kelley writes, "the Russians were the 'new Yankees,' Stalin was the 'new Lincoln,' and the Soviet Union was a 'new Ethiopia' stretching forth her arms in defense of black folk" (100). Thus, the teleology of African American deliverance was shifted from the scale of conflict within national borders and from the traditional discourse of U.S. Constitutional rights and into an internationalist, Marxist paradigm.

While translation between communism's revolutionary promise and the long-held expectation of inevitable deliverance within black culture may have been organic in some instances, *Uncle Tom's Children* further develops this connection: first, by inserting the most terrifying experience of black life into familiar biblical types and then by revising the teleology toward which those types, by tradition, should build. Given the horrors of black life in the South, one can easily imagine a narrative of black life that ends in existential emptiness if not outright nihilism; the violent conclusions of "Down by the Riverside" and "Long Black Song" provide little reason for hope. Imagination is not necessary to access an alternative narrative of black life in which suffering is redeemed by faith alone; that is the fate of Harriet Beecher Stowe's Uncle Tom in the novel to which Wright's cycle responds. Neither option is particularly useful in the struggle to end that suffering. Just as Big Boy's traumatic experience is imbued with some hope by the possibility of deliverance northward, so too are "Down by the Riverside" and "Long Black Song" in the larger context of the cycle. Considered from this perspective, their conclusions are not ultimate and irrevocable ends, but terrifying experiences that might awaken African Americans to the necessity of active resistance. They offer the possibility of ruptures in time and of insights that should provoke action, and when read as types of experience that build toward the ends promised in the final two stories, they contain the possibility of redemption.

Revising the Teleology: The Possibility of Rupture, Revelation, and Rebirth

Like "Big Boy Leaves Home" and "Long Black Song," "Down by the Riverside" offers few obvious reasons for hope on its own. The protagonist Mann shares Silas's Jeffersonian dream of agrarian independence, as well as his fate: the dreams of wealth and patrimonial lineage are ended by the dissolutions of their families and, ultimately, their deaths at the hands of white men. Rather than fleeing the rising waters of the Mississippi, Mann chooses to remain at his home with his pregnant wife, son, and mother-in-law, hoping to gain an advantage on other farmers who might have left. This fateful decision—individually focused, capitalist in nature, evincing a faith in the yeoman fantasy—proves calamitous. Though he manages to row his family to safety in a stolen boat, his wife Lulu dies in childbirth, as does the infant. Along the way, he encounters Heartsfield, the white owner of the stolen boat; the two men exchange gunfire, and Heartsfield is killed. Mann is subsequently conscripted into the flood fight by the National Guard (echoing the real events of Greenville, Mississippi during the 1927 flood), and in a tragic twist of fate, he is sent to rescue Heartsfield's family, who ultimately turn him in to the Guardsmen following their successful rescue. Mann attempts to escape, and when cornered, begs for help from other black people around him. No assistance comes, and he is ultimately shot dead.

The story is a tragic inverse of the Noah narrative in Genesis: Mann shepherds others to safety during the deluge, but his own life and his line of progeny is effectively ended. In this awful series of trials, Mann's story comes also to resemble that of Job. Indeed, much like the Book of Job, each of the stories in *Uncle Tom's Children* requires the reader to wrestle with the incommensurability of suffering. In Robert Alter's estimation, Job offers "a revelation of the contrast between the half-jaded truths of cliché and the startling, difficult truths exposed when the stylistic and conceptual shell of cliché is broken up" (66). While these truths are indeed bleak, hope emerges from the possibility of and revelation and insight. In this mode, Apocalypse still functions to negotiate uncertainty, but not the uncertain moral status of another person. Instead, it works to explain the inexplicable—that is to say, the suffering of the innocent, the faithful, and the powerless.

Several moments of "Down by the Riverside" hint at the possibility of rupture—that is, at cataclysmic breaks in history that make possible the revelation of such difficult truths. Elsewhere, I have written about the capacity of natural disasters, including the flood in "Down by the Riverside," to expose repressed realities about both social and built structures.[9] The possibility is made evident early in the story, at the very base of the physical manifestation of Mann's agrarian dream. As he walks across the front room, Wright writes, "the half-rotten planks sagged under his feet. He had never realized they were that shaky" (62). Mann, like Silas, has avoided questioning the ideological foundations of his agrarian project. At multiple points in the story, Mann experiences more intensely uncanny ruptures in time: after fleeing the Heartsfield house and well out of earshot, he continues to hear "echoes" of the mother's and son's cries (81); when he is informed of the deaths of his wife and unborn child, a doctor tells him, "Well, boy, it's all over" (88). Later, working his way through the flooded landscape, he watches a house floating through the street. "[I]t seemed like a living thing, spinning slowly with a long, indrawn sucking noise," Wright writes, "its doors, its windows, its porch turning to the light and then going into the darkness" (106). Watching, Mann feels "himself suspending over a black void," outside of space and time (108). Finally, when he returns to the Heartsfields' home, Mann is overwhelmed by "a feeling of unreality" (114).

Perhaps the most important allusion to time in "Down by the Riverside" is also the most innocuous. In the hospital, after learning of Lulu's death, Mann becomes aware of a ticking clock. Time is passing, but it is empty time. "It seemed that he wanted ever so much to say something, to

---

9. "'They're Trying to Wash Us Away': Revisiting Faulkner's *If I Forget Thee, Jerusalem [The Wild Palms]* and Wright's 'Down by the Riverside' after the Flood," *Mississippi Quarterly* 63.3–4 (Summer–Fall 2010): 537–54.

do something," writes Wright, " but he did not know what" (89). In this regard, Mann is representative of Wright's African American subject, not simply because of the inevitably awful circumstances in which he is placed, but because he is "destitute of a theory about the structure, direction, and meaning of modern society," and thus rendered "a lost victim in a world he cannot understand or control" ("Blueprint" 45). Indeed, Mann views time spent considering his circumstance as time wasted; as he leaves the house on the stolen boat, rowing against the current, he "lower[s] his chin and determine[s] not to think," trusting in God and his own physical strength (83). For Wright, that failure to think, to move beyond the hope of divine intervention, inevitably proves fatal.

Fascinatingly, the clock Mann hears is just the first of six similar images that appear in *Uncle Tom's Children*. In each story save "Big Boy Leaves Home," clocks appear in moments in which characters face potentially transformative decisions or are offered significant insights. In "Long Black Song," for instance, the broken eight-day clock initiates the critical conversation about time. While Mann may refuse to recognize the meaning of time or find the possibility of revelation or change in its ruptures, other characters in *Uncle Tom's Children* are moved to take action in these moments.

In the penultimate story of the cycle, "Fire and Cloud," the chimes of clocks twice signal the gravity of decisions faced by the protagonist, Reverend Dan Taylor. Before he ultimately heeds these chimes, Taylor relies upon a fairly conventional, even conservative sense of time and history. He shares the Jeffersonian agrarian dreams held by Mann and Silas, and even romanticizes that hopefulness, as Sarah does. The "hopes of those early years" were once felt in "the plow handles trembling in his calloused hands," and a "surge of will, clean, full, joyful" followed in the sounds of "the earth cracking and breaking open, black, rich and damp" (160). This hopefulness, however, "crumbl[es] in his hands, right before his eyes" as the county is overtaken by drought and the plantocracy refuses to end price-fixing strategies that leaves both poor whites and blacks hungry. In Taylor's worldview, any solutions will not come from black people, who are "los in one big white fog" (157); instead, action can only be taken by "the white folks," who "done conquered *everything*." Black people might be able to convince, cajole, or even frighten white people into action, but only if God intervenes and provides some sign that will provide direction out of the fog. Absent both, Taylor is convinced of his own helplessness: "Here Ah is a man called by Gawd t preach n whut kin Ah do?" he asks (158). "Hongry folks lookin t me fer help n whut kin Ah do?"

Indeed, beseeching God to intervene is, at least initially, the only public response to the drought that Taylor seems willing to make. He offers a lengthy, apocalyptic prayer with his congregation:

"Lawd, Yuhs a rock in tha tima trouble n Yuhs a shelter in the tima storm!"

he is he is

"Lawd, Yuh said Yuhd strike down the wicked men who plagued Yo chillun!"

glory t gawd

"Yuh said Yuhd destroy this old worl n create a new Heaven n a new Earth!"

wes waitin on yuh jesus. (167)

The prayer is grounded in black religion and its millennial expectation of deliverance and salvation. Taylor does not ask for the power to act or change circumstances, but begs God to "ack in us n well obey! . . . Wes helpless at Yo feet, a-waiting fer Yo sign!" Taylor has no expectation that he or any of his congregants should act to alleviate this suffering. Instead, he falls back on a belief that God's intervention is imminent. Thus, when one of the congregants implores him, "Please, Reveren, cant yuh do *somethin?*" he quietly leaves the room (169).

For Wright (as perhaps for any committed Marxist), Taylor's choice to passively wait on God is a manifestation of the perniciously problematic consequence of religious belief; again, in his analysis, once black religion "began to ameliorate and assuage suffering and denial," it became implicated in the oppression of its believers ("Blueprint" 39). Through the choice faced by Taylor, "Fire and Cloud" dramatizes the juxtaposition of faithful waiting and committed action. Once at his home, he must confront a divided congregation, some of whom implore him to lead, while others, including the "black Judas" Deacon Smith (161), who hopes to curry favor with the white elites; a delegation from the town's white leadership, demanding that he take action to prevent a rumored march; and "the Reds," a group of Communist organizers who seek his help in organizing an integrated rally. In each private meeting, he maintains the position expressed in his public prayer, equivocating as he awaits God's guidance. Neither the town's white leadership nor the Communists accept this: the mayor and his cronies ultimately threaten his life, and the Communists make it clear that the minister nonetheless has both the ability and responsibility to act. The white organizer Hadley tells him, "Then the demonstrations going to be smashed.... *You* can stop it! You have the responsibility and the blame!" (175). Taylor, however, refuses that responsibility; he rejects any action that resembles "war" or "makes blood," and he tells them, "Gawd knows Ah ain t blame" (176).

Crucially, this is the first moment in *Uncle Tom's Children* in which a black character is not simply reacting to the awful, inevitably tragic suffering wrought by Jim Crow. Instead, Taylor is here endowed with real agency, which he initially rejects. This equivocation, couched in the terms of Christian peace and his responsibility to protect his congregation, is sharply contrasted with the impatience of his son Jimmy, who tells his father, "We jus as waal git killed fightin as t git killed doin nothin" (163). The gravity of Taylor's circumstance is once again signaled by the appearance of a clock. As Taylor moves through the home and between the various groups, who are not necessarily aware of the presence of their rivals in the house, Taylor notes his own eight-day clock, which "boomed six times; he looked and his eyes strayed up and rested on a gleaming, brass cross" (171). This is not the empty time that Sarah experiences, but rather, an instance fraught with the sort of apocalyptic, world-changing possibility implied by the symbol of Christ's sacrifice.

The transformative consequences of Christ's death and resurrection are invoked in Taylor's subsequent violent confrontation with representatives of the white power structure, who kidnap and brutally beat him. Though horrifying, this assault is not a hopeless episode of black suffering. Rather, it is the moment in the cycle in which the historical agency of the black subject is finally renewed. With each blow, something of Taylor seems to be burned away, and Wright refuses to spare the reader Taylor's pain:

> Each flick came straight on his back and left a streak of fire, a streak that merged with the last streak, making his whole back a sheet of living flame....
>
> There was a pause. Then the blows came again; the pain burned its way into his body, wave upon wave.... Each blow weakened him; each blow told him that soon he would give out. Warm blood seeped into his trousers, ran down his thighs. He felt he could not stand it any longer; he held his breath, his lungs swelling. Then he sagged, his back a leaping agony of fire; leaping as of itself, as though it were his but he could not control it any longer. The weight of his body rested on his arms; his head dropped to one side. (199)

As Taylor nears a total collapse, the sheriff mocks the preacher by demanding that he recite the Lord's Prayer between blows. Taylor stumbles on the phrase "Thy will be done," however; simply waiting on Christ's return and the restoration of God's kingdom on earth may be pointless in the face of this sort terrorism.

That is not to say that Taylor's suffering is meaningless, however. In Wright's worldview, the full confrontation with pain and suffering is a necessary step toward resistance. From it emerge the possibilities of rupture and of revelation. And indeed, Taylor is transformed by this brutal assault—not terrified as the sheriff intends, but awakened to the necessity of direct resistance. In constructing his model of the *death-bound subject*, JanMohammed suggests that an antidote to the social-death of slavery and subjection, as formulated by Orlando Patterson, and the actual death to which resistance might lead is a *symbolic death*, a painful process that begins when the subject faces "his powerless position, the genealogical isolation, his lack of control over any aspect of his present and future life" as well as his or her own complicity in that isolation (21). Then, JanMohammed writes, "the individual must destroy or effectively overcome his own formation. In short, he will have to annihilate his old self and (re)form another one" (22). Having already survived the physical trauma of his own beating, Taylor can only survive the psychic trauma by destroying the self that was complicit in the infliction of pain—the self that, despite praying the Lord's Prayer and dutifully waiting for God's will to be done here on earth, has never been delivered from evil. Once he confronts the very real possibility of his death, he gains the authority to determine the direction of his life, which had been previously circumscribed by the counterclaim posed by the threat of lynching, so evident in "Big Boy Leaves Home." Time has been ruptured, but its consequence is neither stasis nor dislocation. Instead, Taylor gains a new sense of history in which he has the agency necessary to alter its direction.

Again, the chimes of a clock mark a rupture in time. Wandering the streets and still groggy from the beating, Taylor hears "a clock striking so faintly that it seemed to be tolling in his own mind" (202); once he counts the number of strikes and determines the hour, he begins to gain his bearings and to make sense of his circumstance. Though this process begins in the conventional terms of human time and space—he ascertains the late hour, his location, and the danger posed in these combined circumstances—his effort soon moves to the plane of morality and metaphysics and into a prophetic sense of time. "Like a pillar of fire he went through the white neighborhood," writes Wright (204). "Some day theys gonna burn! Some day theys gonna burn in Gawd Awmightys fire!"

The image of the pillar here both recalls the fiery pain he endured during his beating and invokes the pillars of cloud and flame from the Book of Exodus. These manifestations of God's presence led the Hebrews through the wilderness during their flight from bondage in Egypt. However, Taylor is not a figuration of Moses in this instance, being led *toward* deliverance, but the pillar itself, preparing to lead others. Likewise, the flames are not as benign as those in Exodus, but the all-consuming, destructive flames of apocalyptic judgment. Taylor thus beseeches God, not for a sign, but for the strength to act: "Gawd, ef yuh gimme the strength Ahll tear this ol buildin down! . . . Tear it down like Samson tore the temple down!" The notion of a minister tearing down a temple is striking, as is the revelation to Taylor that follows. Learning from Jimmy that his unexplained absence after his beating has provided Deacon Smith, with the opportunity to usurp his position at the church, the fire that "seethe[s]" from him "inside and out" becomes a "fire of shame" for his failure to act earlier (206). "Seems like Gawds done left me!" he tells his Jimmy (208).

This final sense of abandonment by his God and his congregation initiates the final steps of Taylor's transition toward a collectivist cosmology that looks toward "the people" as the source of transcendence and deliverance, rather than an individual relationship with God, as evangelical Protestantism demands. "Its the *people!*" he tells his son Jimmy. "Theys the ones whut mus be real! Gawds wid the people! N the peoples gotta be real as Gawd t us!" (210). Emboldened by this new faith, Taylor fully becomes the scriptural pillar of fire—not an agent of judgment, but a sign for others to follow. He returns to the church and shares his story with the congregants: "Ah done seen the sign. . . . Ah done felt it! Its *fire!* Its like the fire that burned me last night! Its sufferin! Its hell," he tells them (218). "Gawds done sent His sign. Now its fer us to ack. . . . " The congregation erupts into song, describing the Israelites' journey out of bondage. They have not abandoned their faith; rather, they have reconfigured its messianic eschatology to announce a demand for justice in *this* world. Their (re)visionary invocation of the apocalyptic imaginary, like those of the activists chronicled by Robin D. G. Kelley, fits the particular textures of African American spiritual traditions, as does Dan Taylor's assumption of a prophetic role within a prophetic sense of time.[10] By refusing to wait,

---

10. As Houston Baker notes, "the preacher generally identifies himself as the person

by choosing to *act*, they restore themselves to a meaningful relationship to history. Critically, this embrace of a collectivist eschatology does not require them to abandon their faith. Taylor seems to caution Jimmy from wholly accepting the gospel offered by "the Reds" (210), and as he takes the first steps of his march, he thinks to himself, "Gawd ain no lie!" (220). What has emerged from Dan Taylor's experience is an entirely new cosmology, one that draws upon the revolution possibilities of both Marxism and the prophetic historical vision of African American religion.

If the original ending piece, "Fire and Cloud," offers the possibility of resistance, then Wright's addition of "Bright and Morning Star" adds a call for and recognition of the importance of sacrifice and even martyrdom—themes that are, of course, crucial to Christian theology. In the story, Wright makes the connections he seeks to draw between the eschatologies of Christian and Marxist thought explicit, if not more complicated, through Sue's changing worldview or, as she refers to them, her three *visions*. Sue's original vision is the faith in Christ she developed within the institution of her church; her two sons, both Communists, have at least attempted to awaken her class consciousness.[11] The original vision, in Wright's formulation, has clearly failed Sue and her community, helping them to cope with the trauma of their lives but nearly paralyzing them: "Long hours of scrubbing floors for a few cents a day had taught her who Jesus was, what a great boon it was to cling to Him, to be like him and suffer without a mumbling word" (224). Though her suffering is unspoken, it is still experienced, and the structures of oppression—"the white folks and their laws"—are manifest within the vision as "a cold white mountain," a figuration of authority that perhaps recalls Moses's reception of the Commandments on Mount Sinai (224). Sue understands her desire to actively challenge the mountain as "temptation, something to lure her from the Lord, a part of the world God had made in order that she might endure it and come through all the stronger," and so she attempts to put it out of her mind.

The continued psychic disruption caused by the image of the mountain, however, leaves her ripe to accept an alternative. Indeed "the new and terrible" vision of class resistance offered by her sons Sug and Johnny-Boy seems a ready-made replacement for its predecessor: "The wrongs and sufferings of black men had taken the place of Him nailed to the Cross; the

---

chosen by God to herald a fiery end of time that will come unless his listeners repent" (51).

11. Lowe contends that the activists have encouraged her to trade in the "Bright and Morning Star" of her hymnal—that is, Christ—for another star, that of the Soviet flag (59).

meager beginnings of the party had become another Resurrection; and the hate of those who would destroy her new faith had quickened in her a hunger to feel how deeply her new strength went" (225). However, the psychic residue of the former vision lingers, and Sue guiltily finds herself singing "The Lily of the Valley" as she works: "But sometimes like tonight, while lost in the forgetfulness of work, the past and the present would become mixed for her; while toiling under a strange star for a new freedom the old songs would slip from her lip with their beguiling sweetness" (226).

Wright's choice of the word "vision" to designate Sue's view of the world has a scriptural antecedent. St. Paul's conversion on the road to Damascus is couched in terms of *vision*, *sight*, and *blindness*, and the awakening of class consciousness clearly parallels the Christian notion of conversion. The term 'vision' is equally appropriate within the context of Apocalypse, as the Book of Revelation is St. John's record of a dream vision. The writer of apocalyptic narrative casts him or herself into the role of interpreter, taking on the job of organizing the vision of signs, messages, and images into a coherent narrative (Zamora, *Writing the Apocalypse* 15). Interpretation is a crucial element of Wright's vision: as he argues in *Black Boy*, the dogmatic teachings of the CPUSA failed to attend to the realities of black experience in the United States. Much as Kelley's black Alabama communists took it upon themselves to create a Marxism that spoke to their lives and their culture, Sue finds agency once she actively engages the possibility of resistance and charts her own historical vision. Operating under the principles offered by party dogma, Sue attempts to challenge the authority of the sheriff, who has come to her house, seeking Johnny-Boy:

> Hotly, something ached in her to make them feel the intensity of her pride and freedom; her heart groped to turn the bitter hours of her life into words of a kind that would make them feel that she had taken all they had done to her in her stride and could still take more. Her faith surged so strongly in her she was all but blinded. (240)

She "gropes" to turn her feelings into "words," but she cannot; she believes she sees the world as it truly is, but she is blinded. This vision offered by party organizers has failed her by further obscuring the truth.

Once she has been betrayed by the Judas figure, Booker, Sue recognizes a final vision, in which she finds "focus" (253) and "the strength to live and act" (252). This third vision is initiated as Sue returns to the hymn "The Lily of the Valley":

... Mired she was between two abandoned worlds, living but dying without the strength of the grace that either gave. The clearer she felt it the fuller did something well up from the depths of her for release; the more urgent did she feel the need to fling into her black sky another star, another hope, one more terrible vision to give her the strength to act and live. (252)

Though Sue is emboldened by her second vision—that offered by the Communist Party—it is a limited epistemology, inadequate to represent the particularities of African American experience. Johnny-Boy "believes so hard hes blind," Sue thinks, and he himself claims not to see race but only class (234). Sue's agency comes at the moment in which she recognizes that her resistance does not necessitate the complete abandonment of her culture and her community. The attempt to do so is impossible, in fact, and leaves one "mired" between the two. Instead, Sue gains agency once she begins to *interpret* these visions and to use them both toward a single end.

Although Wright remains our ultimate apocalyptist, Sue is the collection's final interpreter of the signs of the times. Just as she finds a space to integrate the ideological material of both visions, Wright continues to adapt the Christian myth: Sue is at once a figuration of God, the Blessed Virgin, and Christ. In the context of the story, however, her sacrifice—after she shoots Booker—allows her to define the meaning and consequences of her own suffering and death. According to Lowe, Wright subverts the threat of the ritual violence against African Americans by locating the wounded and maimed bodies as the "generative ground for the new 'word' [i.e., Gospel] of Communism" (59). It is not a by-the-book communism that shapes the form of Wright's cycle, however. Through the intertextual exchange between the secular historical vision of the Left and the sacred historical vision of the apocalyptic imaginary, Wright's narrative renews the black subject by restoring it to a meaningful teleology. This self is made whole, at least provisionally, by redirecting it toward a telos that exists outside the reaches of the regimes of white authority.

The story, and the cycle, ends with Sue staring up at the stars above "the doomed living and the dead that never dies" (263). The *doom* the living face might be a lynching yet to come, but it is just as easily and logically the course that the institutions of race and class—not fate or God—have determined for them. "Blueprint for Negro Writing" provides useful context for this final line and, specifically, for Wright's notion of *doom:* "at the moment when a people begin to realize a *meaning* in their suffering, the civilization that engenders that suffering is doomed" ("Blueprint" 41). *Doom*, it seems, need not have the horrific connotation which we normally ascribe to it—and which it seems to have in *Light in August*. Indeed, from the doom of Apocalypse emerges a renewed world. When Sue joins the resurrected victim of "Between the World and Me" and countless other brutalized and murdered African Americans as part of "the dead that never dies," their deaths are to be relived by others. Their spirits, however, need not haunt the survivors. Instead, they might spur them to action and to find a meaning in their doom.

Conclusion: Writing New Endings

In addition to rarely considering *Uncle Tom's Children*, the long scholarly project of reconciling Wright's often contradictory statements, presentations, and uses of black religion often fails to account for a crucial biographical fact: for much of his childhood, Wright did not attend a conventional black congregation, but rather, his grandmother's Seventh-day Adventist church. This transracial denomination had very few black members in Mississippi during his childhood.[12] While his grandmother's congregation was most certainly an African American one, affiliation with the Adventists would have isolated the young Wright from the majority of his peers and perhaps removed him from some of the spiritual sustenance of more conventional black congregations. Historian Holly Fisher specifically contrasts the social conservatism of Adventist belief with the liberation theology of African American religion (113). Though the Adventists preached racial equality, the church envisioned it as an equality before God rather than men. Thus, while the Adventist Church reached out to African Americans in the South, their Michigan-based leadership did little to encourage the integration of congregations or church leadership in the region. And, like those of many other white fundamentalist Protestant groups, the Adventist eschatology did not encourage worldly involvement or political activism, as Calvin Rock, a current African American leader in the Seventh-day Adventist Church notes: "Certainty that the world would end any day or hour made serious plans for change unrealistic" (57).

---

12. According to Calvin Rock, the Seventh Adventist Church counted just 3,500 black members in all of North America in 1918, when Wright was ten years old (21). This membership was concentrated in urban areas of the Northeast (Bull and Lockhart 278).

Despite his frustration with its precepts, Wright's worldview shares something important in common with the Adventist faith. According to Malcolm Bull and Keith Lockhart, Seventh-day Adventism positions its members as separate and apart from any nation, including the United States. Furthermore, its prophetic vision imagines "America [as] the ultimate eschatological adversary." For the early Adventists, "Not only was the world about to end, but America . . . was actually a diabolical monster bent on the destruction of the saints" (246). Their prophetic belief holds that American will be "toppled" through divine intervention (248). As Delbert W. Baker notes, early Adventist leader James White (the husband of Adventist founder and prophetess Ellen G. White) even argued in 1862 that the institution of slavery was yet another sign that the United States was doomed (130).

Despite such statements, the Adventist belief in the imminent return of Christ and its inclination against political involvement did little to facilitate the realization of this revolutionary vision[13]—a point at which the materialist historical vision of *Uncle Tom's Children* departs. Nonetheless, one cannot help but speculate how intimate experience with this specific eschatology informed Wright's broader interpretations of other prophetic visions, including that of black religious culture. Indeed, while they might condemn the actions of the United States, black writers like Frederick Douglass and Martin Luther King, Jr., still offered variations of the American jeremiad and called for a national, democratic renewal. If Wright's cosmology rejects anything, then, it is not religion, as Coleman suggests, but the possibility that black people could be delivered by the political institutions of the United States of America.

Furthermore, Wright's experience with the Adventist Church would have almost certainly have required him to take a comparative approach to the very notion of Apocalypse and even the narrative function of endings. In his youth, he likely would have had direct engagement with the unique eschatology of Seventh-day Adventism, the millennial hope of African American religion, the civil religion of the Lost Cause espoused by so many white Mississippians, the millenarian nationalism of the U.S., and the revolutionary eschatology offered by communism. Ultimately, Wright would adhere to none of these; his body of work reveals an evolution in

---

13. Baker cites Ellen G. White's 1908 pronouncement that "We are not to be in haste to define the exact course to be pursued in the future regarding the relation to be maintained between white and Colored people. . . . Men may advance theories, but I assure you that it will not do for us to follow human theories" (130).

eschatological and apocalyptic thinking, moving away from the prophetic visions offered African American faiths and by communism in favor of a narrative drive toward the chaotic collapse of a modernist and existentialist end of meaning. The engagement with the southern apocalyptic imaginary in *Uncle Tom's Children* still exists in the aesthetic of later works—in the blighted apocalyptic or even post-apocalyptic urban landscapes of later existentialist works like *The Outsider* and *Savage Holiday*, in which words and actions alike seem increasingly meaningless and through which protagonists march toward their inevitable dooms. However, *Uncle Tom's Children* fascinates, not simply because it is a step in the development of the aesthetic of later works, and not because the cosmological and ideological foundation of this aesthetic is so evident in this nascent stage. Instead, the prophetic vision of this early work is worth study because its use of those elements is so powerful and the attempt to negotiate the contradictions between them in order to create a revolutionary historical vision of black liberation is so effective. In *Uncle Tom's Children*, the Apocalypse is suddenly and violently not what the audience expects—though, like other apocalyptic visions, it remains both a cause for alarm and for rejoicing, for fearful repentance and resolute action.

Indeed, the revision of Apocalypse is perhaps the most subtly subversive move any writer can make. According to Lois Parkinson Zamora, "Apocalyptic narrative moves toward an *ending* that contains a particular attitude toward the goals of the narration, and toward an *end* that implies an ideology" (*Writing the Apocalypse* 12). While the telos toward which the apocalyptic narratives of *Uncle Tom's Children* drive is unquestionably different from that envisioned by African American religious tradition, neither the aim nor the result of his engagement with the apocalyptic imaginary differs greatly from those of the churchgoers he depicts. Writing on the eschatology of African American music, Gilroy observes that "by posing the world as it is against the world as the racially subordinated would like it to be, this musical culture supplies a great deal of the courage required to go on living in the present" (36). The revision of ends is not limited to contemporary writers but rather is a crucial element of the African American apocalyptic imaginary. Gilroy describes African American millennialism as representative of a "politics of fulfillment," which he defines as "the notion that a future society will be able to realise the social and political promise that the present society has left unaccomplished" (37). This discourse provides "a medium in which demands for goals like non-racialised justice and rational organisation of the productive process can be expressed." The same can be said for the apocalyptic imaginary.

Certainly, it allows us to revise and rewrite our endings and, thus, to direct events and experiences toward a new telos. Moreover, it is discursive space open to possibilities denied by conventional systems of meaning, as I will show in the next chapters.

Part II

3

"Some Say Ain't No Earthly Explanation"

Excavating the Apocalyptic Landscape of Randall Kenan's Tims Creek

> And I feel Old Earth a-shuddering—
> And I see the graves a-bursting—
> And I hear a sound,
> A blood-chilling sound.
> What sound is that I hear?
> It's the clicking together of the dry bones,
> Bone to bone—the dry bones.
> And I see coming out of the bursting graves,
> And marching up from the valley of death,
> The army of the dead.
>
> And the living and the dead in the twinkling of an eye
> Are caught up in the middle of the air,
> Before God's judgment bar.
>   —James Weldon Johnson, "The Judgment Day"

THROUGHOUT this book, I have argued that expressions of a southern "sense of place," aiming for something just short of prophesy, are inextricably bound up with the apocalyptic world view offered by southern religion. "[A]n overdeveloped eschatological sense is one of the more enduring characteristics of the southern literary tradition," writes Scott Romine. Citing exchanges between Allen Tate and Robert Penn Warren, Romine states, "the southerness of place, it seems, is always in danger of expiring" (26). In other words, the South, in its most frequent manifestations, is brought to life out of the fear of its own inevitable disappearance. This brand of Apocalypse promises both the End of Time and the End of this

World; as the events of history finally play themselves out, the geographies in which they take place are ultimately used up.

In the novel *A Visitation of Spirits* as well as in the subsequent short story collection *Let the Dead Bury Their Dead and Other Stories*, Randall Kenan assumes the eschatological burdens of southern literature some sixty years after the Agrarians took their stand. *A Visitation* is framed on one end by a section entitled "ADVENT: or the Beginning of the End," which laments the increasing infrequency of hogkillings—events that once transcended agricultural necessity, fulfilled the ritual function of sacrifice, and culminated in a communal feast. The frame is closed by "A Requiem for Tobacco," Kenan's mythic elegy for the shared labor around which the collective identities of communities like his fictional Tims Creek once coalesced. While Tate, Ransom, Warren, and the rest would perhaps have joined in Kenan's memorialization (albeit, from a safe, segregated distance), they would likely have rejected what is contained within this frame[1]: the story of sixteen-year-old Horace Cross, struggling to understand how his queer desire can exist within the geography of his southern African American community.

Facing the incongruity of his existence within the cultural and social spaces of family, church, and the rural community of Tims Creek, North Carolina, Horace seeks escape in the unlimited, unseen geography of the southern apocalyptic imaginary. By conjuring this invisible, otherworldly realm into the existence of *this* world, Horace threatens to initiate a cataclysm that will realize in an explosive instant what was envisioned by the Agrarians as a slow, regrettable decline. Kenan's novel, like Faulkner's *Light in August*, juxtaposes the creeping expiration of a community with the possibility of violent eruption within it. While *A Visitation of Spirits* laments the loss of traditional forms of community, mourning alone is an insuffi-

---

1. Or at least kept quiet. Homosexuality should be anathema to the Agrarian platform; as Gary Richards writes, "there seems to have been little legitimate place for same-sex desire in the Christian South imagined by Agrarians," given the biblical injunctions against sodomy and the patriarchal society idealized by their platform (216). However, in an autobiographical essay about his time as a tenant and employee of the aging Agrarian John Lytle, John Jeremiah Sullivan effectively outs the author—and perhaps the entire movement. Sullivan writes that, by the time he boarded and worked for Lytle in the 1990s, the author's queerness was "more or less an open secret" in the community around Sewanee (95). Sullivan describes Lytle's efforts to seduce him, summarizes Lytle's stories of being propositioned by Allen Tate, and cites the old writer's frequent contention that "the idea of there having been a homoerotic side to the Agrarian movement itself." Sullivan continues, noting "Robert Penn Warren's more-than-platonic interest in Tate" and reminding the readers that the "rarely mentioned" Agrarian Stark Young was openly gay.

cient response to the novel's central event—Horace's suicide. Rather, his death is an opportunity for exhortation: Horace's trials and ultimate death disrupt the romantic, idealizing veil of grief, reveal the original sins that have doomed the community, and expose the horrific consequences that will follow the continuing refusal to tell that history. The southern apocalyptic imaginary provides Kenan with the narrative and discursive space adequate for experiences that disrupt the bivalent, heteronormative ways of speaking that dominate his community. From the apocalyptic imaginary, revelation about this southern and black past can proceed.

A *Visitation of Spirits* eschews a conventionally sequential chronology. Instead, it explores the causes and consequences of Horace's death by shifting between the dates of his vision and death, April 29–30, 1984, and the journey of three surviving family members—his grandfather, Zeke Cross; his great-aunt, Ruth Cross; and his cousin, Rev. James "Jimmy" Greene—to visit a dying cousin over a year later, on December 8, 1985. While these sections are located temporally with great specificity, they are separated by Jimmy's chronologically dislocated first person "Confessions." Despite the precise chronological markers, the text moves fluidly: the Crosses slip in and out of time, consistently returning to the family and the community's history in order to make sense of what they witness and what they have experienced, thus producing deep spatial and temporal maps of their landscape. The result is a work of magical realism[2] that elides any easy distinction between communal myth, familial legacy, historical fact, and individual hallucination.

This chapter will examine the role of the apocalyptic imaginary in Kenan's Cross/Tims Creek narratives—A *Visitation of Spirits* and the short

2. *Magical* (or, *marvelous*) *realism* has been most often associated with Latin American writers; indeed, Terry McMillan has famously called Kenan "our black Marquez" (Betts 17). According to the *Oxford Companion to English Literature*, works of magical realism "have, typically, a strong narrative drive, in which the recognizably realistic merges with the unexpected and the inexplicable and in which elements of dreams, fairy story, or mythology combine with the everyday, often in a mosaic or kaleidoscopic pattern of refraction and recurrence." The aims of magical realism are closely associated with the revelatory aspects of the apocalyptic as I have outlined them. Lois Parkinson Zamora notes, magical realism's primary concern is "the nature and limits of the knowable" ("Magical Romance/Magical Realism" 498), which it often explores by flaunting the limitations of conventional representations of reality. As Alejo Carpentier writes, "The marvelous begins to be unmistakably marvelous when it arises from an unexpected alteration of reality (the miracle), from a privileged revelation of reality, an unaccustomed insight that is singularly favored by the unexpected richness of reality, or an amplification of the scale and categories of reality perceived with particular intensity by virtue of an exaltation of the spirit that leads it to a kind of extreme state" ("On the Marvelous Real in America" 85–86).

story "Let the Dead Bury Their Dead"—with particular attention to how apocalypse functions to contain and conceal histories that would trouble the stability of family and community. Unbounded by the laws of time and chronology, these works expose the contradictions implicit in the southern and the African American imaginaries. Throughout both, the voices of millennial victory, so central to black spirituality, are tragically confounded by the rhetoric of apocalyptic condemnation: while a coherent, narrowly defined sense of collective identity has allowed this community to survive and even thrive, despite the oppressive forces upon it, a refusal to change now threatens to doom its members. However, Kenan abandons neither place nor the apocalyptic imaginary. Instead, his work interrogates the complicated ethical implications of eschatological elements of place, and it takes manifestations of Apocalypse as discursive markers of concealed historical knowledge. Ultimately, Kenan's jeremiad offers hope and suggests that, through the revelation and recovery of the past, expiring communities can be reinvigorated and an affirmative claim to a legacy of triumph in the face of oppression.

Tims Creek and the Eschatology of Place

Not unlike Lena Grove's entrance and departure in *Light in August*, the frame of mourning in *A Visitation of Spirits* locates and contains the cataclysmic energy that threatens to overwhelm the novel. It also establishes *place*—the practices and regular rhythms of human interaction and exchange that occur in Tims Creek—and introduces its eschatological quality, even before the apocalyptic madness begin. Barbara Ladd understands the "sense of place" as a contradictory "sense of stability amid flux" ("Dismantling the Monolith" 46); in this definition, stability should be neither privileged above flux nor confused with stasis or stagnation. Movement can occur within stable patterns, and indeed, the regular reoccurrence of events—sunrises and sunsets, the phases of the moons, tides, birthdays, holidays, and even hogkillings and tobacco harvests—allow us to make sense of the otherwise infinitesimal passage of time. Thus, this opening frame is filled with seasonal and temporal images: the "winter rye grass that just begun to peek from the stiff earth"; the barbeque pit is "a hole as deep and wide as a grave" (*A Visitation* 7).

Critically, these seasonal/temporal images, along with the description of the seasonal ritual of the hogkilling, are not offered by any individual character but rather by a collective voice, which addresses the reader directly and intimately. The hogkilling functions as a rite of passage for the adolescent male, who is allowed to pull the trigger and kill the animal for the first time. He becomes an adult; the community welcomes a new member, and with him, the ascendance of a new generation, who will continue their mission. Within this ritual, the members of the community easily assume their roles, determined by age and gender, almost as if by instinct. Of course, it is not instinct but rather the process of acculturation that informs the passing of the gun from an old man to the boy. However, the collective knowledge of the process and its origins are repressed—pushed back into the unconscious until the ritual becomes an ontological certainty. Here (as elsewhere) *flux* is rejected as an element of place; the community craves stability, both at its center and along its margins.

In *The Production of Space*, Henri Lefebvre investigates this impulse toward stability. He contends that "the material conditions of individual and collective activity" are the foundational elements of human relation to place, preceding any and all systematic efforts to establish and maintain a coherent sense of that place (71). In Lefebvre's estimation, the secondary abstraction of a place as a singular and stable entity "represses the reality of human labor" (289). Wesley A. Kort surmises that Lefebvre worries that "such constructed wholes" can be mobilized as "a surrogate reality, an agent that particular and economic interests can employ in order to validate themselves" (177). Kenan's concern about the problematic of place echoes Lefebvre's worries. In the opening frame and the concluding "The Requiem for Tobacco," Kenan does not mourn shifts in agricultural practice, but rather the gradual expiration of social relationships that developed through these practices, as well as the community's subsequent failure to adequately adapt them or develop new forms of community in their place. At the moment described by the narrator, gatherings like the hogkilling are increasingly infrequent: why go through with it—why even raise hogs—when, as Kenan writes, "folks . . . go to the A&P for their sausages, to the Winn Dixie for their liver pudding, to the Food Lion for their cured ham" (9)? An older generation clings to traditions that seem antiquated, and reject the possibility that their traditions might evolve to address new circumstances. They demand stasis beyond the passing of one generation to the next, and they fail to recognize the distinction between the particular tasks of work and its beneficial social consequence. As a consequence rituals, along with its sense of collective identity and mutual obligation, simply fade away.

However, Kenan's work does not reject *place* as a wholly negative construct. In this regard, his approach to place has less in common with

Lefebvre's than with Kort's: rather than narrating place as stable entities, configured around issues of inclusion and exclusion, Kort formulates places "as repositories of meaning" and "sites of social relationships" (196). The contradictory elements of place, at once restricting and empowering, is evident in Kenan's description of the community as "bound by this strange activity"—i.e., the harvesting of tobacco (*A Visitation* 257). "Bound" consolidates the contradictions of place into a single verb. Certainly, the word calls up the collective strength of solidarity and the value of obligation; here, it also calls up *boundaries*, the problematic processes of inclusion and exclusion necessary to configure the community as a coherent entity. The ritual of the gun and the shared experience of farming tobacco provide milestones that, in part, designate full membership into the community. However, the material conditions and historical exigencies under which these rituals emerged have been concealed by the "constructed whole" of place: they now are enacted simply to maintain the community as it exists in memory and to distinguish its members from the rest of the world. Because the result—the binds of community—is never dissociated from the action that fosters it, place seems to drawing to an inevitable end, rather than a transformative moment. This view of place is limited, however, because it fails to account for the legacies of survival, mutual obligation, and collective triumph that are equally a part of the community and its rituals. In order to restore the nourishing possibilities of place and community, Kenan's work suggests, the genealogies of rituals like the hogkilling must be investigated and the meaning concealed by the "constructed wholes" of place must be reclaimed.

Kenan's fiction recognizes the difficulty of this task. *A Visitation of Spirits* makes plain the appeal and power of a stable sense of place, particularly for the members of the Cross family. Their ancestral patriarch Thomas Cross established the village's most significant institution, the First Baptist Church, where Horace's grandfather, Ezekiel (or Zeke), wields great authority as the eldest member of the deacon board, and his cousin Jimmy is the new pastor. For Zeke in particular, Tims Creek is an empowering place, where he has access to much of what Jim Crow sought to deny. He has acquired an expansive farm and maintains a generational lineage generally unimpeded by the white world. In this small universe, he has the incredible authority offered by what he believes to be a totalizing knowledge of its geography: at one point, he assumes that he can identify the customers at the local gas station in a given moment by simply surveying the cars out front (46). In the story "Let the Dead Bury the Dead," Kenan further develops the town's history through Jimmy's uncompleted ethnography. His research investigates the town's development, beginning with a maroon community of escaped slaves who established a permanent, stable existence and were able during Reconstruction to officially lay claim to their own town. As such, the legacy of Tims Creek—and thus, the legacy asserted by Zeke—offers a powerful oppositional black subject position. While the southern place-narrative of the plantation (manifest in *A Visitation* via the production of an inane plantation musical, *Ride the Freedom Star*, for which Horace serves as a stagehand) elides the efforts of maroon communities and self-contained African American communities to map their experiences onto the geographies of the South, the black-owned places of Tims Creek, the Cross farm, and the First Baptist Church provide the social spaces in which histories of black expression and black life can be articulated.

This sense of exceptionalism is something of a tautological construction: the Crosses have a special status *because* they exercise the rights and authority of (white) men, and because they exercise these rights and authority, they have proof of their special status. Jimmy, for instance, views both Horace and himself as specifically chosen to continue that exceptional mission—as destined to bear their burdens and achieve the successes of Tims Creek and the Cross family. His ministry at the First Baptist Church, specifically, becomes a birthright—not something to which he is necessarily entitled but an achievement that realizes his great-great-grandfather Ezra Cross's "dream that one of his own progeny would stand before the altar as His, and his, minister" (*A Visitation* 115). The fulfillment of this "familial, dynastic hope" establishes the Crosses as "worthy," according to Jimmy, and thus eradicates the emasculating, vitality-sapping shame of slavery and Jim Crow.

However, something has gone wrong—something so awful that it leads Jimmy to frame the contemporary struggles of the black community as an apocalyptic attrition of a generation. "Why are we sick and dying now?" he asks in the confession that follows the earring episode. "All the sons and daughters groomed to lead seem to have fled. . . . How, Lord? How? The war is not over" (188). Jimmy alone seems cognizant of this crisis; his confessions articulate a prophetic vision of the dissolution of the structures of community and family. Though Jimmy struggles to determine the cause of this problem, the novel offers a clear diagnosis through Horace's struggle: the best of his generation has left in order to *survive*. The community rejects difference within its boundaries[3]; anyone who does not fit

---

3. Zeke, in particular, is representative of this worldview, which imagines "Tims Creek

within its strictly bivalent epistemology leaves or, like Horace, risks their sanity.

While the discursive regulation, concealment, and even expiation of difference in Tims Creek shares much with the collective response to ambiguity in *Light in August*, Zeke is no Doc Hines, and Tims Creek contains no Percy Grimm. Despite the difference in time, both Tims Creek and Jefferson are threatened by undifferentiation and ambiguity, inasmuch as such presences demand a confrontation with the essential instability and permeability of both the boundaries of community and the bivalent categories that configure those boundaries. While the white residents of Faulkner's Yoknapatawpha violently maintain these collective boundaries to ensure their individual positions (as white) within the racial order, the maintenance of the boundaries of community has historically been practiced as a means of collective self-preservation against white oppression by the African American residents of Tims Creek. Thus the instability in Tims Creeks is perhaps more ethically vexing, particularly for an outsider to this culture.

Such questions of identity and self-preservation are posed by the family's reaction to the earring Horace wears to Thanksgiving dinner. The scene itself, rendered as drama rather than prose, seems on its face to be a fairly conventional intergenerational family squabble, indistinct from thousands of other conversations adolescents have had with their elders over earrings, long hair, fashion, or make-up. However, this particular argument is notable as it marks the convergence of two discourses that are often ruthlessly and unfortunately kept distinct: race and gender. The earring registers first as a contravention of gender norms, and Horace's great-aunt Jonnie Mae states the piercing makes him look "[l]ike some little girl. Like one of them perverts" (184). However, Horace's transgression of racial divisions becomes the dominant theme of the evening. Ultimately, Zeke forbids his grandson from associating with his new white friends with whom Horace got the piercing as a sign of solidarity. "But they're my friends," he protests, "But they're different. They aren't from around here" (186). Here, Horace implies that, by virtue of their northern and western backgrounds, his friends exist outside the divisions that define the southern places and histories that the Crosses inhabit. Responding almost as a chorus, his aunts

---

and the Cross family as impermeable spaces with established racial and gender borders" despite the inevitable appearance of the "uncanniness of difference," according to Lindsey Tucker (315).

immediately restore the binary divisions destabilized by Horace's assertion of undifferentiation:

RACHEL: They're white, ain't they?
HORACE: Yeah, but—
REBECCA: You black, ain't you?
HORACE: But they don't—
RUTHESTER: He's just foolish. He just don't understand.

Specifically, what he does not understand, according to his aunt Rebecca, is "all the white man's done to us." When Horace reacts by proclaiming his disapproving family members "bigots," Jonnie Mae sternly rebukes him with by narrating the history of bigotry she and the generations before him have faced: "Do you have any idea how many white men have called me girl and aunt? Out of disrespect? Out of hatefulness? How many white men called your late Uncle Malachi—God rest him—boy and uncle?" (187).

Like the ultimate confrontation between Horace and Jimmy, this episode is presented in Jimmy's Confession as a dramatic exchange, complete with stage directions. There is no mediation and no comment on the confrontation until it is over and Jimmy's narration resumes. The reader is left alone to observe and to sit as a judge weighing the merits of the various positions. Given both Horace's position as the protagonist and the dramatically ironic knowledge of his homosexuality, the reader is perhaps inclined to sympathize with Horace. However, Jonnie Mae's conclusion of the dispute reminds the reader (and Horace) of the stakes of African American solidarity at moments in which lynching might be the consequence of a violation of the boundaries of race. Indeed, the Crosses, along with the community of Tims Creek, have thrived precisely because they have sought to distance themselves from white people as much as possible and to strictly regulate necessary or unavoidable moments of contact. While they have been relatively successful in their efforts to create a black-controlled space, that space is itself ultimately restrictive. Once the regulation of difference was a matter of self-preservation; now, it is necessary to preserve their senses of themselves. The Crosses can neither brook ambiguity along the margins of their community nor tolerate any threat to the purity and stability of its center—that is, to the patriarchal legacy that designates Horace as "[s]omebody who's gone make us proud," as Jonnie Mae says (187) and as "a son of the community, more than most," in Jimmy's words (188). And while Jonnie Mae's rebuke responds to Horace's violation of racial boundaries, it is articulated as a reinforcement of gender roles: among the worst crimes of white oppression, she makes clear, were the restrictions levied upon her ability to express her femininity and the emasculation of the now-dead Malachi.[4]

Thus, in counteracting the marginalizing power of white domination, the Crosses have constructed their family and their community as unified wholes, complete with collective boundaries that distinguish them from an imagined Other and keep them separate from the evil it poses. Like nearly all forms of apocalypticism, this is a radically bivalent view, imagining existence in terms of an ongoing conflict between a chosen few and those who oppress them. This eschatology is both patriarchal and messianic, in which past suffering and sacrifice are redeemed by the ultimate victory of the community, perpetuated and led by its male heir. While the solidarity fostered by this eschatological vision was perhaps necessary in the face of Jim Crow, the ongoing reproduction of a stable collective identity—particularly one centered on a patriarchal lineage—"denies or represses the heterogeneity of social difference," according to Iris Marion Young. "It denies the difference among those who understand themselves as belonging to the same group; it reduces the members of the group to a set of common attributes" (335). In particular, the production of a stable black identity often fails to account for the presence of homosexuality: "Men who love men and women who love women disrupt this system along many axes," she writes, but not simply because they challenge a Levitical injunction. Rather, she contends, "the need to make homosexuality invisible is at least as much existential and ontological as it is moral" (335–36); in order to survive, communities have demanded a rigid sameness, which severely limits the potential for empowerment and political movement that the group identity offers by denying someone like Horace full access to its sustaining power.

---

4. As Albert Raboteau notes, the spiritual nourishment offered by the black church was bound up with the exercise of gendered citizenship rights from the earliest moments. He cites Bishop Daniel Alexander Payne of the African Methodist Episcopal (A.M.E.) Church's assessment that slaves "'found freedom of thought, freedom of speech, freedom of action, freedom for the development of a true Christian manhood.' Significantly, Payne and other black clergymen linked 'True Christian manhood' with the exercise of freedoms that sound suspiciously like civil and political rights. The ineluctable tendency of the black evangelical ethos was in the direction of asserting 'manhood' rights, which were understood as a vital form of self-governance" (94). This notion of masculinity and citizenship strikingly—and troublingly—converges with the conflation of citizenship and rape that informs the discourse of lynching as it is modeled by Robyn Wiegman.

Apocalypse as Alternative Discursive Space

The Crosses' brand of black millennialism, it seems, imagines victory specifically as the establishment of a new patriarchal order and a generation legacy. Its terms, then, are ineluctably heteronormative, leaving Horace in a difficult position: reject his most intimate self, or abandon all that has sustained him. Horace's struggle to determine how he can exist within this place—how he can lay claim to this empowering but limited collective identity—leads him away from the narratives of millennial victory and to Apocalypse—that is, to the discursive space, within an otherwise bivalent worldview, through which he can articulate the experiences of ambiguity and undifferentiation. Well before he conjures a demonic vision, he imagines Tims Creek as fraught with apocalyptic signs and images. Contemplating the "transformation" he hopes will provide an escape, Horace imagines the land, "the soybean fields surrounding his grandfather's house, the woods that surrounded the fields, the tall, massive long-leaf pines. . . . He thought of the sky, not a blue picture-book sky with a few thin clouds, but a storm sky, black and mean, full of wind and hate, God's wrath, thunder, pelting rain" (14). This image is not just Horace's: after his death, the narrator offers a winter sky that is "white-grey and desolate, stretched like the hand of God, high and wide" (45). Horace's interest in the quantitative, methodological engagement with nature offered in his science courses does not suspend his belief "in an unseen world full of archangels and prophets and folk rising from the dead, a world preached to him from the cradle on, and a world he was powerless not to believe in as firmly as he believed in gravity and times tables" (16).

While the denizens of this world might be invisible, their existence is integrated into the maps of community constructed in memory and narrative. Thus, abstract concepts like evil and judgment are tangible and projected onto people and place. In the discussions of older men in barbershops and the fields, "the evils of the world had been put before [Horace], solidly and plainly," and located in the figure of "the white man" (89). And it is not just residents who formulate the landscape in this manner. In his confession, Jimmy recalls his expatriated siblings begging him to "Leave North Carolina. Get out. As if it were on fire. As if, like Sodom or Gomorrah, the Almighty would at any moment rain down fire to punish the wicked for all the evil done on Southern soil" (35). An apocalyptic sense of place is evident in even ostensibly secular narratives of the region: according to his brother Franklin, Jimmy has been "brainwashed and pussywhipped" into joining his wife Anne, a "high-minded, high-yalla, rich, militant-talking Northern girl," on the frontlines of a delusional holy war for social justice in "the big bad, bloody South" (35). Horace's visions thus amount to more than a hallucinatory conjuring of the "unseen world of archangels in prophets" into visibility; the visitations of the past make apparent all of the overdetermined associations of judgment and cataclysm layered upon imaginary landscapes of southern places. In the various articulations of Horace's sexuality, the convergent nature of *evil* and *ambiguity* is painfully apparent. He is variously "possessed of . . . a wicked spirit" (28); an "aberration"; sick and "diseased" (160); and even "curse[d]," "doomed to hellfire and damnation" by the desire he cannot escape (101). Even Horace's masturbatory fantasies end with a "thunder[ing]" deity: "this God bellowed in his head when the need arose and Horace had conjured up the pornographic images he had seen of women and men in unholy congress." Again, Horace does not conjure these images out of a vacuum but rather appropriates them from the apocalyptic discourse of difference specific to his environment.

Horace confronts the apocalyptic elements of place via the vision initiated by his entry into the church. Here, Horace is visited by (or perhaps visits, depending on one's reading) the memory of Rev. Barden's sermon on Romans I and the biblical injunction against homosexuality. Barden uses the scriptural language of pollution and uncleanness; moreover, he recites a familiar argument by locating the source of the pollution *outside* of his community in the fallen culture of the modern world threatening them via mass media (here, an afternoon talk show). The sermon constructs Tims Creek as isolated, culturally and temporally, but Barden counters any argument that would position him "behind the times": "Brothers and sisters, there is no time but now, and I am telling you: It's unclean" (79). The sermon amounts to a rhetorical display of purity and unity via a refutation of the ambiguity posited by homosexuality and to a call for steadfast, absolute maintenance of the borders—cultural, spatial, and temporal—that preserve the coherence of the community. "See, the soul is a valuable thing," Barden tells the congregation. "And it's our responsibility to keep it up, like a house. . . . You got to lock the door when you go to bed at night or you might find somebody there when you wake up that you didn't leave there when you went to sleep" (80). Barden ascribes cosmic significance to the maintenance of these boundaries and applies the discourse of sin to delineate the margins of community. However, it is vision fraught with cosmological contradiction, as it seeks to both claim the community of the church as the source of divinely ordained stability amid the earthly chaos and situate this same community on the precipice of a cataclysmic dissolution. The result is a collective paranoia—a demand for the obsessive maintenance of boundaries via the individual display of purity.[5]

In the vision he experiences in the church, Horace is both horrified and thrilled by the cataclysmic consequences of the disruption of community: the scimitar-wielding demon demands that Horace kill Barden. When he fails to do so, the demon takes matters into his own hands, beheading the pastor and, thus, unleashing the possibility of cataclysm. The floor rumbles, and the baptismal font below explodes "as if it were alive—like a wave, sending splintered wood, chairs, lamps, Bibles, plants, tatters of carpet, and hymnals in a moist conflagration, wet fire, into the air" (83). The threat to community posed by Horace, it seems, is so complete that the church—its central physical structure—cannot withstand his presence. However, the church does not collapse; instead, the focus of the cataclysmic inertia is redirected, as it inevitably is, back upon Horace. Barden reappears, head on shoulders, to lead a baptism—Horace's. And though he wants to accept the redemptive waters, he fears that he will "fall, crack his skull on the cold concrete and turn the purifying water to scarlet," thus polluting the holy, healing water (84). After he relents, he stands at the front of the church, haunted by the realization that he cannot take his inherited place there and "overwhelmed" by the desire to be like his grandfather and the knowledge that he never will. The parishioners hurl homophobic invectives at him until he flees—out of the church doors and back into the world of "unholy elves and imps and griffins and werewolves and pale-faced phantoms" (87).

Though he does not know it, he becomes like Zeke in this very desire. Just as he does, his grandfather and his cousin are both troubled by their perceived failures to live up to the legacy of the Cross men. In his youth, Zeke imitated his father, "his way of standing, his talk, his talk," but, "in the end, he didn't grow up to be more like him . . . and that was a hard thing for him to settle to square with himself, for in a strange way he was

---

5. Barden's sermon engages the same preacherly tradition assumed by Rev. Dan Taylor in Wright's "Fire and Cloud." Houston A. Baker, Jr., writes that while "God was generally viewed as the exclusive agent of the apocalypse" in spirituals and hymns, in sermons, the black preacher "generally identifies himself as the person chosen by God to herald a fiery end of time that will come unless his listeners repent" (*Long Black Song* 51). However, the ends to which Barden deploys the rhetoric of apocalyptic prophesy have more in common with those of Faulkner's Doc Hines: rather than leading his community toward social change or offering hope of deliverance, Barden uses Apocalypse to stabilize the racialized, gendered boundaries of community.

glad" (53). While Zeke imagines Horace as "foreign to me," this is hardly an anomaly within the Cross lineage; the stability of community and patriarchy, it seems, is tenuous at best. Consequently, they must be actively maintained through a variety of strategies including the imitation of the previous generation; rites of passage, such as depicted in the hogkilling; and, indeed, by the election of individuals, like Jimmy and Horace, to the status of "Chosen Nigger." Rather than confronting the challenge Horace's behavior and ultimate suicide pose to the patrimonial narrative, Zeke locates his grandson as "foreign," discursively exiling him from the space of family and expiating the existential threat that his difference poses. Indeed, he is all but absent from Zeke's internal monologue and is never mentioned during the conversations in the car. The script of abjection is thus enacted in order to preserve the coherence of Zeke's "surrogate reality." Though Horace's homosexuality poses a seemingly insurmountable contradiction to his familial legacy, his suicide ironically enacts the sacrificial associations invoked by their last name and links him to Faulkner's Joe Christmas, another source of collective existential angst. In death, both Horace and Joe are removed from the communal bodies that their existences so trouble. Consequently, Zeke can retrospectively exile his grandson to the margins of family and community and designate him as "foreign." In Tims Creek, as in Jefferson, the center, at least rhetorically, holds steady once the threat is removed.

Of course, the distinctions between center and margin affirmed by Zeke are destabilized for the reader who, unlike the old man, is privy to Horace's dissolution. Unfortunately, Horace imagines these boundaries of community and family as no more permeable or dynamic than his grandfather does. Instead, he internalizes the incongruity and locates himself as the source of instability. Kenan seems to take Eudora Welty's counsel to writers—to be careful to locate characters within places, lest they "fly to pieces"—not as a warning but rather as a road map for Horace's descent into incoherence, which parallels the dissolution of Joe Christmas (122). In fact, the multitude of demonic voices visited upon him, as well as his own visitations to the past, are indicative of the dissolution of Horace as a unified self that moves sequentially through time and space. Rather than challenge the location of his queer desire outside the boundaries of community, he seeks to conjure the "unseen world" of archangels and demons of this plane into visibility, hoping that coherence will be possible in this seemingly limitless supernatural possibility of this realm. So powerful is the hold of this "surrogate reality" and so entrenched are the boundaries of community that Horace attempts to escape into a fantastic, unseen world that is freed from the inviolable laws of physics, rather than questioning the instability of the structuring narratives of this realm. Social or communal change is far more implausible, in Horace's view, than his transformation into a hawk. He imagines this bird of prey and its hunt of a rabbit in explicitly apocalyptic terms:

> Talons would clutch the thrashing critter tighter than a vise, its little heart would beat in sixteenth notes, excited even more by the flapping wings that beat the air like hammers and blocked the sun like Armageddon. Then the piercing of the neck, the rush of hot, sticky blood. The taste of red flesh. He felt a touch of empathy for the small mammal, its tail caught in the violent twitching of death thralls, but he was still thrilled. (*A Visitation* 15)

While Horace's fantasy begins by identifying with the predatory, his focus moves in short order onto the prey, and his own feelings of incoherence are displaced onto the torn flesh of the rabbit. The fantastic existence of the bird is "thrilling," not just in this displaced violence but also because, he imagines, it offers the possibility of sailing above the terrain, "unfettered, unbound and free" and without having to leave. Indeed, he chooses a red-tailed hawk because it is indigenous to North Carolina (14). Even in fantasy, Horace cleaves to his grandfather's farm and to the community that has granted him chosen status; he even believes he will be reunited with his family at the Rapture, the moment at which the faithful will bodily ascend to heaven (22). In the next world, he imagines, the contradictions and confusion that plague him in his human form will simply melt away.

The apocalyptic elements of Horace's visitations only become more specific and more elaborate. As he stands on the football field, for instance, another denizen of the unseen world comes into view, who is described as "a manlike figure, dark, clad in what appeared to be thick, black robes, wearing a silver helmet and armed with a gleaming scimitar" (165). As he watches him, the voices he hears begin to speak:

> *For behold, the day cometh, that shall scorch as an oven;* whispering whispers, *and all the proud, yea, and all that do wickedly, shall be stubble,* Come, come. Horace, afraid to do otherwise, stepped forward slowly. Come. The voices whispered whispering, *But unto you that fear shall the Sun of righteousness arise with healing in his wings,* whispered, whisperings, whispered, Come.

The words the voice speaks are from scripture. Specifically, they are from Malachi 4:1–2, the final chapter of the final book of the Christian Old Testament, and they offer a prophecy of the coming of the Messiah. The nature of the figure in front of him is not clear: is it a demon? An angel? Christ himself? The text offers little illumination, and perhaps, it is of no consequence. The vision is quickly broken up by the appearance of several white teens who see that Horace is armed and naked and come after him. Believing himself to be in cosmic battle, Horace runs and then opens fire. If the "day cometh," Horace must fight for its healing promise.

The possibility that Horace might maintain coherence—albeit, in non-human form—is quickly ended. During the course of the April night, his alienation from place becomes so complete that he does indeed "fly into pieces," losing himself amid the voices of the demons and in the memories that leap up from the terrain. After he conjures the demons, Horace moves across the Tims Creek landscape and becomes dislocated from time and place in a manner not unlike Joe following the fire at the Burden place in *Light in August*. While Faulkner shifts his narrative perspective away from Joe before he finally falls to pieces, Kenan allows the reader to experience Horace's descent into incoherence. The conventionally-perceptible landscape of Tims Creek fades into the background as the heretofore unseen geographies of the apocalyptic imaginary increasingly dominate the landscape. These images loom larger and larger, increasingly dominating the space through which Horace moves until they ultimately overtake him completely.

This process of dissolution culminates in a confrontation with a grotesquely costumed doppelgänger he finds in a mirror at the Crosstown Theatre, the site of the previous summer's "lavish" production of *Ride the Freedom Star* (213). The play is an inept epic historical musical written, produced, and funded by the last scion of the white Cross family, Philip Owen Cross; its comically banal version of the region's plantation past offers more in the way of elaborate fireworks and sumptuous costuming than historical accuracy. Crucially, this specifically antebellum southern narrative is situated as *national:* it draws upon the rhetoric and iconography of the Revolution and early Republic, recasts the plantocracy as the Founding Fathers, and disconnects the word "freedom" from the African American experience. Though far from view, Horace's work as a stagehand is the closest *Ride the Freedom Star* comes to incorporating the presence of *black* Crosses. The play's black characters fail to transcend the familiar stereotypes, eliciting the white audience's laughter with their buffoonery and inspiring awe with the "raw and dynamic singing" of black spirituals and faith through a minister's sermon, "which was the most passionate, hell-raising moment in the play" (214).

Nonetheless, Horace's experience with *Ride the Freedom Star* is empowering as it offers his first exposure to the possibility of a community open to the expression of queer desire. The cast features eleven "young, ambitious" professionals brought in to perform the lead roles, many of whom are gay (215), including both Horace's lover Antonio and the object of his desire, the bourgeois African American co-star, Everett Church Harrington IV. While the members of the troupe openly express their desire, it is a desire that seems, at best, vacuous and fleeting and offers none of the transformative, healing possibilities Horace seeks. The emancipatory possibilities offered by the troupe are further tempered by their work on stage, which seeks to reinscribe the plantation myth as the region's singular historical and sociospatial narrative, thus silencing the story of the black Crosses. The script is so crass, however, that it only serves to empower Horace by reminding him of both the difficulty and the success his family has faced to maintain their story. "Damn, you know, I never put two and two together. That's *your* fucking family too, isn't it?" Antonio asks Horace, assuming that he must be seething with anger (224). That is hardly the case: "It's funny. I'm kind of proud, too. You know. Not about the slavery stuff, but to know where we've gotten, you know?" The legacy of the black Crosses is an enormous source of strength for the adolescent, and he seeks to insert himself into its narrative as "the next generation," the Chosen Nigger: "You know, I often think of how I'm going to make my family proud of me." Antonio's amused response—"Look out world. Superfag is on the move"—disgusts Horace, and he rejects the attempt to locate him as "fag," as he did with his first lover, Gideon. The confines of the Cross patriarchy offer no space for queer desire, it seems.

On the night of Horace's death, these memories loom up from the Theatre. Ultimately, they yield the stage of Horace's consciousness to his doppelgänger who is costumed as a clown, "white-faced" and applying the make-up of black face (220). In the figure of the doppelgänger, who offers and then demands that Horace put on his make-up, Kenan conjures all of the overdetermined associations of minstrelsy and elides any easy distinction between the silencing of the black claim to place and the silencing of Horace's queer desire by the narrative through which that claim is made.[6] Though Horace cannot transcend the heteronormative boundar-

---

6. Minstrelsy evokes a wide-raging "antinomy of responses," according to Eric Lott, including a "disdain . . . for the incorporation of black culture fashioned to racist uses" as

ies of the Cross legacy, this visitation nonetheless embodies the normally abstracted and fragmented creation of cultural and discursive borders in a single matrix of marginalization and cultural amnesia. Moreover, the consolidation of this matrix in the doppelgänger suggests the necessity of an individual's complicity with their own silence. Thus, Horace's rejection of the possibility of queer desire is no less a masking than the educated, bourgeois Everett Church Harrington IV's performance as a buffoonish slave in service of the play's "conflagration of counterfeit glory" (211).

When the phantasm finally speaks, it offers the tube of make-up as a "way" out and an escape from the demons that embody Horace's queer desire. The rejection of the doppelgänger falls short of an affirmation of self; rather, it is the ultimate and traumatic dissolution of Horace as a unified subject. The result of this dissolution, presented earlier in the dramatic confrontation with Jimmy, is Horace's disappearance into a persona of the demon, which claims to be in possession of his physical form. In his final attempts to resist this possession, Horace invokes the hope of Apocalypse: *"Where will it end? Will it end?"* he asks. Here, he begins the chain of apocalyptic associations by imagining an end to the narrative of his own existence: a grave, and its promise "[n]o more, no more ghosts, no more sin, no more, no more" (231). This conclusion is the specifically personal End of death, not the world-shaking End of cataclysm, and it is articulated only after he forgoes the possibility of individual transformation, either through the supernatural metamorphosis into something nonhuman or the expression of queer desire. His dismissal of possibility of escape through conjure is preceded almost immediately by the visitation of the memory of the cast's drunken, drug-fueled orgy in the cemetery the prior summer. Frustrated by his inability to confess his love to Harrington (or ECH IV, as he is known), Horace follows his lover Antonio to the graveyard where the orgy develops almost organically. The experience is hardly transformative; in fact, it is not even a positive. Instead, it is rendered in unmistakably supernatural, even wicked terms—"like witches in a coven" (230)—and is fraught with the "strange inevitability" that is characteristic of Apocalypse. However, Horace is removed from the moment, observing "as a true scientist—clinical, clean, objective." His assessment: the moment is empty, existing as almost a last recourse for the participants who lack an appropriate space to express their desire; they therefore conjure the moment "in

---

well as "a celebration of an authentic people's culture, the dissemination of black arts with potentially liberating results" (17). See also Robert C. Toll, *Blacking Up: The Minstrel Show in Nineteenth-Century America*.

lonely inarticulateness." Despite the language of sorcery, the orgy is "not the otherworldly event he knew it should be," Kenan writes. "The moon did not change color or phase, lightning did not flash, the earth did not quake, the sun did not rise. They were left only tired and stoned and dirty and smelly and empty" (230–31). The orgy announces a subversive claim to space, boldly refusing the location of their desire outside margins of gender and community by violating those boundaries—indeed, enacting that desire in extreme—in a public space. However, for Horace the orgy amounts to little more than this. It fails to offer the human intimacy of family and community from which his desire threatens to exile him; it fails to end, transform, or reveal anything.

What sort of transformation does Horace anticipate? A personal one, an awakening of a queer self that will be unconcerned with all that pains him, that will be able to leave behind the old realm of Tims Creek for the new world offered by the troupe? Or a transformation of the space he inhabits via a cataclysm which would end that world that cannot contain him and create a new realm in which the contradictions between the various subject positions he occupies would simply be erased? Regardless, in the wake of the failure of the transformation to come, it is those boundaries transgressed by his desire that seem unshakable and impervious to the efforts of the orgy to collapse them. Horace is thus only more certain in the location of the instability in himself, and he thus envisions his removal from those boundaries as the only solution. Physical exile, however, is insufficient; indeed, the possibility that Horace might simply leave Tims Creek is never mentioned. Even elsewhere, he remains located within the narrative of familial legacy as the "next generation" of Cross.

Horace does not imagine his death as a sacrifice necessary to maintain that order but rather as the only available escape. His invocation of various apocalyptic narratives marks a final attempt to find solace in the traditional African American faith so crucial to the Cross identity, and delineates Horace's loss of faith when the apocalyptic salvation it promises fails to materialize. While that narrative's hold upon his family and himself remains intractable, Horace recognizes that its failure for him is not unique but rather symptomatic of the African American experience. The narrative is broken up by the apocalyptic assertions of African American hymnology—*God showed Noah the Rainbow Sign . . . Said it won't be water, but fire next time*—that are never realized.[7] "[T]he gods have new names

---

7. Fire, of course, is a central trope of apocalyptic, evoking the torment of hellfire, as well as the possibilities of purification, renewal, and sexual passion. Thus far, this project

and sit high and look low, but never reach down" (233). Despite the promises, "there is no Pentecost, no Ascension, no Passover," Horace eventually comes to believe (233); cataclysm is not a matter of God's imminent judgment but rather is a threat posed by "men breath[ing] hateful fumes and . . . try[ing] to unleash God's own sun." Horace's vision moves from his own memories to images from the collective traumatic memories of African American people, "[w]omen and children big-eyed and big-bellied, no food" (234), people without "voices" to articulate and counteract their oppression, with neither the possibility of purifying rains and fire from above nor a savior on their horizon. The only End that Horace can initiate is to end his own life, and so he does.

The Possibility of Revelation: Excavating Apocalypse

A Visitation of Spirits concludes on April 30, 1984, at 7:05 A.M.—immediately after Horace's death. The narrator inhabits the perspectives of none of the Crosses but a detached, observant story-teller who ultimately rejects any effort to determine the reality of Horace's possession. Such concerns are "irrelevant" (253), the narrator tells us, in the face of the unquestionable reality of Horace's pain and death, which are alternately rendered clinically and awfully. "Most importantly," the narrator says of the night's events,

> the day did not halt in its tracks: clocks did not stop. The school buses rolled. The cows mooed. The mothers scolded their children. Plows broke up soil. Trucks were unloaded and loaded up. Dishes were washed. Dogs barked. Old men fished. Beauticians gossiped. Food was eaten. And that night the sun set with the full intention of rising on the morrow. (254)

---

has documented the ritual burnings of lynchings in Wright's "Big Boy Leaves Home"; the "pillar of fire" which Rev. Dan Taylor becomes in "Fire and Cloud"; the "roman barbeque" at the Burden place in *Light in August*; and Bone's fiery fantasies of nascent sexual desire and retribution in *Bastard Out of Carolina*. Here, Kenan calls up both the African American spiritual "God Gave Noah the Rainbow Sign"—a central expression of black apocalyptic spirituality—as well as James Baldwin's succinct 1963 examination of U.S. racial politics, *The Fire Next Time*, which drew its title from this song. Indeed, Kenan's most recent work, *The Fire This Time* (Hoboken: Melville House, 2007) is a twenty-first-century response to the Baldwin text.

In other words, the Apocalypse does not come. What, then, are we to make of Kenan's engagement with Apocalypse? Does A *Visitation of Spirits* amount to a refutation of the formative faith traditions of Kenan's youth as, at best, offering false hope, and, at worst, agents of oppression? In its plea for the necessity of remembering, the "Requiem for Tobacco" suggests otherwise. The consequence of Horace's death is the destabilization of the absolute boundaries of community and its patriarchal center. Kenan implores the reader to remember the actual practices, obligations, and responsibilities that constituted the *binds of community* rather than the narrative of patriarchy and patrimony that narrated the *boundaries of communities*.

It is, however, insufficient simply to memorialize these binds. Rather, Kenan suggests that it is necessary to excavate them—to dig up the past and bring what has been concealed into the light and what has been silenced into speaking. This, in fact, is how Jimmy responds to Horace's death in Kenan's revisitation and reexamination of the Cross narrative in the titular story of his subsequent collection, *Let the Dead Bury Their Dead and Other Stores*. The story is an elaborate and playful exploration of genre, presented in the form of an ethnography composed by Jimmy from research conducted during graduate work toward a degree in history at the University of North Carolina and published after his death in a car accident in 1998 (Kenan's story was published in 1993). The story includes a foreword from fictional anthropologist Reginald Gregory Kain, who both shares the author's initials and is a member of the faculty at Sarah Lawrence College, where Kenan taught at the time of the story's publication. Setting oral and archival histories alongside one another, the text moves between the unmediated transcript of Zeke's account (including the various interruptions of a skeptical aunt Ruth) of the maroon origins of Tims Creek as "Snatchit" and later "Tearshirt"; the narrative counterpoint offered by the cotemporaneous diary of Rebecca Cross, the nineteenth-century matriarch of the white branch of the family, and the letters of her son, Phineas; and finally, Jimmy's own meditations on his place within the family. All save the latter contain voluminous footnotes, referencing actual and fictional historical and anthropological research.

Derided by Ruth as merely a "haint" story and as a bunch of lies, Zeke's tale begins at a specific site—a curious mound, according to Jimmy's footnote, located six miles outside of Tims Creek—and moves outward, spatially and temporally, to narrate the creation of the community and the beginning of its evolution from a maroon community of escaped slaves into an organized municipality. Central to the story is the conflict between the legacy of its founder, the runaway slave and conjurer Pharaoh, and the subsequent leadership of his successor, a Christian Preacher of gargantuan gastronomic and sexual appetites. Despite its generic trickery, "Let the Dead Bury the Dead" is perhaps best described as a parable—one that prompts the reader to consider the powerful histories of African and African American resistance that have been silenced by dominant historical discourses and necessarily forgotten by the descendants of slaves as they seek to engage in those discourses.

As Jimmy comments in a footnote, "Not enough has yet been written about maroon activity in the southern states" (283); indeed, research of marronage has almost entirely focused on the Caribbean. Herbert Aptheker, one of Jimmy's sources, conducted the pioneering studies on U.S. maroon communities beginning in the late 1930s. Maroon communities, writes Aptheker, were a "seriously annoying" and "ever-present feature of antebellum southern life," providing "havens for fugitives" and "bases for marauding expeditions against nearby plantations" and even "supplying the nucleus of leadership for planned uprisings" (151). In his groundbreaking 1939 article "Maroons Within the Present Limits of the United States," Aptheker suggests at least fifty distinct maroon communities existed in the U.S. South between 1674–1864. Of these, a community in the Dismal Swamp of Virginia and North Carolina seems to have been the most "settled," complete with homes and successful agricultural efforts. "It seems likely that about two thousand Negroes, fugitives, or the descendants of fugitives, lived in this area," Aptheker writes. "They carried on regular, if illegal, trade with white people living on the borders of the swamp" (152). Indeed, the swamp provided Harriet Beecher Stowe with the setting for the follow-up to *Uncle Tom's Cabin*, the maroon novel *Dred: A Tale of the Great Dismal Swamp*.

In its explicit concern with contradiction, and specifically, with what has been concealed by dominant historical discourses and what other forms might yet reveal, Kenan's faux-ethnography proves to be the ideal text to demonstrate the apocalyptic model I have sought to develop. Multigeneric and polyphonic, the many voices evident in the text—the nineteenth-century white Crosses, the editor Kaine, Zeke, Ruth, and Jimmy himself as both an ethnographer in the footnotes and as a member of the community in the reflective components—allow Kenan to contrast not just the variances among individual interpretations of experiences but also the limits and boundaries of conventional historical narrative. For instance, several of Kaine's additional footnotes effectively contradict Zeke's story: "There is no documentation of a town or community named Tearshirt in any state or federal files or records" (304 n17). Yet, in every other way, Jimmy's work supports its existence; his own footnotes frequently point to the incomplete nature of the historical record, and his recovery of Rebecca Cross's diary and Phineas Cross's letters operate to fill in those gaps through the conventional methodologies of an archival historian.

In fact, the story of Tims Creek's maroon origins is made all the more powerful by its persistence in the face of documentary evidence; its vitality is suggestive of the possibilities, even necessities, of different sorts of knowledge in order to come to grips with the appearance of contradiction. Barbara Webb argues that the novels of Caribbean writers like Alejo Carpentier and Wilson Harris explore the figure of the maroon and maroon communities "in order to bring the repressed knowledge of the past into historical consciousness" (58). Kenan employs marronage similarly: dominant racial and historical discourses sought to silence narratives of U.S. marronage almost immediately, as the very existence of such communities, as Aptheker shows, posed a dangerous threat to the white plantocracy and to narratives of racial inferiority. Aptheker was not careless with his words when he described marronage as a "feature of antebellum Southern life" (151), for runaways and maroon communities existed as *an aspect of*, rather than as *an alternative to*, the plantation system. In Richard Price's words, maroon communities were "a ubiquitous presence" in and "a chronic plague" on New World plantation life, which served to make the possibility of black resistance "embarrassingly visible" (2).

A century later, Zeke Cross's story serves to challenge the officially sanctioned brand of history and its repression of African American resistance. The narratives of dynastic republican glory and enlightened patriarchal mastery upon which Philip Quincy Cross bases the play *Ride the Freedom Star* fall apart when confronted with the existence of a self-sufficient maroon community. These communities have been ignored by the historical record, and their existence has even been denied in order to maintain the surrogate realities that map such geographies as spaces of white domination. The boundaries of the plantation, static and hermetically sealed in the play's romantic imagination of moonlight and magnolias, are so destabilized by the knowledge of the interaction and exchange between the plantations and Tearshirt that they ultimately dissolve away. Indeed, while the concealed maroon community exists on the geography of the plantation, it would be free from the structures which produce it as the locus of black oppression.

However, the contradictions posed to dominant historical narratives by marronage are not the only such opposition being worked out in "Let the Dead Bury Their Dead": Jimmy's ethnography works also to uncover the repression of the Africanist elements of slave culture. While it is clear in *A Visitation* that Zeke's identity is inexorably bound up with both the moral vision of his Christian faith and the institution of his church, this story engages the conjure traditions of African cosmologies and African American folk religion. Pharaoh is presented as conjure man endowed with various otherworldly abilities, and his proselytization of traditional African religious practice is positively characterized. Upon his death, Pharaoh is buried with an unknown book, access to which he expressly forbids prior to his demise. The mysterious Preacher arrives to fill the absence of leadership. Calling Pharaoh's teachings "the sure way to hell and damnation" (319), he demands absolute adherence to the Christian gospel and an immediate disavowal of all Africanist elements of the community. The relative harmony that coincided with Pharaoh's holistic spirituality almost immediately dissolves into chaos: three young girls and two boys lose their minds and are ultimately killed, either at their own hand or by the townspeople. Each child, Zeke believes, had been sexually abused by the Preacher. Finally, the Preacher demands that Pharaoh be exhumed and the secrets of the book—perhaps, he tells the townspeople, a map to treasure—be revealed. This act results in the resurrection of the town's dead, who have returned to life to exact retribution upon their kinsfolk and neighbors. The Preacher appears to lead the living dead against the town, but he is beheaded by the returned Pharaoh, who declares, "Damnation and ruin. What began as good has ended in evil. We are not ready" (332). Pharaoh takes a baby, whom the Preacher had earlier captured, and leaves; following his departure, "fire rained down from the sky, just like Sodom and Gomorrah and none of the wicked escaped . . . ," Zeke tells Jimmy. "When it died down, wont nothing left. Nothing. Just that mound you asked about, smoking hot."

Zeke's story is prompted by Jimmy's (unrepresented) inquiry as to the origins of the mound near Tims Creek. As the tale's central chronotope,[8] the mound serves as the physical feature of landscape upon which the spatial and temporal maps of the community most obviously overlap. Just as important, however, is Pharaoh's book, which signifies the lacuna within both the oral and textual histories of African Americans. The story itself

---

8. The most succinct English definition of *chronotope*, famously formulated by Bakhtin in the essay "Forms of Time and Chronotope in the Novel," can be found in Michael Holquist's and Caryl Emerson's glossary in their translation: "A unit of analysis for studying texts according to the ratio and nature of the temporal and spatial categories represented. . . . The chronotope is an optic for reading texts as x-rays of the forces at work in the culture system from which they spring" (Glossary to *The Dialogic Imagination*, 426).

articulates this lack, but it fails to preserve what is lost; consequently, the book exists only as a present absence. This absence is so central to the community's collective identity that the possession of the text is a source of immense authority: once the Preacher has sole control of the narrative of the past, he can control the past and even activate it *against* the community. If we consider this ethnographic record alongside *A Visitation*, it seems that Jimmy is prompted by Horace's death to investigate the origins of the collective narrative in which his cousin Horace could not exist. The parable here poses two central questions: what has been erected to fill the place of the absent text, and is its preservation worth the cost of continued forgetting? The first question is relatively easy: the contents of the text, along with the structures of utopian community preached by Pharaoh, have been replaced by a narrative of patrimonial legacy, which both resists and mirrors the very white history that seeks to silence it—the history narrated in the *Ride the Freedom Star*. That history contains some of the same absences, as Jimmy learns from the unrestrained queer desire expressed in the letters of his white nineteenth-century cousin Phineas Cross.

The second question might be more difficult to answer. In a footnote, Jimmy Greene cites various speculations into the book's origin: "an Arabic version of the Koran," a Carthaginian text "stolen from the library at Timbuktu," the text of a Zoroastrian creation myths, "a book of spells, the Book of Life, the Book of the Dead," and even "a time-travel device." But his speculations focus on a single hypothesis: that the book is "a transliteration from the one of the traditional Yoruba *oral* libraries" into either English or "an approximation of the Yoruba tongue," an act that amounts to blasphemy in the oral traditional of Yoruba culture (287n6). Regardless of which, if any, might be true, the text nonetheless signifies an absence—the gaping hole left by knowledge of an African past that is no longer accessible within African American culture. In the introduction to the collection *Maroon Societies*, Price argues against the notion that maroon cultures were structured around a common "collective memory" of a pan-African past (26). Such models elide the particularities of African cultures as well as the "nascent but already powerful plantation-forged" African American culture. Instead, Price presents the Africanist presence in maroon cultures as a matter of rhetorical and ideological commitment. Rejecting the notion that slave and maroon cultures "mechanistically" developed as a "mosaic" of strands of European culture with some common, base-line African culture that organically and unselfconsciously adapted to the necessities of New World life, Price posits "commitment to 'things African'" (27) and to a "'home-land' ideology" (28) as the means by which maroons negotiated the diversity of African cultural practices. Thus, this commitment was "the cement" that allowed it all to cohere. While the various social practices that characterize marronage necessarily included Western forms of knowledge and the experience of slaves, runaways, and freed persons of color within various New World cultures, this commitment to Africa configured the unmapped geographies of the maroon community as a space in which black suffering could be articulated.

Despite what Price calls "commitment to 'things African,'" the particularities of African experience were inevitably lost; according to Webb, "even among maroons, knowledge of an African past is, at best, incomplete" (55). In the production of a grand new syncretic culture, which allowed these groups to survive and even thrive, something was inevitably lost: while many particular elements of African American cultures have traceable African origins, "no maroon social, political, religious or aesthetic *system* can be reliably traced to a specific tribal provenience," writes Price (29). Interestingly, he further argues that, generally, the cultures furthest removed from "the vital African past" often display the most "tenacious fidelity" to the *idea* of an African past. While Price is unwilling to specifically locate the phenomenon of marronage "along a continuum of forms of resistance" (23), the "fidelity" of this ideological commitment is unequivocally, if not quantifiably, a resistant act.

In Wesley Kort's sociospatial terms, the maroon community functions as a "repositor[y] of meaning" (196) that Kenan, like Glissant and Wilson, seeks to recover. However, the exact forms of the social relationships that generate this meaning are not accessible or perhaps even knowable by the conventional methodologies of an archival historian. That does not mean that, even when concealed, these forms of knowledge are not useful. In Kenan's story, the maroon origin of Tims Creek affirms its latent but still accessible emancipatory legacy and offers the possibility of alternative cultural forms and systems of knowledge that would threaten the oppressive and repressive production of southern spaces and places. The recognition of maroon culture destabilizes the borders of the plantation as the governing spatial construct of a static narrative of southern history that would silence both the victories and suffering of African Americans. Likewise, it requires that African Americans consider the stability of their own collective and communal boundaries by prompting reconsiderations of the ontology of their own culture and revisitations of the experiences that they too have ignored. The discourse of marronage provides a model for syncretism and for the negotiation of cultural difference.

Though *A Visitation* and "Let the Dead Bury Their Dead" are two separate works, it is useful to consider them together. In this context, we discover that Horace is the lacuna in Jimmy's ethnography—the absent presence to which Zeke and Ruth pointedly do not refer. Snatchit and Tearshirt are perhaps logical destinations in Jimmy's attempt to wrestle with the death of the boy he describes as having "been created by this society" and "a son of the community, more than most" (*A Vistation* 188). Scott Tucker notes that "maroon societies were, like the constructions of gender and race . . . , a function of the hegemonic institutions that seemingly excluded them" (314). They were also spaces within which difference had to be negotiated, as neither exile nor scapegoating would be possible under such circumstances. Unfixed on any map and unrecorded by the documents of history, maroon communities function as the repository of historical contradiction for Kenan and, thus, are the apocalyptic space *par excellence*. Just as Zeke's story does for Jimmy, Kenan's writings implore us to revisit the past and demand that we confront the inherent instability of the locations of center and margin, not so that we might bring place to an end but rather so that we might open it up to those who have been denied its nourishment and to those whose claims to it have been silenced. Again, Apocalypse becomes the site for our explanation, a signal of deferral, of trauma, and of productive instability. The unmistakably apocalyptic nature of Zeke's story—the dead rise to mete out justice upon their kin—is appropriate in the context of a maroon community. As Paul Gilroy writes, "creolisation, métissage, metizaje, and hybridity" constitute "a litany of pollution and impurity" (2)—imminent concerns of the apocalyptic, as we have seen. However, Gilroy formulates *pollution* as a threat to the hegemonic position of dominant narratives of history. While Zeke's tale certainly destabilizes the official narrative of regional history, the story cannot be considered an attempt to regulate or conceal a threat to the plantation narrative; it is, after all, an *African American text* that is transmitted orally within an *African American community*. The impurity that it seeks to regulate, then, must constitute a threat to the *African American* historical narrative of Tims Creek. Its maroon genealogy destabilizes a collective identity bound up with the institutions of church and patriarchal order: the possibility of hybridity troubles the ontology of a homogenous blackness and its component rigid black masculinity, which has been imagined as the only available avenue of survival in the face of oppression. Once again, Apocalypse signals a site in need of excavation. Despite the terrific ending to Zeke's story, the community of Tearshirt does not end in a bang, or even a whimper, but rather persists as Tims Creek and in Zeke's story. Likewise, Horace's death in *A Visitation* does not bring about the cataclysms of which they dream. Once again, even when the End does not come, the apocalyptic imaginary remains the culturally specific space in which undifferentiation and uncertainty might be confronted.

The Uses of the Past

By painstakingly excavating the consequences of those boundaries that are not readily accessible, Kenan begins to work through the contradictory possibility of place in fiction and in public discourse. This is difficult work: as a gay black man writing the story of a gay black teenager, Kenan seems nothing if not the consolidation of the sort of radical social change that the sense of place, when formulated as a desire for stability instead of flux, can be mobilized to lament and even reject (Ladd, "Dismantling the Monolith" 52). As such, the sense of place in southern literature would ostensibly seem to have little to offer either Kenan or Horace. And yet, Kenan can make no move more subversive than claiming place as the matrix through which he can articulate an empowering subject position.[9] The implications of affirming Horace's homosexual identity *in* Tims Creek, rather than exiling him from it, are far more radical than moving him anywhere else.[10]

9. McRuer suggests as much in taking exception with Henry Louis Gates, Jr., over the novel. In a 1991 interview, Gates told Charles Rowell that he hoped Kenan would "take Horace to the big city in his next novel"—that is, to one of the urban centers historically more amenable to the expression of homosexual identities and, indeed, in which gay men have claimed their own spaces in neighborhoods such as New York's Greenwich Village or the Castro in San Francisco. "What Gates elides in his suggestion to Kenan is the fact that taking Horace *to* anywhere also entails taking him *from* somewhere," McRuer writes (185).

10. Indeed, in Robert McRuer's estimation, by locating Horace at the center of this southern place, the place where he might be least likely to come out, Kenan advances the goals of queer theory articulated by Michael Warner and "confront[s] the default heteronormativity of modern culture with its worst nightmare, a queer planet" (194). Such a confrontation is certainly valuable within the context of this project. However, my aims are somewhat different from Warner's. In excavating the apocalyptic as a discursive site of concealment and revelation, this book seeks to confront the default resistance to progressive political movements held by U.S. political and religious culture with the challenging and even liberating possibilities of Apocalypse, and thus, to activate the emancipatory potential of place. I am less interested, then, in how Horace's particular presence challenges and disrupts the heteronormativity of Tims Creek than how the telling of his story, along with the oral history of the community's maroon origins in the story in "Let the Dead Bury Their Dead," can transform Tims Creek into a more open and accessible matrix for the expression of an oppositional, resistant subjectivity.

Furthermore, by embedding Horace so deeply within his community, Kenan creates a space for meaningful discussion of the possibility of difference within community. The literary map of Tims Creek confronts the instability of the community's boundaries; the consequences of the boundaries' long maintenance suggest the necessity of moving away from a formulation of margins as borders to change and instead prompt the reader to investigate them as sites of dynamic exchange between the self and the other, between the local community and the world outside, that are informed by the experiences and folkways framed within. The ethics of Kenan's fiction require the remembrance of the past, not in order to maintain a stable identity but rather in order to create a usable history that will guide these exchanges and that will be accessible to all who wish to claim it. In this effort, Apocalypse is our site of excavation, the proverbial "X" marking the spot: both Horace and his cousin, Jimmy Greene, turn to Apocalypse in order to understand the contradictions to community and family posed by, among other things, the presence of homosexual desire. The otherworldly discourse of Apocalypse functions as a narrative space in which the unspeakable can be addressed indirectly and where contradiction is negotiated through deferral to a cosmological myth. Where it occurs, something has been silenced.

4

"An't It Time the Lord Did Something?"

Vindication and the Practices of Place in Bastard Out of Carolina

> Went back home Lord, My home was lonely
> Since my mother she had gone
> All my brothers, sisters crying
> What a home so sad and lone
> Can the circle be unbroken
> Bye and bye, Lord, bye and bye
> There's a better home a-waiting
> In the sky, Lord, in the sky
>
> —The Carter Family, "Can the Circle Be Unbroken"

IN A 1993 conversation published in the *Village Voice Literary Supplement*, Randall Kenan and Dorothy Allison held forth on a wide-range of topics, including snakes, their shared Carolina backgrounds, and ultimately, the political imperatives of their work. "What can you write about more urgently than some 70-year-old woman depending on her social security check?" asks Kenan, who rejects the attempt to locate this hypothetical woman "on the so-called margins" (27). Such people don't exist on "the fringe of society," in Kenan's estimate; rather, "They *are* society." Allison agrees: "People think that society is, like, Kathie Lee Gifford. No, she's one of the ghosts on the edge of society. My sisters are society."

Allison and Kenan, products and chroniclers of the South's marginal spaces, have produced some of the most compelling writing about the region in the last generation. Along the margins, regional literature is not genre defined by old conventions and tropes, which are left only to be parodied; the decline of an idealized old South is not mourned, but celebrated.

From the vantage point of the margins, regional identity and history are the social forces to which—and against which—these writers respond. In this conversation, Kenan and Allison—a gay black man and white trash lesbian from the Carolinas—remind us that the aim of their work is not a feel-good multiculturalism in which diverse self-identified communities exist alongside one another in plural, utopian bliss. Rather, Allison and Kenan seek to recover the historical meaning that is silenced by the efforts to regulate the configurations of sex, race, and class. Both demand that in mapping social spaces—including the southern places in which their fiction is located—attention be paid to those people who have been exiled to the discursive margins and whose experiences have been concealed by the various surrogate realities of place.

Allison's writerly concern with narration and revision is difficult to ignore. In her performative memoir *Two or Three Things I Know For Sure*, she writes, "Behind the story I tell is the one I don't. . . . Behind the story you hear is the one I wish I could make you hear" (39). Indeed, much criticism and scholarship of *Bastard Out of Carolina* has focused on storytelling, whether through formal approaches to revision and narrativity or approaches that examine the book through the lens offered by trauma theory. However, no treatment has heretofore acknowledged or explored the role evangelical and apocalyptic discourse plays in the narrator's efforts to understand and articulate her experiences—stories that defy the conventional southern discourses of place, class, and gender. Much like Richard Wright, Allison appropriates and reconfigures the apocalyptic narratives and images of southern religious culture in order to offer a historical vision in which her characters suffering is not silenced, but instead, given meaning by an ultimate victory. In *Bastard Out of Carolina*, the apocalyptic imaginary is central to Allison's efforts to make us hear her story—almost from the very beginning.

While the bulk of the novel presents Bone's increasing alienation from family and self, her individual voice is almost indistinct from the collective narration of familial history in the lyrical first chapter. Here, Bone introduces her family and herself through the recollection of stories so often repeated among her family that authorial attribution is impossible; the stories are never static and never remain long in the past but rather are conjured up, constantly revised and retold, to fit the needs of the family at a given moment. Among the family stories told in this opening chapter, the recollection of a catastrophic fire at the Greenville County Courthouse stands out—not because of the damage wrought by the flames, but because of the joy the family finds in its destruction. A specific psychic need instigates the Boatwrights' laughing recollection of the fire and leads someone, perhaps Bone, to ascribe to the fire the qualities of wish fulfillment. Presaging the painful visions of retribution that will haunt Bone, the collective voice remembers Anney's apocalyptic fantasy: "An't it time the Lord did something, rained fire and retribution on Greenville County? An't there sin enough, grief enough, inch by inch of pain enough? An't the measure made yet? Anney never said what she was thinking, but her mind was working all the time" (14). As the county's central public space, the courthouse holds the documentary evidence of Greenville's communal history—a history that categorizes Bone as a bastard and the Boatwright men as petty criminals. Moreover, it functions as the symbolic consolidation of collective identity, as it is the central structure in which many of the county's most significant events would have occurred. The Boatwrights' access to this history, however, is restricted: they can neither edit nor add to the documents of history (including Bone's birth certificate) or the discourses of law and class that enact the script of abjection. In the historical narrative offered from the marginal spaces in which the Boatwrights live, the destruction of the courthouse is a liberating event, not a moment of destruction. For the Boatwrights, this story provides an opportunity to revise their own history, to cast their experience into a narrative in which they are not damned but, in fact, will ultimately be vindicated. Like so many of the apocalyptic narratives introduced in *Apocalypse South*, this story provides order and meaning to pain, suffering, and trauma that would otherwise seem chaotic or incoherent.

Heretofore, I have proposed that the southern apocalyptic imaginary has been harnessed to often contradictory ends: just as it is used to regulate moments of undifferentiation and hybridity that contradict the dominant discourses of race and power in southern places and spaces, its historical vision nonetheless offers hope to oppressed communities when it is most needed. In both of these applications, Apocalypse signals the presence of concealed or displaced meaning—of the sort of stories Allison wishes she could tell directly. In *Bastard Out of Carolina*—as in Kenan's Tims Creek narratives—Apocalypse signals the presence of a voice that has been silenced or a history that has been expunged, and, thus, a site to be excavated. Allison's Bone endures experiences so ultimately horrifying and so contradictory to dominant systems of representation that they do not yield to easy articulation. These experiences—rape and incest and abuse—threaten the coherence of southern places and spaces, unsettling the discursive boundaries that are used to define fundamental entities like family and community, as well as the stable limits of the self. In order to articulate her stories from the margins, Allison's Bone turns inevitably to Apocalypse and to the cleansing and purging fires of Revelation, which she hopes will bring an end to an experience so awful that no narrative available offers the space adequate to contain it.

While the novel does not engage eschatological concerns with the consistency of the major works that I have examined thus far, Bone's narrative is framed by Apocalyptic visions on either end: the vision of the flaming courthouse that begins it and a fiery, cataclysmic voice of condemnation and justice that concludes it. This chapter will interrogate the ways in which this frame and other manifestations of the apocalyptic imaginary map the apocalyptic possibilities of cataclysm and judgment onto southern spaces and places in *Bastard Out of Carolina*. The chapter will begin by exploring the restrictions and limitations placed on her and her family by the gendered, classist discourses of southern spaces and places, and then it will address the Boatwrights' various attempts to stake their own claim to those spaces by revising and retelling their own histories. The failure of these attempts leads Bone toward the apocalyptic imaginary: much as it does for Wright's Aunt Sue and for Kenan's Horace, the apocalyptic imaginary provides an alternative discursive space, open to possibilities beyond those offered by the dominant spatial and platial discourses. In the final section of this chapter, I will examine how Bone's engagement with the apocalyptic imaginary allows her to provide narrative coherence to her story—and thus, herself—and how Allison's engagement, more broadly, stakes its own claim to the landscape of the South and refuses to be located along its aberrant margins.

The Limits and Restraints of Southern Spaces

Before her audience can even approach the text of the novel, Allison demands they confront the limits of their own definitions of southern identities and southern places. The title, *Bastard Out of Carolina*, both locks her story into a place—Carolina, or more specifically, Greenville, South Carolina—and lays an affirmative claim to an identity, *Bastard*, that has been declared aberrant and pushed to the margins of that place. This initial invocation of place is indicative of the juxtapositions and contradictions that characterize the subsequent attempts of her narrator, Ruth Anne "Bone" Boatwright, to locate her traumatic past within the physical terrain that is coterminous with the social spaces that would restrict her story. As the second chapter opens, Allison's narrator, the adult Bone, conjures up her childhood by invoking the idealized, even Edenic southern space of her aunts' homes: "Greenville, South Carolina, in 1955 was the most beautiful place in the world," she says.

> Black walnut trees dropped their green-black fuzzy bulbs on Aunt Ruth's matted lawn, past where their knotty roots rose up out of the ground like the elbows and knees of dirty children suntanned dark and covered with scars.... Over at the house Aunt Raylene rented near the river, all the trees had been cut back and the scuppernong vines torn out. The clover grew in long sweeps of tiny white and yellow flowers that hid slender red-and-black striped caterpillars and fat gray-black slugs—the ones Uncle Earle swore would draw fish to a hook even in a thunderstorm. (17)

To access the memories of her family, Bone imaginatively reconstructs the places in which they existed—the physical geography upon which her cousins played and in which her uncle Earle collected grubs for bait. Both cognitive psychologists and literary scholars have long noted the spatial elements of memory: J. Gerald Kennedy writes that as "we reconstruct the past largely through the imagery of place . . . memory is less the retrieval of bygone time than a recovery of symbolic space" (500). This insight is complicated by Bone's inability or unwillingness to linger upon the idyllic landscape of her childhood. Moving from Ruth's and Raylene's homes, Bone recalls her Aunt Alma's yard, which had been rendered a "smoldering expanse of baked dirt and scattered rocks" by the spendthrift landlord who "had locked down the spigots so that the kids wouldn't cost him a fortune in water bills" (17–18). Even in the imaginative landscape of memory, the *places* that give shape and context to her past can offer only limited *space* for her to articulate an empowered self; the textures of place are configured by the social and economic forces that shame Bone and ascribe the status of "poor white trash" to her family.

"I was born trash in a land where the people all believe themselves natural aristocrats," Allison writes in *Two or Three Things I Know for Sure*. "Ask any white Southerner. They'll take you back two generations, say, 'Yeah, we had a plantation.' The hell we did" (32). Allison is less interested in why or how these hypothetical white southerners can make such claims of lapsed aristocratic origins than in the ways in which these claims are used to marginalize her. "I have no memories that can be bent so easily. I know where I come from, and it is not that part of the world." Here, almost as if by force, Allison counters the production of social *space* that, configured in terms of inclusion and exclusion, would alienate and even exile her from *place*. Refusing to yield to the imposition of placelessness, she locates her experience on the very southern geographies that reject her presence. Just as she demands that her audience acknowledge her claim to a southern past, so too does *Bastard* insist that we consider Bone's story in its *place*, that is, in the rural edges and seedy apartments of Greenville in the '50s. However, these places refuse to yield the space necessary to tell her story. It is a story that insists the listener confront the Boatwrights as more than legendary, hell-raising, hard-drinking men; more than women who endure until their bodies are broken; and more human—fraught with neither the degeneracy nor the sentimental nobility that representations of poverty often include.

In the previous chapter, I mentioned Scott Romine's suggestion that much southern writing displays a peculiar eschatological anxiety—a constant worry that "the South is always expiring" (26). The geography of Greenville County is not that which these earlier generations of southern writers mourned, and, indeed, Allison's novel betrays little interest in that brand of southern apocalypticism (or even the elegies offered by Kenan in *A Visitation of Spirits*). Indeed, her "sense of place" is quite different from her predecessors, as Minrose Gwin has compellingly argued. Gwin situates Bone's narrative within the "convergences of material, textual, and cultural spaces" (416)—in particular, the material and cultural space in which a southern patriarchal power is enacted, *home*. Because the space of the home is the crucial site through which the formative memories of childhood are accessed, Gwin contends, the oppression and abuses suffered by women in that space are all the more troubling and oppressive for the female subject. For Gwin, *region*, like home, is a product of both *material* space (i.e., the physical geography) and *cultural* space (416)—that is, it exists in the ideologies and practices layered onto the southern landscape.[1] In Gwin's reading, *Bastard* exposes the oppressive consequences of southern cultural practices: inextricably connected to and determined by an ideology of absolute patriarchal rule, these practices restrict and regulate the movement of women within the social spaces of the region.

Geographers often distinguish *space* and *place* by degree of specificity; Wesley A. Kort "defines *place* in contrast to *space* as particular in contrast

---

1. Interestingly, Gwin employs the term "region" rather than "place." I infer that this is an implicit recognition—and rejection—of the formulation of place as resistant to progressive political movement and to the generally "positive orientation" of the "sense of place" within the more traditional, conservative discourses of southern literature and southern literary studies (Romine 24).

to general" (14). In this formulation, non-specific concepts like *home* and *hometown* are spatial discourses that configure cultural practices and social interactions within particular and locatable places, such as Alma's house or Greenville. These places, writes the geographer Linda McDowell, offer particular "living histories of past and current social relationships" (4). Thus, an invocation of a specific place does not simply reference a set of coordinates. Instead, it draws upon both a spatial discourse that inform and regulate social interactions at a category of location to which the site belongs (for instance, hometown) *and* the specific experiences that occurred in that location (that is to say, in Greenville). These experiences may either support the dominant spatial discourse, or they may challenge or disrupt its continued production. Allison's claim to "know where I come from" denies the spatial discourse of the plantation as an adequate signifier of her southern experience and disrupts any effort to locate that particular experience as a geographic or cultural aberration. The subsequent exclamation, "The hell we did," rejects the plantation myth as an accurate signifier of any southern place. Ultimately, this statement boldly clears out a space for Allison within the geography of the South: her experiences happened there, and she demands that they be included.

Another example from *Two or Three Things* offers some insight into the formulation of place, space, and margins. Midway through her fourth grade year (probably 1957 or 1958), a new teacher, "right out of college and full of ideas" (7), was assigned to Allison's class. Her first attempt to encourage creative and critical thinking among her charges—a current events project—draws complaints: "the nightly news," Allison tells us, "was full of Birmingham and Little Rock, burning buses and freedom marchers." These images are probably too complex for eight- and nine-year-olds to grasp, but, more immediately, they are issues that their parents undoubtedly wished to avoid or ignore. In search of a safe solution, the idealistic teacher requires the students to create family trees and recommends that they look to family Bibles as sources. Allison describes her mother's reaction to the assignment as a look of "exasperation," as if she "was ready to throw something." Her Aunt Dot, on the other hand, responds with amused sarcasm: "I can just see all those children putting down Mama's name, and first daddy's name and second daddy's name. Could get complicated" (10). Allison's aunt and mother work to reconstruct the family's past from their incomplete and often contradictory memories. Nonplussed, Dot finally asks her sister, "What you think? Should we get a family Bible?" (11).

In Dot's assessment—"This girl an't from around here"—*here* does not refer to the South or even to Greenville County, but rather to the diffuse community of farmers, mill workers, truck drivers, and diner waitresses on the margins of Greenville County whose children this elementary school serves. Allison's mother reacts with exasperation because the assignment requires her daughter to bend their family history to the bourgeois narrative forms of the family tree and the family Bible. In many ways, the well-meaning teacher's mistake is understandable; after all, as I have noted, southern religious culture is nothing if not Bible-centered. Thus, its use as the central document of family life—as a text that situates the individual within the earthly history of family and within the otherworldly narrative of sacred history—is appropriate to place, if we understand it as nearly synonymous with region. The problem posed by the assignment: their family history doesn't fit into the blank *space* the Bible provides. Their genealogy does not match the form in its first pages and can be forced into that space only by simplifying certain elements and forgetting or denying others.

Similarly, the fictional Anney Boatwright's engagement with the public spaces of Greenville County in the first chapter is indicative of the limited discursive, physical, and class mobility available on the margins of the community. In the county hospital, Bone is declared a "bastard" upon her birth, as her Aunt Ruth and her grandmother cannot agree on the identity of her father. From there, the forms are transmitted onto another public space, the courthouse, where the frustrated clerk rejects the pleas of the Boatwright women and "certifie[s]" Bone's illegitimacy. Again and again, Anney seeks to have a certificate issued without the red "illegitimate" stamp, attempting to "deny what Greenville County wanted to name her," but each time her request is rejected with moral condescension. "The facts have been established," the clerk informs her (*Bastard* 4). Bone's Uncle Earle counsels Anney to abandon her efforts: "The law never done us no good," he tells her (5). Earle's statement is not inaccurate, for neither the institutions nor the discourses of justice are accessible to the Boatwrights. Likewise, they are denied access to the physical places that characterize the collective experience of southern communities—the plantations, the town squares, or the courthouses. Even the access to their own homes is restricted, as Alma's scorched yard attests. In these southern spaces, they are located as "aberrant," placed on the margins of what the community considers acceptable, and denied the right to speak through that discourse. In the narrative of the community, the Boatwrights are white trash.

Bone's mother Anney struggles with the Sisyphean task of pushing away the appellation and the associations it calls to mind: "*No-good, lazy, shiftless.* She'd work her hands to claws, her back to a shovel shape, her mouth to a bent and awkward smile—anything to deny what Greenville

County wanted to name her," Bone recalls (3–4). "Trash" elicits these moral qualities for Anney, but it is inescapably bound up with waste—material byproducts that are first contained for the health and purity of the community and then removed and confined to its outer edges. The Boatwrights are, in Patricia Yaeger's terms, "throwaway bodies"[2]: the necessity of their presence is recognized, but the family cannot be considered an integral part of the community. Thus, their interaction with the larger community must be regulated. Only by keeping the Boatwrights at a safe physical and discursive distance can the rising middle class of 1950s Greenville County narrate its own triumph, or even delineate its difference from any other group.

The Boatwrights' Attempts at Narrative Resistance

The script I have outlined above should be familiar: it is the same process of collective, narrative self-creation that occurs in Faulkner's Yoknapatawpha and in Kenan's Tims Creek. The limited social space through which the Boatwrights can move may offer more freedom that the horrifying racialized regulation of space in Wright's Mississippi, but it is nonetheless similarly circumscribed. Like Wright's work, and unlike Faulkner's and Kenan's, *Bastard Out of Carolina*, does not offer the perspective of those who seek to confirm their own position at the center. Instead, the novel focuses wholly on the perspective of the marginalized, and neither the fictional Boatwrights nor the Gibsons in *Two or Three Things* easily yield to their systematic abjection. In Allison's memoir, Dot's dismissive response to the genealogical assignment implies that, in the geographic and discursive margins of Greenville, people found alternative narrative spaces to articulate their family histories. From these marginal spaces, both Allison's family and their fictional counterparts narrate stories (like the burning of the courthouse), telling and retelling them in an ongoing effort to counteract efforts to restrict their movement and to silence their experiences.

In addressing the novel's interest with telling and retelling, most critical work engages the scholarly discourse of trauma studies. Rightly so:

---

2. Yaeger defines the throwaway body as "women and men whose bodily harm does not matter enough to be registered or repressed—who are *not* symbolically central, who are looked over, looked through, who become a matter of public and private indifference—neither important enough to be disavowed nor part of white southern culture's dominant emotional economy" (68).

Bone's story is composed of events so horrible that they defy the victim's ability to articulate their meaning. Because it contradicts the prevailing discourses of place, gender, and family, this story has been silenced. For this reason, Allison's reliance on the strategies of realistic fiction—brutally real, in fact—are perhaps surprising, as they seem to enact the very forms that serve to silence the expression of trauma. Queer theorists have long noted the similar limitations of realism as an appropriate discourse to the articulated queer stories and queer subjectivities, which are silenced by linear, realistic narrative conventions.[3] Though the chronology of the novel is fairly conventional (and by that, I mean that it moves sequentially), the stories embedded in the text—the "relentless linear narratives" (King 122) through which Bone seeks to narrate a coherent identity that will make sense of the abuse she has suffered—are anything but conventional. "Bone must rewrite—and in some cases simply reject—the names and stories that make her vulnerable to violence," according to Vincent King. We may also conceive of this spatially: lost in the family's never-ending cycle of eviction and moving into new but sterile rental properties and alienated from her mother by Anney's failure to prevent Glen's sexual abuse, Bone becomes displaced—unhinged from family and from place. In response—in order to grant weight to her existence—Bone assumes exciting new personae and backgrounds at her new schools.

This ability to inhabit different identities transcends that conventional playacting of childhood and instead points to an effort to work through the stigma of her "white trash" class position and the traumatic sexual abuse inflicted by her stepfather, "Daddy Glen" Waddell. His failures precipitate both his violent rages and the family's repeated moves from one rented home to another, and these events leave Bone displaced, feeling "ghostly, unreal and unimportant" (65)—a nonperson in nonplaces. Bone assumes new identities as she enters new schools, creating detailed but fictional personal histories that locate her outside the boundaries of Greenville. "It scared me that it was so easy—my records, after all, had not caught up with me—that people thought I could be Roseanne Carter from Atlanta, a city I had never visited. Everyone believed me, and I enjoyed a brief popularity as someone from a big city who could tell big-city stories" (67). When

---

3. Katrina Irving describes realism as "an interesting choice on Allison's part, since it has been argued that the representational double-bind in which queer artists currently find themselves—the desire not to provide the dominant culture the marginal subjects it demands ('positive images'), coupled with the desire to avoid collusion in the dominant culture's 'ghosting' of the deviant—cannot be slipped within the parameters of the realist form" (94).

Bone's stories are localizable to Greenville, they are necessarily constrained by the same sociospatial discourses that characterize her experience; an imagined Atlanta, on the other hand, offers limitless possibility.

Bone is initially thrilled with the freedom of being *unplaced* but is quickly terrified by the dissociation from place that ultimately constitutes an alienation from the self. Bone struggles between a claustrophobic desire to escape the marginal spaces inhabited by the Boatwrights (which results in alienation from the family) and a longing for a communion with them. In her isolation, however, she does not recognize that she has in fact imbibed the family's legacy of resilience—particularly, the use of narrative as a mechanism of resistance among the Boatwright women. Her fantasies have much in common with the collective effort of her mother and aunts to revise and retell stories in order to transcend those confining spaces. Lamenting their financial struggles, Anney and Raylene find some solace—and laughter—by retelling and reliving their sister Alma's refusal to yield to the sheriff's efforts to repossess her furniture. Bone overhears Raylene recounting Alma "screaming to the neighbors how they were trying to rob her" (188). In their memory, Alma's resistance is both dramatic and comic. Her fearless, even shameless, manipulation of gender and class codes emasculates the sheriff, who in Anney's account "like to peed in his pants when he saw her [Alma] throwing her clothes out the window and yelling, 'Take it all, why don't you? Take the kids too, take it all.'" When the sisters debate whether Alma actually disrobed and threw her housedress at him, it becomes apparent that neither witnessed the event; the story has been told so many times that its details are no longer clear. However, both agree that the inclusion of the image of Alma, standing defiantly in her underwear, is an acceptable addition, as it not only makes the story better but also accurately represents the spirit of Alma's resistance.

In retelling the story, Anney and Raylene attempt to narrate their own resistance and their own refusal to yield to the restrictions of class. In their telling, the repossession is understood as a robbery and thus becomes a metonym for the sort of intrusive abuses that disrupt their efforts to claim space within the geography of Greenville. However, the limitations of Alma's opposition quickly become clear to Bone. The story turns from Alma's resistance to the shame with which her daughter Temple responds to it: Temple, Anney says, "just didn't want the neighbors to think they couldn't keep up the payments." Formulating the event in this manner shifts the moral characterization of the event from a violation of Alma's home—her intimate personal space—to a failure on her part to maintain that place. Importantly, it is not the failure itself that concerns Temple but the neighbors' knowledge of it. Thus, she does not seek to *prevent* the repossession but rather attempts to silence it so that it might not be used to *name* her or her family. Anney and Raylene are quick to differentiate themselves and their sister from their niece and her attempt to silence this event: like her sisters, Alma "knows who she is," Anney says. Bone realizes that she possesses neither this self-awareness nor the sense of collective identity that exists among her mother and aunts, and she wishes to "be more like them, easier in my body and not so angry all the time" (190).

Though the communion that exists among these women seems enviable from Bone's position of alienation from self and family, she is aware of the costs necessary to reach an easy position in place: " . . . Through the steam they both looked older—two worn, tired women repeating old stories to each other and trying not to worry too much about things they couldn't change anyway." Bone—and the reader—are left to ponder the implications of the sisters' knowledge of "who they are": is this a defiant statement of the refusal to yield to the sheriff's, the furniture salesman's, and the neighbors' efforts to name them, or does it amount to an acceptance of a "white trash" identity that allows only limited oppositional possibilities and little opportunity for meaningful resistance? Though Anney and Raylene delight in a story of defiance, enacting their own narrative resistance in its telling and retelling, how much space does it afford them to grow, change, and challenge their own subjection? What is the distinction between knowing "who" you are and "where" you belong?

Like Horace Cross and even Jimmy Greene in *A Visitation of Spirits*, Bone struggles mightily with the gendered notions of inheritance and legacy. She is profoundly ambivalent about what it means to be a Boatwright, and more specifically, a Boatwright woman. She wants to belong among them, to have a position for herself alongside her mother and her aunts, but she fears their legacy and the future to which it dooms her. These contradictory impulses are expressed both spatially and temporally: Bone wants to fit into the social space of family but is afraid of the limited outcomes that are possible within it—a restricted number of potential histories, each of which seems to end in stasis, suffering, or oblivion. In this regard, Bone shares much with many of the central characters in the works I have considered. Joe Christmas refuses to be located in the bivalent racial system of the South; the adolescent self that Wright describes in *Black Boy* realizes at any early age that he must struggle for his very life to live "in a country in which the aspirations of black people were limited, marked off" (169); Horace invents and ultimately becomes lost in the worlds he creates to escape the restrictions of his position in his family and community.

Recoiling from the Boatwright history, Bone attempts to insert herself into different narratives in a continuing project to generate a narrative that will give coherent form to her experiences of abuse. In this attempt, Bone displays an "instinctive" understanding of the postmodern insight "that her identity, far from being stable or fixed, is transactional," according to King (126). That is not to say that Bone is not affected by the identities and names that others impose upon her; indeed, she obsesses over her physical appearance and over how she is perceived, particularly by Glen. "When I saw myself in Daddy Glen's eyes, I wanted to die," she says. "He looked at me, and I was ashamed of myself" (*Bastard* 209). Though she despises him, she mourns his absent affection and ascribes to it the properties of a psychic and emotional panacea. "Love would make me beautiful; a father's love would purify my heart, turn my bitter soul sweet, and lighten my Cherokee eyes. If he loved me, if only he loved me. Why didn't he love me?" Bone does not realize—at least, explicitly—that, through this agonizing longing for patriarchal acceptance, she joins the other Boatwright women in a communion of suffering.

Terrified of the future to which she believes that being a "Boatwright woman" destines her, Bone becomes fascinated with the seemingly unrestricted social spaces occupied by the men in her family. "Men could do anything," she says, "and everything they did, no matter how violent or mistaken, was viewed with humor and understanding. . . . What men did was just what men did. Some days I would grind my teeth, wishing I had been born a boy" (23). She is not alone: Glen is thrilled by the possibility that he might "marry Black Earle's sister, marry the whole Boatwright legend, shame his daddy and shock his brothers" and that, like them, he might "carry a knife in his pocket and kill any man who dared to touch" his wife (13). For Bone and Glen both, the Boatwright legacy of "white trash" offers an identity that openly and defiantly enacts the very behaviors that have been ascribed to them in order to affect that marginalization. As J. Brooks Bouson argued, the Boatwright legacy follows "a socially scripted and stereotypical role: that of the shamelessly defiant and angry white trash poor" (108). While this behavior "flaunts" the ascription of shamefulness, it is "is not to be without shame." Instead, the Boatwrights enact a sort of feedback loop, internalizing their shame with each defiant display of shameful behavior. The "stubborn 'pride' and the defiant shamelessness of poor whites like the Boatwrights function to cover their social shame—their feelings of social powerlessness and inferiority," writes Bouson (108), but never to counteract it or to offer the possibility of actual empowerment. Thus, when Bone visits Earle in prison, she seizes upon his concealment of a knife as an emblem of nearly superheroic opposition: "We're smart, I thought. We're smarter than you think we are. I felt mean and powerful and proud of all of us, all the Boatwrights who had ever gone to jail, fought back when they hadn't a chance, and still held on to their pride" (*Bastard* 217).

Bone, it seems, has accepted the abjection of the family and even fashioned it into a subversive and empowering identity: if the family must live on the margins, at least the margins are theirs. In this sense, Bone's white trash experience seems to exist on the same terrain as bell hooks's childhood in the black community that existed on the edges of "a small Kentucky town." "To be in the margin is to be part of the whole but outside the main body," hooks writes. "This sense of wholeness, impressed upon our consciousness by the structure of our daily lives, provided us an oppositional world view—a mode of seeing unknown to most of our oppressors, that sustained us, aided us in our struggle to transcend poverty and despair, strengthened our sense of self and solidarity" (ix).

However, while the margins may offer an empowering vantage point, enacting the script of one's own abjection offers a limited victory at best; at worst, this exacerbates the process of domination. Thus, in Raylene's assessment, the knife is hardly an indication of Earle's ingenuity: "All you kids think your uncles are so smart. If they're so smart, why they all so goddam poor, huh?" (*Bastard* 217). By shamelessly living out the abject practices that delineate the marginal spaces afforded them, the Boatwright men only reinforce its boundaries. Furthermore, this feedback loop of shameful behavior silences the experiences of the Boatwright women and, ultimately, the abuse Bone suffers. In seeking to counteract the shameful emasculation wrought by his father's rejection, Glen Waddell asserts a violent, masculine authority and assumes an identity that works, ultimately, at cross-purposes with his efforts to throw off the shame. His parents and siblings do not register his actions as a rejection of them or their social mores; instead, they view them as further evidence that he is a failure. Glen seeks to establish his own coherent identity in and through the series of rented homes through which the family moves in with regular and fairly rapid succession. As Minrose Gwin points out, while the space of the home is frequently characterized as maternal, it is also the site at which the discourses of legal ownership and patriarchal authority converge (419); a mother may maintain a space, but a father remains its master. For Glen, emasculated by the authority of his own father, the material success of his brother, and his inability to hold a job, the patriarchal mastery over family is all that stands in the way of utter impotence. Even in the home space, this limited power is provisional at best, frequently disrupted by the demands of the landlord. Consequently, he works to silence any threat to this integrity, hoping to forestall its imminent collapse. He "whine[s]," according to Bone, when Anney takes Bone and her sister Reese to the Parsons, Reese's paternal grandparents and the parents of Anney's tragically dead husband, and he upsets the relationship between the girls and the Parsons by making a claim to their land on behalf of "our girl" (*Bastard* 56). Glen is further threatened by another source of potential disruptive narratives—Anney's own mother, who, he tells Reese and Bone, "is the worst kind of liar" (52). "I'll tell you what's true," he tells Bone, his grip emphasizing his authority. "You're mine now" (52).

In Katrina Irving's reading of the novel, Glen's statement of possession is indicative of "a patriarchal system that needs marginal subjects in order to demarcate and suture its own boundaries" (95). Again, we turn to spatial formulations. For instance, in order for the Waddells to claim a place within the hegemonic, "moonlight and magnolia" narratives of southern places, they must be able to turn away someone at the plantation gates—that is, they must cast themselves against people like the Boatwrights who cannot access that narrative space. Likewise, in order to claim his own narrative space, Glen must locate someone as the object of his authority. Thus, the boundaries of his power are located in Bone and Reese: they constitute the furthest reaches of his claims of possession. However, when that authority appears to be on the verge of collapse, Glen seeks out a scapegoat—Bone. As I discussed earlier, instances of social crisis inevitably involve the failure of dominant discourses of authority, whether intricate cosmologies, secular narratives of nation, or, as in the case of Glen Waddell, a belief in one's authority. Individuals in such cases, writes René Girard,

> are disconcerted by the immensity of the disaster but never look into the natural causes; the concept that they might affect those causes by learning more about them remains embryonic. Since cultural eclipse is above all a social crisis, there is a strong tendency to explain it by social and, especially, moral causes. . . . But, rather than blame themselves, people invariably blame either society as a whole, which costs them nothing, or other people who seem particularly harmful for easily identifiable reasons. (*The Scapegoat* 14)

Bone is "easily identifiable" in her alienation from family, her frequent escapes into books and imagination, and her resistance to Glen. In the terms I have employed elsewhere, her presence constitutes an instance of undifferentiation that cannot be tolerated: though Bone exists within the physical place of the home, she will not yield to Glen's authority. Thus, she disrupts the discursive configuration of the home as a patriarchal space. Glen does not seek to sacrifice her as a literal scapegoat but rather to erase the contradiction she poses by demanding his dominion over her in the most extreme and absolute manner imaginable.

The Alternative Narrative Space of Apocalypse

The psychic effect of Bone's location within these geographies of power and patriarchy is suggested by the initial description of Alma's scorched yard: even the spaces that she inhabits in memories afford a radically restricted sense of mobility and freedom. Likewise, most of the stories she tells end with the Boatwrights' subjection to the law. Confinement and containment are thus the hallmarks of Bone's narration. It should not surprise us, then, that these geographies are destroyed in the elaborate, apocalyptic fantasies she creates. While Apocalypse is frequently formulated temporally as the end of Time, that end occurs in a specific geographical location; it results in the destruction of the limitations of place and space and the end of the division between the world and the divine realm of heaven.

In her initial masturbatory fantasies—images of burning straw that threaten to consume her as she struggles to escape—Bone does not seem to be aware of the destructive, purging, or cleansing qualities of fire. Indeed, if she does already feel tainted by Glen's abuse, she nonetheless struggles to preserve herself from the flames. These images do not occur in a vacuum; rather, they are foreshadowed and perhaps informed by the retributive fantasy of the courthouse's destruction that Bone attributes to her mother and by the story of her uncles reveling in the actual fire. In this context, it becomes clear that Bone's daydreams engage an extant discourse of retribution and that her familiarity with it predates even her exposure to scripture. Consider the description of the weather in the collective narration of Lyle Parsons's death—"the devil's rain," an ostensibly pleasant combination of rain and blinding sun that the highway patrolman says, leads to the wreck (7). In the short story "Clarence and the Dead" (*And* What Do They Tell You, Clarence? *and* The Dead Speak to Clarence), Randall Kenan deploys another variation of this saying—"the devil beats[ing] his wife" (3). From this benignly folksy aphorism, two crucial ideas emerge: first, the latent but nearly omnipresent influence of a cosmology that anthropomorphizes Satan and situates him as a presence in the geography of the rural South, and second, the silenced presence of violence committed against female bodies. The abusive potential of the patriarchy and the flames of hell and judgment are sublimated but nonetheless present in the narrative and discursive production of the southern geography that Bone inhabits.

Though fire is a constant within Bone's masturbatory fantasies, it is hardly limited to them. In fact, the fantasy of the courthouse's destruction attributed to Anney in the first chapter presages Bone's emotional response to Glen's middle-class family, the Waddells: "I could feel a kind of heat behind my eyes that lit up everything. It was dangerous, that heat. It wanted to pour out and burn everything up, everything they had that we couldn't have, everything that made them think they were better than us" (*Bastard* 103). Bone recognizes that same heat—"the fire of outrage" (158)—in the eyes of her would-be friend, the albino Shannon Pearl. Shannon Pearl's gruesome but brutally realistic stories of "decapitations, mutilations, murder, and mayhem" engage the apocalyptic discourse of retribution far more specifically than Bone's initial fantastic daydreams: "Shannon Pearl simply and completely hated everyone who had ever hurt her and spent most of her time brooding on punishments either she or God would visit on them" (157–58). As she spends more time with Shannon Pearl's family on the southern gospel circuit, as well as in the various evangelical churches that dot the geography of rural Greenville County, Bone's own fantasies increasingly and more specifically engage the apocalyptic imaginary. The world of southern gospel music seems to offer Bone everything that the familial stories lack: the possibility of financial success; models of independent women who are able to create something positive out of the heartache wrought by their fathers, husbands, brothers, and sons; and perhaps most importantly, the possibility of a divine justice that would deliver her from her abuse and punish Glen for his crimes.

Critical work on *Bastard Out of Carolina* has surprisingly neglected the novel's invocations of Apocalypse. In an otherwise insightful essay, Laurie Vickeroy reduces Bone's obsession with southern gospel music (both in its content and the circuit) as evidence of "her need to be cocooned by narrow, predictable thinking" (154). This condescending assessment fails to recognize the significance of revivalism and southern gospel music among the southern working class of the U.S. South. For Bone, as for many southerners, the revival tent functions as a mobile, unrestricted space in which working-class southerners are able to articulate an identity distinct from the aberrant, "white trash" labels ascribed to them elsewhere.

In the revival tent, individuals can claim an identity as a member of God's Chosen people and articulate their own experiences within the sacred historical narrative of redemption and resurrection—a deep contrast to the shame lumped onto them in the conventional, secular documents of history, such as Bone's birth certificate. Bone's experiences at the revival tent occur during the gospel boom of the 1940s and 1950s, a point at which working-class southerners had created a nearly independent, impressively influential, and financially thriving gospel music industry. This industry offered them a pathway to the middle class successes that they had been denied (Graves and Fillingim, Introduction 10). Prompted by the end of wartime rationing and the new interstate highway system, gospel musicians cut more records, shipped them cheaply, and traveled across the country to promote them; new, nationally broadcast radio ministries transmitted the music ahead of them (Goff 157–59). "By the middle of the twentieth century," Michael Graves and David Fillingim write, "Southern Gospel was an established genre in print, broadcast, and recorded media" (13).

Bone's interest in religion and in southern gospel music, then, should not be reduced to a turn from the complexities of her experiences toward a realm of "narrow, predictable thinking," as Vickeroy contends; rather, it must be contextualized within Bone's continuing exploration of the various discourses available to her and within Allison's efforts to map out the geography of Greenville County. Bone is thrilled by the possibility of deliverance and salvation: she dreams of both saving her family through the earthly, material successes a career as a gospel singer might bring *and* spiritually redeeming them by introducing them to the church. Moreover, she is thrilled by the possibility of being *wanted*. "There was something heady and enthralling about being the object of all that attention," and so Bone comes "close to being saved about fourteen times . . . in fourteen different churches," continually prolonging her flirtation with religion (*Bastard* 149). The state of *being wanted* is deeply gratifying, it seems, and provides a balm for the absence of fatherly love and the awful sting of shame that she feels at the Waddells'. This community's desire for her presence within their boundaries is an antidote for her abjection. Bone only vaguely understands this desire, but Earle seems to be able to articulate it: "They want you, oh yes, they want you. . . . I'll tell you, Bone, I like it that they want me, Catholics and Baptists and Church of Gods and Methodists and Seventh-Day Adventists, all of them hungry for my dirty white hide, my pitiful human soul." Earle, however, remains assured that the world is "irredeemably corrupt" and that no congregation "would give two drops of piss for me if I was already part of their saggy-assed congregation" (148). Despite his protestations otherwise, Bone believes that "the hunger, the lust, and the yearning" that she feels (but which she doesn't understand completely) are also "palpable" in Earle's voice. "As it was, all I could think was how marvelous it would be when he finally heard God speaking through me and felt Jesus come into his life" (149).

Just as there are limitations to the oppositional identity constructed in the family stories of the Boatwrights, the psychic balm offered by a gospel identity is incomplete. Bone never steps forward to declare her faith; rather than feeling "[w]hatever magic Jesus' grace promised," these moments are "cold and empty" (152). It seems that Bone is unable to shake her initial reaction to gospel music—the sense that it is intended to "make you hate and love yourself at the same time, make you ashamed and glorified" (136). The thrill of chosen-ness conjured by the music is contradicted by the awareness of her inadequacy. Again, Earle's explanation of his refusal to accept religion offers insight that Bone, on her own, cannot obtain: "Religion gets you and milks you dry. Won't let you drink a little whiskey. Won't let you make no fat-assed girls grin and giggle. Won't let you do a damn thing except work for what you'll get in the hereafter" (148). In the physical space of the revival tent and in the narrative space of gospel music, the rural poor are free to articulate an identity outside the marginalizing conventions and prerogatives of class shame. Paradoxically, the identity can be claimed only if Bone accepts as shameful the very things that define the Boatwright legacy.

While Earle's explanation appears to be little more than a rejection of the strict moralism of southern evangelical Protestantism, we can begin to further develop the specific limitations of this faith as a vehicle for an oppositional subjectivity by examining it as a statement of the theodicy of gospel music. In stark contrast to slave spirituals and African American gospel, which often locate evil as the consequence of earthly oppression, the southern gospel music of the white working class responds to evil by rejecting the suffering of this world, "emphasiz[ing] the believer's eternal home in heaven," and encouraging "believers to trust Jesus to soothe their affections while waiting for their heavenly reward . . . " (Fillingim 50). By ignoring the material and earthly causes of suffering, this cosmology establishes evil as a matter of human morality, and the responsibility for earthly misery is displaced onto the individual enduring it. By this reasoning, Earle not only deserves the initial pain that is derived from his wife's abandonment but also the ongoing sense of lack he seeks to heal through women and booze. Likewise, the theodicy of southern gospel music serves to further shame Bone and to silence the articulation of her abuse; if evil has no external cause, then she believes that it must be a consequence of her own moral failings.

While Bone ultimately fails to consummate the public assumption of a "glorified" gospel identity, her fascination with the fantastic imagery of apocalyptic, retributive destruction becomes increasingly elaborate. Mourning "the loss of something I had never really had" (i.e., a fixed identity within the gospel narrative), Bone "tak[es] comfort in the hope of the apocalypse, God's retribution on the wicked. I liked Revelations, loved the Whore of Babylon and the promised rivers of blood and fire. It struck me like gospel music, it promised vindication" (*Bastard* 152). Apocalypse provides solace even before she begins to explore the text of John's vision. The vague interest begins with the hope for the courthouse's destruction, attributed to Anney in the first chapter; it develops into the ethereal, if frightening, flames of her masturbatory fantasies, and finally it becomes a wish for some otherworldly force—"God or magic" or even the doctor who sees her wounds—to confront Glen with the truth of his abuse, demand his repentance, and cause him to "weep tears of blood" (116).

This daydream is complicated. In it, Glen's fate is her decision, and Bone is thus endowed with the agency and narrative control his abuse seeks to deny her. However, the fantasy is also self-annihilative and even culminates in her death. Certainly, we might formulate Bone's image of death as simply a fantasy of escape, but its recurrence, as well as her rejection of it following Shannon Pearl's horrific immolation, suggests that elaboration is necessary. Frank Kermode writes that Apocalypse amounts to a macrocosmic figuration of our own deaths—the necessary end of the fiction we use to impart sequence, consequence, and coherence upon a human life (7). Bone's dreams of her own death seem to reverse this: in them, her death ends the threat that she poses to the narrative of a happy family. Unable to articulate a story in which she exists happily within this framework, she internalizes Glen's abusive attempts to locate her as the source of any incoherence within the patriarchal order he seeks to establish in their home. The trauma she endures destabilizes the boundaries of this space, and Bone locates herself as the source of this instability.

Let us return for a moment to the notion, discussed both by Kennedy and Gwin, that memories are accessed by imaginatively reconstructing the geographies in which past events occurred. Certain places—her aunts Ruth's and Raylene's homes, for instance—serves as oases of stability both for Bone and the reader as each moves through the imaginative landscapes of the text. For the most part, however, Bone is alienated from place; the small measure of stability that does exist amid their repeated moves is translated either as a gut-wrenching stasis and immobility, which Bone believes is her birthright as a Boatwright woman, or as the claustrophobia consolidated in the grip of Glen's overlarge hands. This incongruity is profoundly troubling for Bone's developing sense of her self. She either has no place in which to locate herself, or she is confined to places that offer no room to move and no space to speak. Again, we can consider the image of Alma's scorched yard where the spigots serve as constant emblem of the ideological and material forces that weigh upon the Boatwrights as well as their ultimate dislocation from the places which the inhabit. In Bone's memory, the boundaries between place and self are rendered incoherent by the twinned effects of displacement and claustrophobia. For a child, this all translates into a simple idea: she does not fit anywhere.

In her initial apocalyptic fantasy, she imagines herself as the element of dissonance and positions her death as the apocalyptic reconstitution of an originary harmony. Shannon Pearl's death initiates a shift in these self-annihilative fantasies; confronted with the "dull thudding sound of her life shutting down, everything stopping," Bone determines to resist the negation of her own existence (205). At first, she simply integrates the burning courthouse into her masturbatory dreams:

> I thought about fire, purifying, raging, sweeping though Greenville and clearing the earth. . . .
> "Fire," I whispered. "Burn it all." I rolled over, putting both my hands under me. I clamped my teeth and rocked, seeing the blaze in my head, haystacks burning and nowhere to run, people falling behind and the flames coming on, my own body pinned down and the fire roaring closer. (253–54)

Ultimately, Bone abandons the self-annihilative component of the fantasy altogether. Though Glen's climactic rape of Bone seems to be about to happen throughout the text, it erupts onto the page with a startling brutality. Bone, however, responds in an even more startling fashion, abandoning her former silence and discovering the voice necessary to articulate the emotions that have so confounded her throughout the text. That voice is unmistakably apocalyptic, and it is not dissimilar to the angry defiance that Wright's Dan Taylor assumes after his own beating. Like Taylor, Bone no longer awaits deliverance from above. Rather, Bone assumes the role of avenging angel herself, damning Glen for every act he has committed and defying his authority with each blow:

> "You'll die, you'll die," I screamed inside. "You will rot and stink and cave in on yourself. God will give you to me. Your bones will melt and your blood will catch fire. I'll rip you open and feed you to the dogs. Like in the Bible, like the way it ought to be, God will give you to me. God will give you to me!" (285)

Bone defies Glen's attempt at physical possession by demanding a discursive possession of her stepfather, claiming the authority to name him within the divine narrative of redemption and retribution.

Of course, as cataclysmic as the rape is for Bone and for Anney, the Apocalypse is never realized. It is, however, not confined to the realm of Bone's fantasies. Following the rape, Bone cannot tell her story to the sheriff. In the terms of trauma theory, this experience defies assimilation and cannot be represented through language. We can also understand this in terms of the sociospatial process of marginalization and its silencing effects: Bone imagines Sheriff Cole as just "Daddy Glen in a uniform" (296)—that is, as the authority maintaining the very cultural practices that limit her ability to tell her own story. This encounter, confined to the institutional space of the hospital room, simply is not big enough to contain Bone's suffering. Instead, any effort to fit the limited textual spaces of a police report would reduce the enormity of her suffering and would continue the abjection of her family, further exiling them to the aberrant margins of their community. Raylene is once again Bone's ultimate defender, and she surprisingly appropriates the language of Apocalypse:

> "She's just twelve years old, you fool. Right now she needs to feel safe and loved, not alone and terrified. You're right, there has to be justice. There has to be a judgment day too, when God will judge us all. What you gonna tell him you did to this child when that day comes?"
> "There's no need—" he began, but she interrupted him.
> "There's need," she said. "God knows there's need." Her voice was awesome, biblical. "God knows." (298)

Among the commonplace materialist criticisms of religion, generally, and of southern evangelical Christianity, specifically, is the contention that, by stressing an afterlife and a judgment to come, religion defers concerns with the oppression of this world and minimizes issues of social justice. Certainly, that is the critique of religion offered by Wright's work.

Thus, while readers may initially disapprove of Raylene's (and Allison's) reliance upon God's otherworldly judgment rather than immediate, *this-worldly* retribution that they would like to see visited upon Glen, we should not be frustrated or interpret this as an apocalyptic cop-out. Rather, Apocalypse here functions as the only narrative realm sufficient to articulate Glen's crime and Bone's suffering. The discourses of discipline and punishment, the mechanisms of the law, have only worked to enact the abjection of the Boatwrights heretofore. Calling upon them now to mete out their retribution would ultimately reinforce their white trash identity, reinscribe the aberrant, shameful behaviors, including incest, that have been attributed to them, and bulwark the boundaries that restrict them to the community's margins. However, constructions such as *margin* and *center* cease to exist in the apocalyptic narrative Raylene invokes, and the institutional effort to locate the individual is supplanted by divine judgment. The disruption of margin and center is critical to the novel—and perhaps, to Bone's survival. In A *Visitation of Spirits*, Horace Cross turns to the apocalyptic imaginary in hopes of writing some narrative in which he might be able to articulate a coherent sense of himself and his place in the word, in which the contradictions and confusion of his experience might not tear him to pieces. However, he fails to find that narrative, and in the end, he cannot envision anything other than his apocalyptic end. Raylene, on the other hand, provides Bone with a story in which her suffering is given meaning, form, coherence, and a measure of closure, thanks to the divine distribution of justice it promises. In this way, *Bastard Out of Carolina* offers something of a corrective to the broadest implications of a text like "Blueprint for Negro Writing": while discursive resistance alone may not be sufficient to actualize social and political change, the spiritual and psychological sustenance that narrative solutions to suffering provide can be crucial for victims to work through and live beyond those experiences. And their survival *is* necessary for action to happen.

Allison's engagement with Apocalypse is not merely formal, and it is not simply about providing a satisfying end to her novel. By invoking the southern apocalyptic imaginary, Allison lays her own affirmative claim to her native ground, demanding that Bone's story *and* her story be included, not along the aberrant margins of the South, but fully within it. For Allison, then, the South is hardly the grounds for parody; *Bastard Out of Carolina* evokes the textures of place with neither romanticism nor irony but instead with fury, frustration, longing, and love. By defiantly excavating experiences from the marginal spaces of southern community, this post-southern novel articulates a "sense of place" that is, to borrow Barbara Ladd's term, "emancipatory" (48): Allison activates the regional and the particular as vehicle for liberation rather than as a mechanism to resist change. The possibilities for this sort of recovery are rich, and once again, Apocalypse signals a site worthy of investigation.

Epilogue

Apocalypse South, *Redux* — Searching for Meaning after the Flood

> If it keep on rainin' the levee gonna break
> If it keep on rainin' the levee gonna break
> Some of these people don't know which road to take
> . . .
> If it keep on rainin' the levee gonna break
> If it keep on rainin' the levee gonna break
> Some people still sleepin', some people are wide awake
> —Bob Dylan, "The Levee's Gonna Break"

WRITING IN the aftermath of the hurricane and flood that nearly destroyed his city, the New Orleans poet Peter Cooley struggled mightily and profoundly to wrest meaning from devastation:

> I see a city in tears
> abomination of desolation,
> bodies of the drowned afloat in back streets,
> graves of the dead buried above ground spring
> open and skeletons whole and in pieces
> set out to decimate the morning light.
> And he said: that is better. But what else?
> Then I answered: my words are little, poor. (61)

Cooley is hardly alone in his frustration to articulate something coherent and meaningful about Hurricane Katrina and the subsequent deluge; the sentiment of poetic inadequacy that is expressed in "I See a City in Tears" is shared by many of the other poems published alongside it in the 2006 anthology *Hurricane Blues: Poems about Katrina and Rita*. These emotions should not surprise. The images broadcast around the globe in the days and weeks following Katrina do not yield easily to our conventional ways of speaking—in particular, to the discourse of American national identity.

The imagery of this poem—and the images that emerged from the Gulf Coast in August and September of 2005—engage the conventions of Apocalypse. Indeed, while Katrina-writing is recognizable in the frequency of terms like *levee*, *breach*, and *FEMA trailer* and references to now-nationally familiar local geographic identifiers, including the *Industrial Canal* and *Lower Ninth Ward*, one might also designate the genre by its tone, which is frequently if not uniformly, apocalyptic. In his book about Katrina, New Orleans *Times-Picayune* editor Jed Horne describes the view from I-10 in the hours before landfall:

> Within twenty-four hours [of the mandatory evacuation order], mobile signboards would go up at key junctions across the interstate system that converged on southeast Louisiana, the lettering picked out in flashing amber dots against a black background: NEW ORLEANS EXITS CLOSED. Blink. NEW ORLEANS EXITS CLOSED—and suddenly, a name once evocative of elegance and devil-may-care good times, a haven of sophistication in the hardscrabble South, carried overtones of catastrophe: a Babylon, a Chernobyl. Blink. NEW ORLEANS EXITS CLOSED. (40)

Horne's description of the scene is hardly anomalous: a quick Lexus-Nexus search for combination of the terms "Katrina," "New Orleans," and "Apocalypse" or "apocalyptic" since the storm yields 460 articles.[1] *Rolling Stone*'s lead piece on the storm, for instance, was entitled "Apocalypse There" (Taibbi 102–45).

Throughout this book, I have argued that Apocalypse is a site in need of excavation; that it is a discourse capable of condemning outsiders and maintaining stable, hegemonic notions of place, race, and gender; that it offers an alternative narrative space in which oppressed communities can articulate their own prophetic historical visions; that its occurrence suggests the presence of concealed historical meaning; and that its vision of vindication and retribution provides individuals and communities a vehicle to work through traumatic suffering. This examination of Apocalypse would be incomplete if it did not reckon with this recent southern catastrophe—a singular event that inspired each of the four different uses of

---

1. This search was conducted on 10 March 2012.

apocalyptic discourse investigated by this book. In no time in recent years has the landscape of the apocalyptic imaginary come so close to materiality in the South as it did in the Crescent City in late 2005. With the population all but disappeared, the remaining residents endured a hellish, seemingly endless isolation; homes and neighborhoods were inundated with toxic waters; the infrastructure and institutions of civic authority largely collapsed; and a semblance of order was restored finally only through the imposition of martial law. Not coincidentally, the discourses of cataclysm and destruction, rebirth and renewal, judgment and justice have been indispensable in the rhetoric of postdiluvian New Orleans. In concluding *Apocalypse South*, this epilogue will deploy the various models of literary engagement with the apocalyptic imaginary identified in the earlier chapters in order to better understand representations of this historical event. Specifically, it will examine the voices of condemnation and scapegoating that followed the flood, approaches to the flood that fit within the prophetic traditions of the American and African American jeremiads, the possibility of historical revelation suggested by John Biguenet's 2006 play *Rising Water*, and the apocalyptic possibility of hope and deliverance that is central to the cultural identity of New Orleans. My aim is not simply to further argue for the southern apocalyptic imaginary as a viable theoretical model, but rather, to make a case for the utility the works examined herein offer to broader efforts to understand the genealogy of southern catastrophes and cataclysms and even to articulate responses to these events that are grounded in the particular textures of the communities that suffer through them.

"Playing the Blame Game": Condemnation and Scapegoating after the Flood

In the days following the flood, President George W. Bush steadfastly refused to assign fault. "Look, there will be plenty of time to play the blame game," he told reporters with frustration (Curl A04). Despite this cautioning otherwise, the assignations of guilt were widespread, and the phenomena of scapegoating and collective persecution were played out in public comments from officials and activists. Thus, while poets and New Orleanians (Peter Cooley being both) may have struggled to articulate a coherent narrative about the flood, others found Katrina's meaning to be self-evident: a vengeful God had laid this modern Sodom to waste. New Orleans is no stranger to such condemnations; the pamphleteers, proselytizers, and self-proclaimed prophets who rail against the wickedness of the fallen world with a righteous fury, recalling Faulkner's Doc Hines, have become familiar sights on Bourbon Street and elsewhere, particularly during Mardi Gras. One should not, then, be particularly surprised by the blogs, press releases, and emails that were blasted out by media savvy fundamentalist and evangelical political activists. For instance, South Carolina anti-abortion advocate Steve Lefemine told the *Washington Post* article that the image of an eight-week-old fetus was visible in the satellite images of the storm as it landed on the Gulf Coast and that this image proved the storm and flood to be the act of an angry God (A27). The same article also quoted Michael Marcavage of Repent America, who cited the storm's disruption of the annual gay and lesbian event "Southern Decadence" as evidence of God's intentions. "We take no joy in the death of innocent people," Marcavage told the *Post*. "But we believe that God is in control of the weather. . . . The day Bourbon Street and the French Quarter was flooded was the day that 125,000 homosexuals were going to be celebrating sin in the streets. . . . We're calling it an act of God."

Marcavage's willingness to speak for the All-Knowing aside, Bourbon Street and the Quarter remained all but undamaged and quickly reopened for business as usual. In fact, the storm itself wrought relatively little damage to New Orleans—the eastern edge of coastal Louisiana and the Mississippi Gulf Coast bore the brunt of its monstrous impact. These distinctions mattered little to Marcavage and the Rev. Dr. Wiley Bennett, the pastor of Woodland Hills Baptist Church in Tyler, Texas. When evacuees poured into his town, Bennett saw fit to emblazon the church's marquee with a message for them: "THE BIG EASY IS THE MODERN DAY SODOM AND GOMORRAH." "What I was trying to do was point out that the wickedness of the city of New Orleans brought a hand of judgment on that city," Bennett told reporters. "It was never put up there with the intention of saying there are no good people in the city of New Orleans. That was a misunderstanding. People took it wrong" (Falsani A4).

Despite their best efforts, the fame Lefemine, Marcavage, and Bennett garnered receded far more quickly than did the flood waters on Canal Street. And while it may be tempting to dismiss such sentiments as little more than ideological extremism, their echoes are disconcertingly audible in the remarks of public figures with far greater authority and far larger audiences. On October 3, 2005, the Rev. Franklin Graham, son of Billy Graham and heir to his father's ministry, offered a convoluted message at Jerry Falwell's Liberty University. In his speech, Graham did not attribute the destruction to a wrathful deity but refused to dismiss any claim that such punishment might be warranted. "I'm not saying that God used this storm as a judgment," he told the audience, before decrying Mardi Gras, voodoo, and the acceptance of homosexuality as "adverse to Christian beliefs." "There's been satanic worship," he continued. "There's been sexual perversion. God is going to use that storm to bring revival" (Seltzer 1H). Similarly, in his weekly self-distributed column, Alabama state senator and one-time local conservative radio personality Hank Irwin (R-Montevallo) wrote, "New Orleans and the Mississippi Gulf Coast have always been known for gambling, sin and wickedness. It is the kind of behavior that ultimately brings the judgment of God" ("Alabama Legislator: Katrina was God's wrath on sinful coast" A14). Richard Baker, the ten-term Republican congressman from Louisiana's sixth district (which includes Baton Rouge and communities just to the west of New Orleans), offhandedly told lobbyists that public housing in New Orleans had "finally [been] cleaned up. . . . We couldn't do it, but God did" (Babbington A4).

While I have heretofore applied this model of Apocalypse to works of fiction, it proves to be equally useful in an examination of these comments. Echoes of Doc Hines's demagoguery in *Light in August* and Rev. Barden's sermonizing in *A Visitation of Spirits* can be heard in the condemnation and scapegoating that followed the storm. Michael Marcarvage posits Katrina's disruption of the Southern Decadence festival as evidence of the hand of a wrathful, anthropomorphic God, angered by such willful flaunting of Levitical prohibition of homosexuality. Marcarvage cites the French Quarter, where "125,000 homosexuals" would have been "celebrating sin in the streets," as the epicenter of God's wrath. Marcarvage was apparently uninterested in facts that might trouble his contention (for instance, Bourbon Street and the rest of the Quarter remained dry, while the New Orleans Baptist Theological Seminary was underwater, along with hundreds of churches). Likewise, he seemed unconcerned with the difficult theodical questions that such events provoke. Suffering and destruction on this scale unsettle notions of causality and moral order, and Marcarvage's apocalyptic rhetoric, like Hines's and Barden's, displaces the troubling ambiguity of an experience by locating an ambiguous figure as its cause. As long as the aberrant presence can be rhetorically contained, the stable social order for which they nostalgically yearn can still seem divinely sanctioned, and the exceptional status of their community of believers can remain unquestioned.

Like the distorted gospels exhorted by Faulkner's and Kenan's preachers, Marcavage's message represents more than an extreme and exaggerated version of evangelical religious belief. Investigation into the particular operations of his rhetoric provides insight into the implications of scapegoating and collective persecution in secular, ostensibly objective representations and responses to the disaster. More pervasive and perhaps more insidious than these apocalyptic condemnations was the scapegoating perpetrated by the popular media in its overwrought concern with looting and their rush to broadcast rumors of horrific violence around the city. "The events that followed in the wake of Hurricane Katrina were spun into legends even as they were happening," writes historian and former New Orleans resident Douglas Brinkley. "Rumors were folded into the news cycle and repeated as fact before they could be corroborated or checked" (572). For instance, though stories of "rampant murder" in the Superdome persisted, none were committed. In Jed Horne's assessment of media coverage, "The aggregate portrait was of a city gone mad, a black city, a city of depraved men and women who would walk away from asthmatic children and leave them to die, if they didn't violate them first" (108). Enthralled by what Horne calls "the biggest story of their careers," reporters sought to articulate the chaos that ensued in coherent form. With little consideration (and, indeed, little time) for nuance or complexity, they churned out stories that in effect established the victims as the perpetrators of their own suffering. The logic that would assign blame for this event (in the case of Marcarvage) to a gay man on vacation perhaps seems ridiculous in a culture that no longer is predicated upon notions of an anthropomorphic, interventionist God; in the end, it is no more problematic than the criminalization and condemnation of a waterlogged group of people stealing dry shoes. Such was the consequence of the images of looters in the flooded stores along Canal Street, endlessly looping on the cable news channels without sufficient explanation. In both instances, the scapegoating mechanism displaces the deeply, existentially troubling questions of theology, theodicy, politics, and ethics posed by the storm; by the mounting death toll; by the masses stranded at the Superdome and the Ernest N. Morial Convention Center; by the people waiting for help on their roofs; and by the elderly, baking in their attics before finally succumbing to heat exhaustion.[2] As is too often the case, however, these very real, very com-

---

2. The last several years have seen the proliferation of books on the 2005 storms, and each of them contains accounts of episodes like these. The best among these included Douglas Brinkley's *The Great Deluge: Hurricane Katrina, New Orleans, and the Mississippi Gulf Coast* (New York: William Morrow, 2006), Jed Horne's *Breach of Faith: Hurricane Katrina and the Near Death of a Great American City* (New York: Random House, 2006), Chris Rose's *1 Dead in Attic: After Katrina* (New York: Simon & Schuster, 2007), Dave Eggers's *Zeitoun* (New York: McSweeney's, 2009), and Josh Neufeld's comic oral history *A.D.: New*

plicated concerns of politics and policy, of infrastructure and economy, and of morality and human rights, are displaced in favor of a more readily intelligible scapegoat and easy narratives of blame and punishment. As with the townspeople of *Light in August* and the congregation in *A Visitation of Spirits*, those who invoke the apocalyptic imaginary in this manner do so to discursively stabilize nation and community. When Apocalypse is deployed in this manner, the chaos and suffering that followed Katrina seem not the consequence of any policy, but rather, the fault of an aberrant few who must be pushed to the nation's margins.

Katrina and the (African) American Jeremiad

While Marcarvage and his cohort assign blame to a population they consider aberrant, other Katrina apocalypticists avoided the trap of the scapegoat and blamed the nation and the communities to which they themselves belonged. In doing, these figures evoked the long rhetorical traditions of the American and African American jeremiads, and positioned the aftermath of the storm as a divine call for moral, spiritual, and civic renewal. Even New Orleans's then mayor, Ray Nagin, jumped onto the apocalyptic bandwagon. According to James Varney of the *Times-Picayune*, Nagin's unprepared remarks suggested "that a vengeful God smote New Orleans with Hurricane Katrina because of heavenly disapproval of America's involvement in Iraq and of rampant violence within urban black communities" and that New Orleans's black majority would reclaim their "Chocolate City" because God willed it so (A1).

At the same event, according to the *Times-Picayune*, several pastors, representing some of the most devastated neighborhoods, argued that the city "served as an example of divine judgment . . . the Rev. Dennis Watson of Celebration Church decried the area's sins of 'corruption, racism, slavery, violence, division among Christians and Mardi Gras'" (Nolan LIVING4). Watson's remarks suggest the complicated possibilities and pitfalls of apocalyptic rhetoric. The "sins" he enumerates are the very things the apocalyptic judgments of others work to obfuscate and elide—and the very things Richard Wright sought to expose in *Uncle Tom's Children*. By equating social injustice with sin, and assigning the destruction of storm

---

Orleans After the Deluge (New York: Panthenon, 2009). The best writing on the storm and its aftermath continues to appear in the New Orleans *Times-Picayune*, for which both Horne and Rose work.

and flood to the hand of an angry God, he imparts an ultimate urgency to social action: essentially, repent or be destroyed. However, when he exhorts the audience to abandon the revelry of Mardi Gras in favor of an explicitly Christian moral code, he reinforces the bivalent epistemologies for which undifferentation and ambiguity are anathema.[3] This rejection of ambiguity is not limited to sexual licentiousness, but rather pervades Watson's invocation of Apocalypse. While his jeremiad begins by noting that the conditions of post-flood New Orleans are the products of a complicated constellation of material, economic, and social injustices, it ultimately rejects that complexity in favor of a reductive cause-and-effect model rooted in a prophetic tradition: we have failed in moral obligation; some have already been punished for their sins, while punishment awaits others, perhaps to be meted out in the final judgment. Indeed, any number of methodologies might be used to explain the power of the storm, the failure of the levees, and the shameful response by all levels of government. Unfortunately, these various disciplinary discourses—meteorology, hydrology, engineering, economics, education, public policy, partisan politics, ethics, and social justice, among others—are not immediately compatible. Watson's best attempt to generate an intelligible call for justice out of this contemporary Babel is compelling, but ultimately reductive.

Other jeremiahs turned to secular rhetorical traditions in their attempts to make sense of the devastation. Just over a month after the storm, *Vanity Fair* featured a piece by the famed journalist David Halberstam entitled "Hell and High Water—American Apocalypse: New Orleans 2005." "The scenes were at once familiar and unfamiliar," Halberstam begins (385), before immediately invoking several of the standard indices of Apocalypse: chaos, contradiction, hybridity, and the interpretive difficulty they provoke. Halberstam points to the conventional formulas of cable news which shaped coverage of the storm and flood: "First, there are the tragedy and the tears; then, in time, the redemption, the rejuvenation, and the gratitude." Despite their generic packaging, the images that emerged disconcerted even the veteran war correspondent:

> . . . it was unfamiliar as well, because when the damage is this catastrophic, the people so helpless, the government so weak and clumsy, we expect it to take place somewhere else—on the coast of Sri Lanka

3. In fact, such undifferentiation is a hallmark, not just of Mardi Gras, but of the carnivalesque, which, according to Bakhtin, involves the "temporary suspension of all hierarchic distinctions and barriers among men . . . and of the prohibitions of usual life" (*Rabelais and His World* 15).

or Bangladesh, for instance—somewhere distant and poor. We do not expect to see so many fellow Americans overwhelmed, unable to help themselves and unable to escape the disaster. We do not expect to see our government so impotent and indifferent that it is completely paralyzed at the most critical moment. We do not expect to see the story play out so slowly and the cavalry arrive so late.

Was this really us? Was this really an American city coming apart—or drowning—as we watched? Were all these poor people, whose lives were broken, and some of whom looted their own city, really Americans? Aren't we better than this? Aren't we different?

Here, Halberstam troubles the notions of American exceptionalism in a quintessentially American, liberal fashion: he questions whether the nation has lived up to a righteous vision of American nationalism, rather than questioning the righteousness of that vision. For Halberstam, that remains a matter of received knowledge, just as it was for the writers, thinkers, and leaders catalogued in Sacvan Bercovitch's seminal *The American Jeremiad*. These American jeremiahs, like Halberstam centuries later, "simultaneously lament[ed] a declension and celebrat[ed] a national dream" (Bercovitch 180). In this discourse, the institutions of nation may have failed to realize its core principles, but those ideologies (and eschatology) remain true. Thus, while Halberstam makes no specific reference to Apocalypse in the body of the piece, "Apocalypse Now and Then" proved a more apt title than *Vanity Fair*'s editors might have realized: the questions he poses are those of Apocalypse. They are the questions of a citizen seeking to interpret the images before him; to contextualize them within a historical discourse in which they do not easily fit; to make sense of that incongruity; and to discover what previously hidden element of human experience has suddenly come unavoidably into our view in this moment of cataclysm. And they are, in fact, the same sorts of questions posed by the works of Faulkner, Wright, Allison, and Kenan. Rather than consigning blame to an abject few, each work reveals our own implication in some historical reality that does not square with the dominant narrative of their communities.

The Possibility of Revelation and Renewal

Given the frequency of apocalyptic imagery in the reportage of the New Orleans disaster, it should be no surprise that the first long-form literary attempt to grapple with the storm, John Biguenet's 2007 play *Rising*

Water, employs apocalyptic structures and suggests the apocalyptic promises of revelation and renewal. Biguenet's play depicts a middle-aged New Orleans couple, Sugar and Camille, in the late evening and early morning of Monday and Tuesday, August 29 and 30, 2005. In the first act, the rising flood waters drive the couple into the attic of their single-story home; there, they are prompted by forgotten items to reconsider their past. In Act II, Camille escapes onto the roof through a small hole; Sugar, "no longer slender," according to the stage directions (2), can only reach his head and one arm through the hole. Trapped with no means of communication and no source of information, Sugar and Camille are profoundly isolated within the very city that has nurtured them, their relationship, and their family for generations. In their isolation, they are prompted to revisit a past they have long-since ignored and to consider the future of a marriage that has given way to the malaise of middle age. The possibilities of revelation and renewal, then, are located in the domestic space of home and family. Sitting atop her roof in Act II, Camille tells her husband (again, whose head is all that is visible), "In this moonlight, everything looks so strange, so fresh. Maybe it's not the end of the world, this rising water . . . our past is being washed away. It's left us sort of standing on a mountaintop up here, like Noah's Ark coming to rest after all that rain" (52).

However, as Sugar reminds her and as the flood waters attest (and, indeed, as we have seen in the lynching of Joe Christmas, the tragic violence depicted throughout *Uncle Tom's Children*, the abandonment of Allison's Ruth Anne Boatwright, and the suicide of Kenan's Horace Cross), the contradictions of history, which have been buried or repressed in order to maintain coherence, have a nasty way of revisiting themselves upon us. Indeed, the insights of the play are not limited to a single couple. The focus of their conversations frequently shifts from their neglected marriage to the collapse of the neglected and aging infrastructure. The city remains a constant presence in their discussions, and Biguenet's choice of names prompts the audience to locate the characters and their experience in the flood within the complex genealogy of New Orleans: without the cash crop of sugar, there would perhaps be no New Orleans—and certainly not the plantation culture of south Louisiana and the international trade that were based upon it; "Camille," of course, provokes recollections of—and comparisons with—the monster Category 5 of 1969 hurricane that barely skirted New Orleans and instead leveled much of the nearby Mississippi Gulf Coast. In sheer power, Camille dwarfed Katrina, which had been reduced to a Category 3 by the time it reached the Mississippi and Louisiana coasts; Biguenet's Camille prompts the audience to contemplate how lucky the city had been throughout its recent history of near-misses and how much worse the destruction might have been if Katrina had been a more powerful storm. Likewise, the audience is reminded that many New Orleanians, like Sugar and Camille, went to bed on that Monday evening in 2005, believing that their charmed city had once again dodged the proverbial bullet.

Like the various entities charged with protecting the city, Sugar and Camille have too long ignored or avoided the most difficult questions facing them and have been content instead to simply maintain the prosaic rhythms of life in the Crescent City. At first, Sugar contends the flood is perhaps a matter of plumbing or perhaps the failure of one of the city's aging pumps. "Probably the city's pumps backed up. Or maybe one of them went down," he tells his wife (11).[4] Surprisingly, his nonchalant response to the rising flood is predicated on a familiar faith in the city's infrastructure that contradicts his awareness of its decaying condition: "A miracle they work at all as old's they are." Later, however, he becomes less certain. As he explains to Camille, if one of the aging pumps fails, the other pumps will have to compensate, and the additional load might cause the entire system to fail "[u]ntil it floods. . . . That's how everything works down here. One piece fails, the whole thing falls apart" (12). While the failure of the pumping system seems possible, Sugar's faith in the levees is unshakable—at least, in these early moments of the flood: "The U.S. Army built those things. The U.S. Army Corps of Engineers. You think they don't know how to hold the water back. A levee's not just mud. There's steel inside. No way a storm like what we had today could breach a levee." As

---

4. Civil engineer A. Baldwin Wood developed New Orleans's massive pumping system and supervised its installation between 1913–15. The Wood pump, as it became known, drained much of the cypress "backswamp" between the original city and Lake Pontchartrain and thus allowed the first major expansion of the city beyond the original limits—the natural levees and ridges carved by the Mississippi upon which the French Quarter and the Garden District were constructed. According to John M. Barry, the Wood pumps were designed to move up to 47,000 cubic feet of water per second—"roughly half the low-water flow of the Mississippi itself"—through tunnels beneath the city, *uphill*, and over the levees and into the lake (228). Much of the original infrastructure remains in service, and modifications are still based upon Wood's original designs. See also Bourne, "New Orleans—A Perilous Future," 42.

According to Douglas Brinkley, the volume of water pouring into the city through the breached levees quickly overwhelmed the massive pumping system, and operators were evacuated by Monday evening (134). Aaron Broussard, then president of neighboring Jefferson Parish, has received much criticism for evacuating that parish's pump operators *before* the system shut down, when the system might have been able to drain areas not yet as flooded as New Orleans itself (Brinkley 133–35; Horne 99–100).

the most obvious manifestation of federal authority in the community, the levees function as a metonym for the nation. Interestingly, Sugar is far more willing to entertain the failure of the pumps (emblematic of municipal infrastructure) than to consider the possibility that the levees (and, by implication, the institutions of the most powerful nation on earth) have failed.

Thus, while the action on stage is limited to Camille's and Sugar's home and the bulk of the narrative is focused upon the particularities of their relationship, the broader questions of policy posed by the flood remain a constant presence. Even in these first hours of the unfolding disaster, the flood disrupts narratives of millenarian nationalism by confronting U.S. citizens with the catastrophic failures of institutions purporting to protect them. The levees along the Industrial and Seventh Street Canals, designed to insure New Orleans's position as a hub of global trade, were hurriedly constructed with little oversight over corrupt officials and fraudulent contractors and little consideration of the long-term effects of slicing up the wetlands outside the city. These wetlands, which would have absorbed the brunt of storm surge, have disappeared at a shocking rate. Other low-lying areas were drained with the aging pumps to encourage development during oil booms that served to facilitate white flight from the original city, the movement of the black middle class to new suburbs, and ultimately, the reduction of support for the decaying institutions and infrastructures that served the city's poorest residents.[5]

Likewise, while the play does not explicitly engage the apocalyptic narratives of judgment offered by fundamentalist commentators who would posit the destruction of the storm as the consequence of sexual licentiousness in New Orleans, it presents a scenario of abandonment that challenges the fundamentalist belief in the Rapture. Clearly, Camille and Sugar's isolation is no fault of their own but rather a consequence of material fac-

---

5. Craig Colten is the authority on New Orleans's geography, and his book, *An Unnatural Metropolis* offers the most comprehensive account. Barry's *Rising Tide* details the history of the Mississippi levee construction. For specific information on the failure of New Orleans's levees during Katrina, see Horne 145–67; Bourne 32–68. Both Horne and Bourne rely on interviews with Ivor van Heerden, the deputy director of LSU's Hurricane Center. Van Heerden has written his own book (with journalist Mike Bryan), *The Storm: What Went Wrong and Why During Hurricane Katrina—the Inside Story from One Louisiana Scientist* (New York: Viking, 2006). Finally, the most thorough and authoritative investigation remains the Independent Levee Investigation Team's 700-plus-page report, *Investigation of the Performance of the New Orleans Flood Protection Systems in Hurricane Katrina on August 29, 2005* (Seed, Bea, et al., 2006), which is available in its entirety online at http://www.ce.berkeley.edu/projects/neworleans/ [accessed 28 Feb. 2012].

tors neither had ever considered. In direct challenge to any narrative that would blame victims, Camille becomes the play's Jeremiah. She first questions a God that would allow this manner of devastation, but, after the still-faithful Sugar describes the flood as an act of men rather than of God, she offers blistering condemnation of those she believes to be responsible and announces a prophetic call for justice:

> You and me, we've lost everything we own. How many people drowned in their own bedrooms since the sun went down? And it's all because somebody cut some corners, didn't pay attention to some detail, decided things were close enough to right and let it go at that? You telling me that's why we're trapped here in our own attic in the middle of the night with water lapping at the stairs? That's the reason we could die tonight, you and me?
> ... [I]f it's not God responsible, then the men did this to us, I hope they never lie down in bed they don't hear the ghosts of those they drowned tonight crying out for help. If I die tonight, I'll never let them sleep, those murderers, I promise you. (38)

In this moment, the particularities of Sugar and Camille most obviously give way to the broader context of the storm; the political debates that will follow loom up but never overwhelm the characters or seem didactic. Nonetheless, the condemnation explicit here is pervasive, if subtly so, throughout the play and is most obvious in the couple's stark, profound isolation, both in the text and on the stage. In the attic, they are surrounded, even overwhelmed, by the evidence of both the richness and the pain of their personal history.

In the second act, however, they are utterly alone and even separated from one another. Camille ascends to the roof first and reports on the "deadly quiet" of their neighborhood. "Nothing but the sound of water lapping at the roof," she reports to Sugar. "No dogs, no motors, no human voices. Nothing. . . . Not a sound. No wind. No birds. Nobody knocking. Nothing but the sloshing of the water" (47). There is no evidence of community, as if all life has been erased from the surface of the earth. That isolation is not simply a matter of Camille's description but also of mise-en-scène: for two acts, the audience sees nothing other than the couple and the space they occupy. In the claustrophobic space of a small attic, isolation seems perhaps the natural consequence of confinement. In the unrestrained space of rooftop, that isolation quickly becomes desolation. Camille anxiously implores her husband to join her on the roof, but he can fit only his head and one arm through the hole. Consequently, the floodwaters that have isolated them from their community now threaten the integrity of the most intimate interpersonal unit—husband and wife. Furthermore, Sugar himself is all but disembodied on stage: "I'm here with you—just not all of me," he good-naturedly reassures Camille (49). With much of his body concealed, he is a fitting emblem of his hometown.

In the play's final moments, wailing sirens signal the failure of the neighborhood's various water-logged home security systems rather than the coming of any an official assistance. As their climactic scream fills the theatre, the audience is discomfited by the contradiction of their proximity to Sugar and Camille and the insurmountable waters that threaten them: rescue or escape is tantalizingly possible but never comes. Camille and Sugar are alone on the stage with no other structure in sight and no other person audible. And yet, as the sirens remind the audience, they are trapped in the ostensibly safe space of a familiar American neighborhood. The floodwaters even threaten to separate them from each other. The infrastructures of a culture obsessed with personal and public security have collapsed, proving incapable of preserving the integrity of even the small unit of a married couple.

The call for judgment announced by Camille in Act I is continued by these screaming sirens. The misfiring home or automobile alarm is an irritant familiar to modern urban and suburban life, and the usual response is annoyance: who or what set that off, and who will shut it off? In this case, the first part of the question seems simple (the rising water did), but it becomes more confusing in the face of the melancholy response to the second part. That answer—no one—is disconcerting and should prompt the audience to begin to work through the necessary questions of infrastructure, politics, and policy that the flood demands we confront. Biguenet does not employ these flood waters as a metaphor for repressed marital and familial pain or Camille and Sugar's relationship as a metaphor for their destroyed city. Rather, *Rising Water* realizes the apocalyptic nature of catastrophe in its fullness: Apocalypse does not simply provide a familiar vocabulary to represent destruction, but rather, it is a discourse in which the various distinctions between past, present, and future collapse. It is a present moment in which the veil that has concealed the contradictions of the past is ripped away and in which we are prompted to consider the possibilities of a new and unimagined future.

While the play questions and condemns, it neither yields answers nor plots a future. *Rising Water* is a play about the flood, and it is likely that post-Katrina art yet to come will seek to investigate what this play only suggests: the genealogy and possibilities of a city below sea level, ringed by insufficient levees, most of the population of which lives in a poverty that was (and is) ignored within the prevailing political and economic discourse.

Justice, Deliverance, and Resistance

Combating the despair that results when we confront the tragedies, traumas, and catastrophes of late modernity is among the most important tasks facing contemporary artists, including those grappling with Katrina. "The gap between the words we write and read and the need for action is so much greater than any individual has the power to perform—that gap grows too large and I despair," writes the native Louisianan (and famous apocalyptist) Tony Kushner. "Despair is a sin, I really believe that, but I am as I say a miserable sinner, and there are days after some nights I can't even get out of bed" (58–59). Each of the writers with whom I have dealt in this project push and prod us out of our beds in such moments; they provoke the most important questions, and they provide the spiritual and intellectual sustenance that carries us through that process. By appropriating the apocalyptic rhetoric of condemnation to represent condemned people and condemned experiences, these works together constitute a legacy of southern resistance.

Such work is desperately needed now; as writers and artists attempt to wrest meaning from the near-destruction of New Orleans, they can look to Bone and *Bastard Out of Carolina* as a model. To work through this trauma, to make sense of the devastation their city has suffered, they will inevitably have to conjure hope in the face of cataclysm, renewal in the face of destruction, and justice in the face of criminal negligence. Just as the emancipatory potential of Apocalypse exists within the culture that condemns Bone and Kenan's Horace Cross, that energy persists in the cultural DNA of New Orleans. Consider—or reconsider—the often-neglected words to a familiar song:

> We are trav'ling in the footsteps
> Of those who've gone before,
> And we'll all be reunited,
> On a new and sunlit shore,
>
> Oh, when the saints go marching in

Oh, when the saints go marching in
Lord, how I want to be in that number
When the saints go marching in

And when the sun refuses to shine
And when the sun refuses to shine
Lord, how I want to be in that number
When the sun refuse to shine

Chorus
And when the moon turns red with blood
And when the moon turns red with blood
Lord, how I want to be in that number
When the moon turns red with blood

Chorus
Oh, when the trumpet sounds its call
Oh, when the trumpet sounds its call
Lord, how I want to be in that number
When the trumpet sounds its call

Chorus
Some say this world of trouble,
Is the only one we need,
But I'm waiting for that morning,
When the new world is revealed. (Lomax 541)

Like many spirituals, one could find many different variations on "When the Saints Go Marching In" (occasionally, "When the Saints Come Marching In"); Allen Lomax included a similar version in the seminal *Folk Songs of North America* (454). Pete Seeger recorded and regularly performed the lyrics presented above, and drawing from his songbook, The Beatles took it on in early demos. Several blues players, including Mississippian Fred McDowell, have used these apocalyptic verses, and in 2003, Dr. John and Mavis Staples recorded a "minor-key dirge [with] the kind of spooky, midnight-in-the-graveyard vibe," which incorporated several, but not all, of these verses (Swenson). In 2006, while on tour with a raucous unplugged tribute to Pete Seeger, Bruce Springsteen regularly closed shows with this version. The first performance of that tour: the 2006 New Orleans Jazz and Heritage Festival, just seven months after the flood.

Writing about the album of Seeger covers for his column for Springsteen's hometown *Asbury Park Press*, Baptist minister Michael Riley argues that American folk music—familiar songs on the album, like "Ol' Dan Tucker," "Jesse James," and "O Mary, Don't You Weep"—is marked by a "sense of working for the kingdom of God [that] is muted in a lot of modern apocalyptic blather." While the fantastic images out of Revelation might transfix audiences, they amount to "theology as science fiction," according to Riley, and thus miss the point of Apocalypse:

> Apocalyptic literature is written during times of hardship and persecution of those who see themselves as God's people. . . .
>
> And the true message is simply and inevitably this: The world seems to be spinning out of control. Justice is a myth, and life is filled with sin and pain misery. But God still is in charge of history, he still loves his children and is working even now to deliver them from evil and bring them home.
>
> Apocalyptic literature is a tract for hard times, and the message at the heart of it is simply: "Hold on."

Perhaps we have heard "When the Saints Go Marching In" too many times. We hear (or read) *march*, and we think of parades, and perhaps we unconsciously replace it with dancing. But the full lyrics remind us that "When the Saints Go Marching In" resides squarely within the traditions delineated by Riley and that it is a statement of what Paul Gilroy terms "the revolutionary eschatology" of African American religion. This civic anthem is, in fact, a slave spiritual born of the need for hope; it nourished the spirits of those persevering in conditions so oppressive that they would defy any rational investigation and sustained their sense of injustice and deliverance when none came.

The apocalyptic hope of these forgotten lyrics words have been obscured or neglected over time. But when played again, they remind us to peel back the layers heaped onto this particular song and to look behind jazz tourism and beyond the Super Bowl trophy won by the NFL franchise that is its namesake. "When the Saints Go Marching In" is a sturdy artifact; its meaning does not threaten to turn to dust in our hands as we examine it. In fact, the deeper we dig, the more resonant it becomes until it finally becomes an agent of the very revelation it promises. Like those of each of the works this project has considered, its apocalyptic vision offers hope, but it does not suggest that we passively wait for deliverance. Rather, the hope it offers is a matter of persistent interpretive work—that is, of reading the signs of these times, as well as those of the past, in order to bring into the realm of visibility those things that other narratives conceal. In our moments of deepest despair and in a world fraught with crisis and catastrophe, the promises of Apocalypse will get us out of bed in the morning and allow us to march forward.

Bibliography

Adams, Timothy Dow. "Telling Stories in Dorothy Allison's *Two or Three Things I Know for Sure*." *Southern Literary Journal* 36.3 (1999): 82–99.
"Alabama Legislator: Katrina Was God's Wrath on Sinful Coast." New Orleans *Times Picayune*. 29 Sept. 2005. NationalA14.
Allison, Dorothy. *Bastard Out of Carolina*. New York: Plume, 1993.
———. *Two or Three Things I Know for Sure*. New York: Plume, 1996.
———, and Randall Kenan. "A Conversation." *Village Voice Literary Supplement*. Sept. 1993. 26.
Aptheker, Herbert. "Maroons within the Present Limits of the United States." *Maroon Societies: Rebel Slave Communities in the Americas*. Ed. Richard Price. Baltimore: The Johns Hopkins University Press, 1979. 151–68.
Appadurai, Arjun. *Modernity at Large: Cultural Dimensions of Globalization*. Minneapolis: University of Minnesota Press, 1996.
Atkinson, Ted. "The State." In Moreland, 2007. 220–35.
Babbington, Charles. "Some GOP Legislators Hit Jarring Notes in Addressing Katrina." *Washington Post*. Sept. 10, 2005. A04.
Baker, Delbert W. "The Dynamics of Communication and African-American Progress in the Seventh-day Adventist Organization: A Historical Descriptive Analysis." Diss., Howard University, 1993.
Baker, Houston A., Jr. *Blues, Ideology, and African American Literature: A Vernacular Theory*. Chicago: University of Chicago Press, 1984.
———. *Long Black Song: Essays in Black American Literature and Culture*. Charlottesville: University of Virginia Press, 1972.
———. *Turning South Again: Rethinking Modernism/Rethinking Booker T*. Durham, NC: Duke University Press, 2001.
Bakhtin, M. M. *The Dialogic Imagination: Four Essays*. Ed. Michael Holquist, trans. Caryl Emerson and Holquist. Austin: University of Texas Press, 1981.

———. *Rabelais and His World*. Trans. Helene Iswolsky. Bloomington: Indiana University Press, 1984.
Baldwin, James. *The Fire Next Time*. New York: Vintage International, 1993.
Barry, John M. *Rising Tide: The Great Mississippi Flood of 1927 and How It Changed America*. New York: Simon & Schuster, 1998.
Bass, Jack, and Marilyn W. Thompson. *Ol' Strom: An Unauthorized Biography of Strom Thurmond*. Marietta, GA: Longstreet Press, Inc., 1998.
Benjamin, Walter. "Theses on the Philosophy of History." *Illuminations: Essays and Reflections*. New York: Harcourt Brace Jovanovich, Inc., 1968. 253–364.
Bercovitch, Sacvan. *The American Jeremiad*. Madison: University of Wisconsin Press, 1978.
Biguenet, John. "The Aftermath of Hurricane Katrina." Plenary lecture given at the Seventh Biennial Conference of the Association for the Study of Literature and the Environment. Wofford College, Spartanburg, SC, 15 June 2007.
———. *Rising Water*. Unpublished manuscript, 2007.
Biles, Roger. *The South and the New Deal*. Lexington: University of Kentucky Press, 2006.
Boles, John B. "The Southern Way of Religion." *Virginia Quarterly Review* 75.2 (1999): 226–47.
Bone, Martyn. *The Postsouthern Sense of Place in Contemporary Fiction*. Baton Rouge: Louisiana State University Press, 2005.
Bourne, Joel K. "New Orleans—A Perilous Future." *National Geographic*. 212.2 (2007), 32–67.
Bouson, J. Brooks. "'You Nothing but Trash': White Trash Shame in Dorothy Allison's *Bastard Out of Carolina*." *Southern Literary Journal* 34.1 (2003): 101–23.
Boyer, Paul. *When Time Shall Be No More: Prophecy Belief in Modern American Culture*. Cambridge, MA: Belknap Press of Harvard University Press, 1992.
Brinkley, Douglas. *The Great Deluge: Hurricane Katrina, New Orleans, and the Mississippi Gulf Coast*. New York: HarperCollins, 2006.
Brooks, Cleanth. *William Faulkner: The Yoknapatawpha Country*. Baton Rouge: Louisiana State University Press, 1963, 1991.
Bull, Malcolm. "On Making Ends Meet." *Apocalypse Theory*. Ed. Malcolm Bull. Oxford: Blackwell Publishers, 1995. 1–20.
———. *Seeing Things Hidden: Apocalypse, Vision and Totality*. London: Verso, 1999.
———, and Keith Lockhart. *Seeking a Sanctuary: Seventh-day Adventism and the American Dream*. 2nd ed. Bloomington: Indiana University Press, 2006.
Caldwell, Deborah. "Did God Send the Hurricane?" *Chicago Sun-Times*. 4 Sept. 2005. CONTROVERSY4.
Caron, Timothy. *Struggles Over the Word: Race and Religion in O'Connor, Faulkner, Hurston, and Wright*. Macon, GA: Mercer University Press, 2000.
Carpentier, Alejo. "On the Marvelous Real in America." *Magical Realism: Theory, History, Community*. Ed. Lois Parkinson Zamora and Wendy B. Faris. Durham, NC: Duke University Press, 2005. 75–86.
The Carter Family. "Can the Circle Be Unbroken." *20th Century Masters: The Best of the Carter Family*. Mercury Nashville, 2005. CD.
———. "No Depression (in Heaven)." *20th Century Masters*, 2005. CD.
Caruth, Cathy. *Unclaimed Experience: Trauma, Narrative, and History*. Baltimore: The Johns Hopkins University Press, 1996.

Cash, W. J. *The Mind of the South*. New York: Vintage Books, 1991.
Chavers, Linda. "The Spot in the Mirror: The Role of Gender in Richard Wright's *Black Boy*." *Reconstruction: Studies in Contemporary Culture* 8.4 (2008). http://reconstruction.eserver.org/084/chavers.shtml. Accessed 14 Feb. 2012.
Cobb, Michael. "Cursing Time: Race and Religious Rhetoric in *Light in August*." *boundary 2* 32.3 (2005): 139–68.
Coleman, James W. *Faithful Vision: Treatments of the Sacred, Spiritual, and Supernatural in Twentieth-Century African American Fiction*. Baton Rouge: Louisiana State University Press, 2006.
Colten, Craig. *An Unnatural Metropolis*. Baton Rouge: Louisiana State University Press, 2005.
Cooley, Peter. "I See a City in Tears." *Hurricane Blues: Poems about Katrina and Rita*. Ed. Philip C. Kolin and Susan Swartout. Cape Girardeau, MO: Southwest Missouri State Press, 2006.
Cooperman, Alan. "Where Most See a Weather System, Some See Divine Retribution." *The Washington Post*. 4 Sept. 2005. AA27.
Cone, James H. *The Spirituals and the Blues: An Interpretation*. New York: The Seabury Press, 1972.
Curl, Joseph. "Bush Denies Race Had Role in Recovery; Refuses to Play Katrina 'Blame Game.'" *Washington Times*. 13 Sept. 2005. Nation A04.
Douglas, Mary. *Purity and Danger: An Analysis of the Concepts of Pollution and Taboo*. London: Routledge Classics, 1966, 2002.
Douglass, Frederick. "What to the Slave is the Fourth of July?" *My Bondage and My Freedom*. Ed. John David Smith. New York: Penguin Books, 2003.
Duck, Leigh Anne. *The Nation's Region: Southern Modernism, Segregation, and U.S. Nationalism*. Athens: University of Georgia Press, 2007.
———. "Religion: Desire and Ideology." in Moreland, 2007. 269–83.
Dylan, Bob. "The Levee's Gonna Break." *Modern Times*. Sony, 2006. CD.
———. "The Levee's Gonna Break." Lyrics available on BobDylan.com. http://www.bobdylan.com/songs/the-levees-gonna-break . Accessed: 9 March 2012.
Eggers, Dave. *Zeitoun*. New York: McSweeney's, 2009.
Eliot, T. S. "The Hollow Men." *Selected Poems*. New York: Harcourt Brace & Company, 1930, 1964. 75–80.
Fabre, Michel. *The World of Richard Wright*. Jackson: University Press of Mississippi, 1985.
Falsani, Cathleen. "Pastor's Sign Rubs Salt in Wounds of Downtrodden." *Chicago Sun-Times*. 16 Sept. 2005. RELIGION44.
Faulkner, William. *Absalom, Absalom!* New York: Vintage International, 1936, 1990.
———. "Dry September." *Collected Stories*. New York: Vintage, 1995. 169–84.
———. *Light in August*. New York: Vintage International, 1932, 1990.
———. *The Sound and the Fury*. New York: Vintage, 1931, 1990.
Fillingim, David. "Oft Made to Wonder: Southern Gospel Music as Theodicy." In Graves and Fillingim. 43–56.
Fisher, Benjamin F. IV. "Southern Gothicism." *The New Encyclopedia of Southern Culture, Vol. 9: Literature*. Chapel Hill: University of North Carolina Press, 2008.
Fossett, Judith Jackson. "Sold Down the River." *PMLA* 122.1 (2006): 325–30.
Fowler, Doreen. "Introduction." *Faulkner and Religion: Faulkner and Yoknapatawpha 1989*. Ed. Doreen Fowler and Ann J. Abadie. Jackson: University Press of Mississippi, 1990. ix–xvi.

Frank, David A. "The Prophetic Voice and the Face of the Other in Barack Obama's 'A More Perfect Union' Address, March 18, 2008." *Rhetoric and Public Affairs* 12.2 (2009): 167–94.

Franke, Katherine M. "Becoming a Citizen: Post-Bellum Regulation of African American Marriage." *Yale Journal of Law & the Humanities* 11 (1999): 251–309.

Frye, Northrop. *The Great Code: The Bible and Literature*. New York: Harvest/HBJ Books, 1982.

Fullop, Timothy E., and Albert J. Raboteau, eds. *African American Religion: Interpretive Essays in History and Culture*. New York: Routledge, 1997.

Gaines, Janet Howe. *Music in the Old Bones: Jezebel through the Ages*. Carbondale: Southern Illinois University Press, 1999.

Gates, Henry Louis, Jr. *The Signifying Monkey: A Theory of Afro-American Literary Criticism*. New York: Oxford University Press, 1988.

Genovese, Elizabeth Fox. *Within the Plantation Household: Black and White Women of the Old South*. Chapel Hill: University of North Carolina Press, 1988.

Genovese, Eugene. *Roll, Jordan, Roll: The World the Slaves Made*. 1972. Reprint, New York: Vintage, 1976.

Gilroy, Paul. *The Black Atlantic: Modernity and Double Consciousness*. Cambridge, MA: Harvard University Press, 1993.

Girard, René. *The Scapegoat*. Trans. Yvonne Freccero. Baltimore: Johns Hopkins University Press, 1986.

———. *Violence and the Sacred*. Trans. Patrick Gregory. Baltimore: Johns Hopkins University Press, 1977.

Godden, Richard. "A Difficult Economy: Faulkner and Poetics of Plantation Labor." In Moreland, 2007. 7–27.

Goff, James R., Jr. *Close Harmony: A History of Southern Gospel*. Chapel Hill: University of North Carolina Press, 2002.

Graves, Michael P., and David Fillingim. "Introduction: More Than 'Precious Memories.'" In Graves and Fillingim. 1–22.

———, eds. *More than Precious Memories: The Rhetoric of Southern Gospel*. Macon, GA: Mercer University Press, 2004.

Gwin, Minrose. "Nonfelicitous Space and Survivor Discourse: Reading the Incest Story in Southern Women's Fiction." *Haunted Bodies: Gender and Southern Texts*. Ed. Anne Goodwyn Jones and Susan V. Donaldson. Charlottesville: University Press of Virginia, 1997. 416–440.

Guthrie, Woody. "Blood of the Lamb." Perf. Billy Bragg and Wilco. *Mermaid Ave. Vol. II*. Elektra/WEA, 2000. CD.

———. "Blood of the Lamb." Lyrics available on WoodyGuthrie.org. http://www.woodyguthrie.org/Lyrics/Blood_of_the_Lamb.htm. Accessed 14 Feb. 2012.

Halberstam, David. "Hell and High Water—American Apocalypse: New Orleans 2005." *Vanity Fair*, Nov. 2005: 358.

Harris, Trudier. *Exorcising Blackness: Historical and Literary Lynching and Burning Rituals*. Bloomington: Indiana University Press, 1984.

Harvey, Paul. "God and Negroes and Jesus and Sin and Salvation." In Schweiger and Mathews. 283–330.

Hill, Samuel S. *Southern Churches in Crisis Revisited*. Tuscaloosa: University of Alabama Press, 1999.

Hobson, Fred. *The Southern Writer in the Postmodern World*. Athens: University of Georgia Press, 1991.
hooks, bell. *Feminist Theory: From Margin to Center*. Boston: South End Press, 1984.
Horne, Jed. *Breach of Faith: Hurricane Katrina and the Near Death of a Great American City*. New York: Random House, 2006.
Howard-Pitney, David. *The Afro-American Jeremiad: Appeals for Justice in America*. Philadelphia: Temple University Press, 1990.
Irving, Katrina. "'Writing It Down So That It Would Be Real': Narrative Strategies in Dorothy Allison's *Bastard Out of Carolina*." *College Literature* 25.2 (1998): 94–107.
Irwin, John T. *Doubling and Incest/Repetition and Revenge: A Speculative Reading of Faulkner*. Baltimore: Johns Hopkins University Press, 1975, 1996.
JanMohamed, Abdul R. *The Death-Bound-Subject: Richard Wright's Archaeology of Death*. Durham, NC: Duke University Press, 2005.
Jameson, Frederic. *Postmodernism, or, The Cultural Logic of Late Capitalism*. Durham, NC: Duke University Press, 1991.
Johnson, James Weldon. "The Judgment Day." *God's Trombones: Seven Negro Sermons in Verse*. New York: Penguin Classics, 1990. 53–54.
Jones, Anne Goodwyn. *Tomorrow's Another Day: The Woman Writer in the South, 1859–1936*. Baton Rouge: Louisiana State University Press, 1995.
Jones, Suzanne W., and Sharon Monteith, eds. *South to a New Place: Region, Literature, Culture*. Baton Rouge: Louisiana State University Press, 2002.
Keller, Catherine. *Apocalypse Now and Then: A Feminist Guide to the End of the World*. Boston: Beacon Press, 1996.
Kelley, Robin. *Hammer and Hoe: Alabama Communists during the Great Depression*. Chapel Hill: University of North Carolina Press, 1990.
Kenan, Randall. *The Fire This Time*. Hoboken: Melville House, 2007.
———. "Clarence and the Dead (And What Do They Tell You, Clarence? and The Dead Speak to Clarence." *Let the Dead Bury Their Dead and Other Stories*. San Diego: Harcourt Brace, 1992.
———. *A Visitation of Spirits*. New York: Vintage, 1989.
Kennedy, J. Gerald. "Place, Self, and Writing." *The Southern Review* 26.3 (1990): 496–516.
Kermode, Frank. *The Sense of an Ending: Studies in the Theory of Fiction—With a New Epilogue*. New York: Oxford University Press, 2000.
King, Vincent. "Hopeful Grief: The Prospect of Postmodernist Feminism in Allison's *Bastard Out of Carolina*." *Southern Literary Journal* 33.1 (2000): 122–40.
Kirkpatrick, David C. "The Evangelical Crackup." *New York Times Magazine*. 28 Oct. 2007. 38–66.
Korn, Joel. "'Behind Nature Is God, so God Must Be Angry.'" *Ottawa Citizen*. 25 Sept. 2005. NEWSA1.
Kort, Wesley A. *Place and Space in Modern Fiction*. Gainesville: University Press of Florida, 2004.
Kreyling, Michael. *Inventing Southern Literature*. Oxford: University of Mississippi Press, 1998.
Lackey, Michael. "The Ideological Function of the God Concept in Faulkner's *Light in August*." *Faulkner Journal* (Fall 2005/Spring 2006): 66–89.
Ladd, Barbara. "Dismantling the Monolith: Southern Places—Past, Present, and Future." In Jones and Monteith. 44–57.

———. *Nationalism and the Color Line in George W. Cable, Mark Twain, and William Faulkner*. Baton Rouge: Louisiana State University Press, 1996.

Lefebvre, Henri. *The Production of Space*. Trans. Donald Nicholson-Smith. Oxford: Blackwell Publishers Ltd., 1991.

Levine, Lawrence W. *Black Culture and Black Consciousness: Afro-American Folk Thought from Slavery to Freedom*. Oxford: Oxford University Press, 1977.

Lincoln, C. Eric. *Race, Religion, and the Continuing American Dilemma*. Rev. ed. New York: Hill and Wang, 1999.

Lomax, Alan. *Folksongs of North America*. New York: Doubleday, 1960.

Lott, Eric. *Love and Theft: Blackface Minstrelsy and the American Working Class*. Oxford: Oxford University Press, 1995.

Lowe, John. "Wright Writing Reading: Narrative Strategies in *Uncle Tom's Children*." *Modern American Short Story Sequences: Composite Fictions and Fictive Communities*. Ed. J. Gerald Kennedy. Cambridge: Cambridge University Press, 1995. 52–75.

Malone, Bill C. *Don't Get Above Your Raisin': Country Music and the Southern Working Class*. Champaign: University of Illinois Press, 2002.

Mathews, Donald G. "Lynching Is Part of the Religion of Our People: Faith in the Christian South." In Schweiger and Mathews. 153–94.

———. "The Southern Rite of Human Sacrifice." *Journal of Southern Religion* 3 (2000). http://jsr.fsu.edu/mathews.htm. Accessed 14 Feb. 2012.

May, John R. *Toward a New Earth: Apocalypse in the American Novel*. Notre Dame, IN: University of Notre Dame Press, 1972.

McCarthy, B. Eugene. "Models of History in Richard Wright's *Uncle Tom's Children*." *Black American Literature Forum* 25.4 (1991): 729–43.

McDowell, Linda. "Introduction: Rethinking Place." *Undoing Place: A Geographical Reader*. Ed. Linda McDowell. London: Arnold, 1997. 1–12.

McRuer, Robert. "A Visitation of Difference: Randall Kenan and Black Queer Theory." *Critical Essays: Gay and Lesbian Writers of Color*. Ed. Emmanuel S. Nelson. New York: Haworth, 1993. 221–32.

Melville, Herman *White-Jacket, or The World in a Man-of-War*. In *Melville: Redburn, White-Jacket, Moby-Dick*. New York: Library of America, 1983. 341–770.

Miller, Perry *Errand into the Wilderness*. Cambridge, MA: Harvard University Press, 1965, 1984.

Moreland, Richard C., ed. *A Companion to William Faulkner*. Malden, MA: Blackwell Publishing. 2007.

———. "Faulkner and Modernism." *The Cambridge Companion to Faulkner*. Ed. Philip M. Weinstein. Cambridge: Cambridge University Press, 1995.

———. *Faulkner and Modernism: Rereading and Rewriting*. Madison: University of Wisconsin Press, 1990.

Morrison, Toni. *Playing in the Dark: Whiteness and the Literary Imagination*. Cambridge, MA: Harvard University Press, 1992.

Neufeld, Josh. *A.D.: New Orleans After the Deluge*. New York: Pantheon, 2009.

Nolan, Bruce. "Pastors Pray for Spiritual Rebirth; Many Say Katrina Was God's Judgment." New Orleans *Times-Picayune*. 18 Feb. 2006. LIVING4.

Noll, Mark A. *America's God: From Jonathan Edwards to Abraham Lincoln*. Oxford: Oxford University Press, 2002.

Obama, Barack. *Dreams from My Father: A Story of Race and Inheritance*. New York: Times Books, 1995.

Parini, Jay. *One Matchless Time: A Life of William Faulkner*. New York: HarperCollins, 2004.
Patterson, Orlando. *Rituals of Blood: Consequences of Slavery in Two American Centuries*. Washington, D.C.: Civitas Counterpoint, 1998.
———. *Slavery and Social Death*. Cambridge, MA: Harvard University Press, 1986.
Price, Richard. "Introduction: Maroons and Their Communities." *Maroon Societies: Rebel Slave Communities in the Americas*. Ed. Richard Price. Baltimore: Johns Hopkins University Press, 1996. 1–32.
Ransom, John Crowe, "Reconstructed by Unregenerate." *I'll Take My Stand: The South and the Agrarian Tradition*, by Twelve Southerners. 1930. Baton Rouge: Louisiana State University Press, 1977. 1–27.
Reed, John Shelton. *The Enduring South: Subcultural Persistence in Mass Society*. Chapel Hill: University of North Carolina Press, 1972, 1986.
Richards, Gary. "'With a Special Emphasis': The Dynamics of (Re)Claiming a Queer Southern Renaissance." *Mississippi Quarterly* 55:2 (2002): 209–29.
Riley, Michael. "The Curious Apocalypse of Bruce Springsteen." *Asbury Park Press*. 30 April 2006. http://www.app.com/apps/pbcs.dll/article?AID=/20060430/ENT04/604300399/1031/ENT. Accessed 14 Feb. 2012.
Rock, Calvin B. "Institutional Loyalty versus Racial Freedom : The Dilemma of Black Seventh-Day Adventist Leadership." Diss., Vanderbilt University, 1984.
Romine, Scott. *The Narrative Forms of Southern Community*. Baton Rouge: Louisiana State University Press, 1999.
———. "Where Is Southern Literature?" In Jones and Monteith. 23–42.
Robinson, Douglas. *American Apocalypses*. Baltimore: The Johns Hopkins University Press, 1985.
Sandell, Jillian. "Telling Stories of 'Queer White Trash': Race, Class, and Sexuality in the Work of Dorothy Allison." *White Trash: Race and Class in America*. Ed. Matt Wray and Annalee Newitz. New York: Routledge, 1997. 211–30.
Sartre, Jean-Paul. "On *The Sound and The Fury*: Time in the Work of Faulkner." *The Sound and The Fury: A Norton Critical Edition*. Ed. David Minter. New York: W. W. Norton, 1993. 265–71.
Scarry, Elaine. *The Body in Pain*. New York: Oxford University Press, 1985.
Schweiger, Beth Barton, and Donald G. Mathews, eds. *Religion in the American South: Protestants and Others in History and Culture*. Chapel Hill: University of North Carolina Press, 2004.
Simone, Nina. "Mississippi Goddam!" *Nina Simone in Concert*. Mercury Records, 1991. CD.
Sellers, James. *The South and Christian Ethics*. New York: Association Press, 1962.
Seltzer, Robert. "If Forecast Hinges on Morality, Does Tolerance Make a Difference?" *San Antonio Express-News*. 8 July 2007. VIEWS1-H.
Slotkin, Richard. *Regeneration through Violence: The Mythology of the American Frontier*. New York: HarperPerennial, 1996.
Smith, Lillian. *Killers of the Dream*. NY: Norton, 1978.
Spencer, Jon Michael. *Blues and Evil*. Knoxville: The University of Tennessee Press, 1993.
Springsteen, Bruce, and the Seeger Sessions Band. "When the Saints Go Marching In." Performance. New Orleans Jazz and Heritage Festival, 30 April 2006.
Strozier, Charles B. *Apocalypse: On the Psychology of Fundamentalism in America*. Boston: Beacon Press, 1994.

Sullivan, John Jeremiah. "Mister Lytle." *Paris Review* 194 (2010): 81–98.
Sundquist, Eric. *To Wake the Nations*. Cambridge, MA: The Belknap Press of Harvard University Press, 1993.
Swenson, John. "The Rhythm of the Saints." *Gambit Weekly*. 10 Aug. 2004. http://www.bestofneworleans.com/gambit/the-rhythm-of-the-saints/Content?oid=1243154. Accessed 14 Feb. 2012.
Szkotak, Steve. "Evangelist: Katrina Could Help Clean Up Sinful New Orleans." *Chicago Sun-Times*. 5 Oct. 2005. NEWS5.
Taibbi, Matt. "My Favorite Right-Wing Nut Job." *Rolling Stone*. Nov. 2007. 47–52.
Toll, Robert C. *Blacking Up: The Minstrel Show in Nineteenth-Century America*. Oxford: Oxford University Press, 1975.
Tucker, Scott. "Looking for a City: The Rhetorical Vision of Heaven in Southern Gospel Music." In Graves and Fillingim. 23–42.
Turner, Lindsey. "Gay Identity, Conjure, and the Uses of Postmodern Ethnography in the Fictions of Randall Kenan." *Modern Fiction Studies* 49.2 (2003): 305–31.
Tuveson, Ernest Lee. *Redeemer Nation: The Idea of America's Millennial Role*. Chicago: University of Chicago Press, 1968. Midway reprint, 1980.
Twelve Southerners. *I'll Take My Stand: The South and the Southern Agrarian Tradition*. 75th anniversary edition. Baton Rouge: Louisiana State University Press, 2006.
Varney, James. "Nagin Backpedals, Apologizes; Katrina's Wrath Not God's Will, He Says." New Orleans *Times-Picayune*. 18 Jan. 2006. National1.
Uncle Tupelo. "No Depression." *No Depression*. Sony, 2004. CD.
Walker, David. *David Walker's Appeal, in Four Articles; Together with a Preamble, to the Coloured Citizens of the World, but in Particular, and Very Expressly, to Those of the United States of America, Written in Boston, State of Massachusetts, September 28, 1829*. Ed. Sean Wilentz. New York: Hill and Wang, 1995.
Wallace, George C. "The 1963 Inaugural Address of Governor George C. Wallace." Delivered on 14 January 1963 in Montgomery, Alabama. http://www.archives.state.al.us/govs_list/InauguralSpeech.html. Accessed 14 Feb. 2012.
Webb, Barbara J. *Myth and History in Caribbean Fiction: Alejo Carpentier, Wilson Harris and Edouard Glissant*. Amherst, MA: University of Massachusetts Press, 1992.
Welty, Eudora. "Place in Fiction." *The Eye of the Storm: Selected Essays & Reviews*. New York: Vintage, 1979. 116–33.
White, Hayden. "The Value of Narrativity in the Representation of Reality." *Critical Inquiry* 7.1 (1980): 5–27.
White, Walter. *Rope and Faggot: A Biography of Judge Lynch*. South Bend, IN: University of Notre Dame Press, 2002.
Whitted, Qiana. "*A God of Justice?*": The Problem of Evil in Twentieth-Century Black Literature. Charlottesville: University of Virginia Press, 2009.
Wiegman, Robyn. *American Anatomies: Theorizing Race and Gender*. Durham, NC: Duke University Press, 1995.
Wilson, Charles Reagan. *Judgment & Grace in Dixie*. Athens: University of Georgia Press, 1995.
Wright, Beverly, and Robert Bullard. "Black New Orleans: Before and After Katrina." *The Black Metropolis in the Twenty-First Century: Race, Power, and Politics of Place*. Ed. Robert D. Bullard. Lanham, MD: Rowman & Littlefield Publishing Group, 2007.
Wright, Richard. *Black Boy (American Hunger)*. 1945. New York: Perennial Classics, 1998.

———. "Blueprint for Negro Writing." 1936. *Richard Wright Reader*. Ed. Ellen Wright and Michael Fabre. New York: Harper, 1978. 36–50.
———. *Lawd Today!* Boston: Northeastern University Press, 1993.
———. *The Long Dream*. Boston: Northeastern University Press, 2000.
———. *Uncle Tom's Children*. 1936. New York: HarperPerennial, 1993.
Yaeger, Patricia. *Dirt and Desire: Reconstructing Southern Women's Writing, 1930–1990*. Chicago: University of Chicago Press, 2000.
Zamora, Lois Parkinson. ("Magical Romance/Magical Realism: Ghosts in U.S. and Latin American Fiction." *Magical Realism: Theory, History, Community*. Ed. Lois Parkinson Zamora and Wendy B. Ferris. Durham, NC: Duke University Press, 1995. 497–550.
———. *Writing the Apocalypse: Historical Vision in Contemporary U.S. and Latin American Fiction*. Cambridge: Cambridge University Press, 1989.

Index

African American Christianity. See black Christianity
African American communities. See black communities
African American gay teenagers. See gay black teenagers
African American Great Migration. See Great Migration
African American identity. See black identity
African American modernism. See "black modernism"
African American music. See black music
The Afro-American Jeremiad (Howard-Pitney), 74
Agrarians, 5, 102
alienation, 21; in Allison, 16, 131, 135, 139–44 passim, 150; in Kenan, 116; in Wright, 74–75
Allison, Dorothy, 130–53; *Bastard Out of Carolina*, 16, 131–53, 168; *Two or Three Things I Know For Sure*, 131, 134, 136, 138
Alter, Robert, 86
ambiguity, 30, 32, 33–34, 44, 49, 58, 161
American exceptionalism, 161–62

The American Jeremiad (Bercovitch), 7, 46–47, 162
Angelus Novus (Klee), 54
anti-Semitism, 50n29
antitypes, 82, 83
Appadurai, Arjun, 13
Appeal (Walker), 73
Aptheker, Herbert, 122
Atkinson, Ted, 50n30

Baker, Houston A., Jr., 70, 71, 91–92n10, 113n5; *Long Black Song*, 11n10, 73
Baker, Richard, 158
Bakhtin, Mikhail, 124n8, 161n3
Barry, John M., 164n4
Bastard Out of Carolina (Allison), 16, 131–53, 168
Bebington, David W., 8n7
Benjamin, Walter, 54
Bennett, Wiley, 157
Bercovitch, Sacvan: *The American Jeremiad*, 7, 46–47, 162
betrayal, 66, 71, 77, 93
Bible, 82–86 passim, 136–37. See also Exodus; Job; Malachi; Revelation
"Big Boy Leaves Home" (Wright), 78–85 passim

Biguenet, John: *Rising Water*, 162–68
Biles, Roger, 34
bivalence, 12, 32, 33, 37–43 passim, 55–58 passim, 110, 161
The Black Atlantic (Gilroy), 11
Black Boy (Wright), 62, 63–64, 68, 69, 75–76, 93, 141
black Christianity, 6–10 passim, 26n2, 61–65 passim, 73–77 passim, 81–82, 88–97 passim, 107, 110n4; in Kenan, 113, 119–20, 124. See also spirituals (songs)
black communities: New Orleans, 160; North Carolina, 101–29 passim
black gay teenagers. See gay black teenagers
black Great Migration. See Great Migration
black identity, 43, 48, 56, 110
black modernism, 70
black music, 97. See also spirituals (songs)
blackness, 30n6, 46, 58
black-white relations. See race relations
blame, 156, 159, 160, 162. See also scapegoats
blood, 29–30, 38, 50, 115, 149
"Blood of the Lamb," 21
"Blueprint for Negro Writing" (Wright), 63, 64, 65, 76, 152
Book of Exodus. See Exodus
Book of Job. See Job
Book of Malachi. See Malachi
Book of Revelation. See Revelation
boundaries, 106, 112–14 passim, 119, 121, 143, 144, 150
"Bound for Glory." See "This Train Is Bound for Glory"
Bouson, J. Brooks, 142
Brinkley, Douglas, 159, 164n4
Brooks, Cleanth, 21–22n1, 38
Broussard, Aaron, 164n4
Bull, Malcolm, 5, 11–12, 13, 32–33, 40, 59, 96
Bush, George W., 156

"Can the Circle Be Unbroken," 2, 130
Caron, Timothy, 22, 75–76n6

Carpentier, Alejo, 103, 123
Carter Family, 1–2, 130
Caruth, Cathy, 58n36
Cash, Wilbur J., 5–6, 7, 27n4
castration, 38, 41–42n22, 44
catastrophes, 24, 81, 131, 154–71 passim
Chavers, Linda, 66n2
Christ. See Jesus Christ
Christian fundamentalism, 2–6 passim, 8–9n8, 10n9, 23–28 passim, 54, 64, 80, 83, 95; New Orleans, 157, 163, 165. See also evangelical Christianity
Christianity, black. See black Christianity
"chronotrope" (word), 124n8
civil rights movement, 136
class and classism, 130–40 passim, 146–48 passim
clocks, 67, 72, 86, 87, 89, 90
Cobb, Michael, 22
Coleman, James W., 75
communists and communism, 64, 84, 88–89, 94, 96, 97
Communist Party USA, 66, 68, 93, 94
Cone, James H., 81
contamination, 29–32 passim, 35n13, 41, 42, 46, 112, 127
conversions, 77, 93
Cooley, Peter, 154
crucifixion, 22, 32, 42, 58
"cult of white womanhood," 35n13, 41, 44
cursedness. See damnation; doom

damnation, 29, 36, 48, 81, 112, 124, 151
Darby, John Nelson, 9n8
defiance, 140–42 passim, 150
deliverance, 2–3, 29, 78, 81–82, 91, 147, 151, 170
demons, 79, 113, 114
despair, 39, 69n4, 143, 168, 171
Devil. See Satan
dispensationalism, 9n8
divine judgment. See God: as judge
doom, 23, 47–48, 55–59 passim, 85, 95, 96, 97
doppelgängers, 117–18

Douglas, Mary, 31–32
Douglass, Frederick, 73–74, 96
"Down by the Riverside" (Wright), 65, 77, 81, 84–86 passim
Dred: A Tale of the Great Dismal Swamp (Stowe), 122
Duck, Leigh Ann, 22, 49n27, 51
Dylan, Bob, 154

Eliot, T. S., 52n31, 59
eschatology, 64, 73, 96–97, 101–2, 110, 115–16, 135. See also millennialism
eschatology of place, 104–10
"The Ethics of Living Jim Crow" (Wright), 69
evangelical Christianity, 1–11 passim, 65, 83, 91; in Allison, 147–48, 151–52; in Faulkner, 21–38 passim, 45–48 passim, 54; in Wright, 91; views of Hurricane Katrina, 157–61 passim
evil, 26–29 passim, 33, 38, 57–58, 80, 111, 148–49. See also good and evil
Exodus, 91

Fabre, Michel, 61–62
"fallen woman," 36n14
family abuse, 132–52 passim
Faulkner, William, 138; *Light in August*, 15, 21–60, 81–84 passim, 95, 104, 108, 113n5, 158, 160; *Light in August* compared to Allison, 141; *Light in August* compared to Kenan, 102, 108, 113n5, 114, 116; *The Sound and the Fury*, 50, 52, 54, 58n35
Fillingim, David, 147, 148
fire: in Allison, 131–32, 133, 145–51 passim; in Faulkner, 44; in Kenan, 111, 113, 119, 120, 124; in Wright, 77, 90–91
"Fire and Cloud" (Wright), 87–92, 113n5
Fisher, Holly, 95
floods, 41, 85, 86, 154–71 passim
folk music, 170. See also spirituals (songs)

Frank, David, 74
Frye, Northrop, 82–83
Fullop, Timothy E., 11
fundamentalism, Christian. See Christian fundamentalism

Gates, Henry Louis, Jr., 128n9
gay black teenagers, 102–3, 108–20 passim
gender, 35–37, 38, 108. See also patriarchy
Gilroy, Paul, 11, 73, 97, 127, 170
Girard, René, 11, 38, 40–41, 144
God, 81–82, 90, 91, 112, 148, 166, 170
God as judge, 8, 25, 36n16, 46–47; in Allison, 146, 151, 152; in Faulkner, 33, 37, 38, 46, 51; in Kenan, 120; in New Orleans, 156–61 passim. See also Jubilee; Judgment Day
good and evil, 12, 26, 28, 32, 124; color symbolism, 30n6
gospel music, 16, 146–47, 149. See also "No Depression (in Heaven)"
Gothicism, 14
Graham, Franklin, 157–58
Graves, Michael, 147
Great Code (Frye), 82–83
Great Depression, 1, 2n2, 12, 34
Great Migration, 34, 49n27
Greenville County, South Carolina, 131–40 passim, 146, 147
Guthrie, Woody, 21
Gwin, Minrose, 135, 143

Halberstam, David, 161–62
Harris, Wilson, 123
Hill, Samuel S., 7–9, 25, 26n2
home, 135, 136
homosexuality, 102n1, 109, 112–14 passim, 128, 157, 158. See also gay black teenagers
hooks, bell, 143
Horne, Jed, 155, 159
Howard-Pitney, Davis, 74
Hurricane Camille, 163
Hurricane Katrina, 17, 154–71 passim

hybridity, 33, 37, 127, 132

identity, 49, 108, 134, 139–49 passim.
   See also black identity; white identity
I'll Take My Stand, 5, 6
intermarriage. *See* miscegenation
Irving, Katrina, 139n3, 144
Irwin, Hank, 158
Irwin, John T., 55

JanMohammed, Abdul R., 41, 80, 90
jeremiads, 73–74, 160–62
Jesus Christ, 22, 25, 30, 58, 73, 89, 94, 148
Jews, 50n29
Jezebel, 36, 44, 84
Jim Crow. *See* racism, institutionalized
Job, 85–86
Johnson, James Weldon, 101
Jubilee, 73, 82
judgment, 29, 60, 111, 133, 157, 167.
   See also God as judge
Judgment Day, 8, 11n10, 101
"The Judgment Day" (song), 101

Keller, Catherine, 5n4
Kelley, Robin D. G., 84, 91
Kenan, Randall, 4, 101–35 passim, 138, 145; *Let the Dead Bury Their Dead and Other Stories*, 16, 102–7 passim, 121–24, 128n10; *A Visitation of Spirits*, 102–28 passim, 141, 152, 158, 160
Kennedy, J. Gerald, 134
Kermode, Frank, 31n8, 52n31
King, Martin Luther, Jr., 74, 96
King, Vincent, 139, 142
Klee, Gustav, 54
Kort, Wesley A., 105, 106, 126, 135–36
Ku Klux Klan, 50
Kushner, Tony, 168

Ladd, Barbara, 13, 35, 45, 46, 51, 104, 153

Lawd, Today! (Wright), 70
Lefebvre, Henri, 105
Lefemine, Steve, 157
Let the Dead Bury Their Dead and Other Stories (Kenan), 16, 102–7 passim, 121–24, 128n10
levees, 164, 165
"The Levee's Gonna Break," 154
Light in August (Faulkner), 15, 21–60, 81–84 passim, 95, 104, 108, 113n5, 158, 160; compared to Allison, 141; compared to Kenan, 102, 108, 113n5, 114, 116
"The Lily of the Valley," 93–94
Lockhart, Keith, 96
Long Black Song (Baker), 11n10, 73
"Long Black Song" (Wright), 66–75 passim, 84–85, 87
Lott, Eric, 117–18n6
Lowe, John, 99n11, 94
lynching: in Faulkner, 24, 25, 29–31 passim, 35–44 passim, 48–50 passim, 58, 65–67 passim, 163; in Wright, 77–81 passim
Lytle, John, 102

magic realism, 103
Malachi, 116
Marcavage, Michael, 157–60 passim
Mardi Gras, 157, 160, 161n3
maroons (people), 107, 121–27 passim
martyrdom, 49, 77–78, 92
Marxism, 64, 65, 84, 88, 92
Mathews, Donald G., 11, 31–32, 37
McCarthy, B. Eugene, 81
McDowell, Linda, 136
McMillan, Terry, 103n2
McRuer, Robert, 128nn9–10
media, news. *See* news media
memory, 13, 106, 111, 112, 118, 134, 149, 150; collective, 84, 125
millenarian nationalism, 5, 11n10, 15, 23, 48–54 passim, 63, 96
millennialism, 6–7, 11, 23, 45–54 passim, 71–82 passim, 96, 104, 111. *See also* premillennialism
minstrelsy, 117

miscegenation, 30, 31, 46, 48, 56–57
"Mississippi Goddam!," 61
modernism, 9, 51, 52n31, 59, 97. *See also* "black modernism"
Moreland, Richard C., 58n35, 59
Morning Star (steamship), 77
Moses, 46, 77, 81, 82, 91, 92
murder, 42, 57. *See also* lynching
music. *See* black music; folk music; gospel music

Nagin, Ray, 160
The Narrative Forms of Southern Literature (Romine), 30, 39
nationalism, millenarian. *See* millenarian nationalism
Nationalism and the Color Line (Ladd), 35, 46, 51
New Critics, 6, 21
New England Puritanism, 8, 23, 46
New Orleans, 154–71 passim
news media, 159–61 passim
"nigger" (role), 43
"nigger" (word), 31n7
"No Depression (in Heaven)," 1–4, 6, 8, 12, 72

Obama, Barack, 74
"one drop" laws, 29
orgies, 118–19
outsiders, 44, 45, 53, 56, 108, 136–37, 143

patriarchy, 135–51 passim
Patterson, Orlando, 29n5, 30n6, 34, 38, 40nn20–21, 90
Payne, Daniel Alexander, 110n4
Pentecostalism, 26n2
place and space. *See* space and place
pollution. *See* contamination
"poor white trash" (identity), 134–42 passim, 146, 152
prayer, 26, 61, 88, 90
premillennialism, 9n8
Price, Richard, 123, 125

The Production of Space (Lefebvre), 105
prophecy, 15, 23, 40, 73–74, 82, 97, 116, 161; in Seventh-day Adventism, 96; in songs, 2, 3, 71–73, 75
punishment, 46, 73, 111, 124, 146, 158, 161
purification, 32
Puritanism: New England. *See* New England Puritanism
purity, 25, 30n6, 35, 37, 112

queer theory, 128n10, 139

Raboteau, Albert, 10n9, 82, 110n4
race, 29–30, 33, 38, 132
race relations, 9, 10; in Faulkner, 22–60 passim; in Kenan, 109; Seventh-day Adventist view, 96; in Wright, 87. *See also* civil rights movement; lynching; miscegenation; segregation
racism, institutionalized, 10, 27, 31, 41n22, 49, 52, 65–77 passim
rape, 41–42, 44, 132, 150
Rapture, 9n8, 165
redemption, 45, 46, 84–85, 147, 151, 161
Revelation, 33, 36, 78–79, 93, 133, 149, 170
Richards, Gary, 102
Riley, Michael, 170
Rising Water (Biguenet), 162–68
rites of passage, 105, 114
Robinson, Douglas, 5
Rock, Calvin, 95
Romine, Scott, 5, 6, 30, 39, 42, 56n33, 58, 101, 135
Rope and Faggot (White), 80–81

sacrifice, 25, 27n4, 32, 38–39, 43, 49, 89, 114
salvation, 25–26, 75, 147
Sartre, Jean-Paul, 52, 54, 65
Satan, 28, 145–46
scapegoats, 40, 41, 42, 144, 156–59 passim

Schweiger, Beth Barton, 9, 10n9
Seeger, Pete, 169–70
Seeing Things Hidden (Bull), 5, 12
segregation, 4, 27, 31, 32
Sellars, James, 29n5
Seventh-day Adventism, 15, 62, 95–96
sex, 68, 72, 112. See also miscegenation
sexism, 66n2. See also patriarchy
sexual abuse, 132, 139, 143, 149. See also rape
sexual licentiousness, 36–37, 161
shame, 107; in Allison, 134, 140–43 passim, 147–49 passim; in Wright, 91
sheep, 39n19
Simone, Nina, 61
sin, 25, 29, 103, 132, 158, 160
slaves and slavery, 10–11, 27, 34, 41n22, 47, 73, 82; Seventh-day Adventist view, 96. See also maroons (people)
Smith, Lillian, 27
social class. See class and classism
The Sound and the Fury (Faulkner), 50, 52, 54, 58n35
Southern Agrarians. See Agrarians
Southern Baptist Convention, 7, 8–9n8
Southern Churches in Crisis (Hill), 7–9
Southern Renascence, 5, 6
space and place, 4–7 passim, 12, 13, 31; in Allison, 133–45 passim, 149–51 passim; as evil, 26; in Kenan, 101–17 passim; profanation of, 42. See also eschatology of place
spirituals (songs), 71–75 passim, 82, 148, 168–69, 170
Springsteen, Bruce, 169–70
stepfathers, 139–52 passim
Stowe, Harriet Beecher, 85, 122
Strozier, Charles, 9n8
suicide, 103, 114
Sullivan, John Jeremiah, 102
Sundquist, Eric, 35, 56

taboo, 32, 37, 41, 78
Tate, Allen, 5, 101, 102
"This Train Is Bound for Glory," 78, 81
Thurmond, Strom, 30–31
time, 67–68, 72, 82, 86–87, 89, 90

trauma, 12, 58n36, 90, 132, 133, 138–39, 149, 151, 155
Tucker, Scott, 127
Two or Three Things I Know For Sure (Allison), 131, 134, 136, 138
typology, 82–84

Uncle Tom's Cabin (Stowe), 85, 122
Uncle Tom's Children (Wright), 15, 63–98 passim, 160

Varney, James, 160
Violence and the Sacred (Girard), 30, 38
A Visitation of Spirits (Kenan), 102–28 passim, 158, 160; compared to Allison, 141, 152; compared to Faulkner, 102, 108, 113n5, 114, 116; compared to Wright, 113n5
vomiting, 58

Walker, David, 73
Wallace, George C., 3–4, 6, 8, 9, 12, 30
Warner, Michael, 120n10
Warren, Robert Penn, 5, 101, 102
Watson, Dennis, 160–61
Webb, Barbara, 123, 126
Welty, Eudora, 114
"What to the Slave Is the Fourth of July?" (Douglass), 73–74
"When the Roll Is Called Up Yonder," 71–73, 74, 75
"When the Saints Go Marching In," 168–69, 170
White, Ellen G., 96
White, James, 96
White, Walter, 80–81
white-black relations. See race relations
white femininity, fetishization of. See "cult of white womanhood"
white identity, 49, 134–42 passim, 146. See also "poor white trash" (identity)
whiteness, 30n6
white supremacy, 24, 25, 41n22, 45
"white trash" (identity). See "poor white trash" (identity)

Whitted, Qiana, 62–63, 76
Wiegman, Robyn, 49
Wilson, Charles Reagan, 25, 26n2
womanhood, southern cult of. *See* "cult of white womanhood"
women's oppression. *See* sexism
Wood, A. Baldwin, 164n4
Wright, Jeremiah, 74
Wright, Richard, 61–98, 152; "Big Boy Leaves Home," 78–85 passim; *Black Boy*, 62, 63–64, 68, 69, 75–76, 93, 141; "Blueprint for Negro Writing," 63, 64, 65, 76, 152; compared to Allison, 131, 141, 150; compared to Faulkner, 64, 69n4; compared to Kenan, 113; "Down by the Riverside," 65, 77, 81, 84–86 passim; "The Ethics of Living Jim Crow,"69; "Fire and Cloud," 87–92, 113n5; "Long Black Song," 66–75 passim, 84–85, 87; novels, 62, 70, 97; *Uncle Tom's Children*, 15, 63–98 passim, 160

Yaeger, Patricia, 138n2
Yeats, W. B., 52n31
Young, Iris Marion, 110

Zamora, Lois Parkinson, 97, 103n2

LITERATURE, RELIGION, AND POSTSECULAR STUDIES
Lori Branch, Series Editor

Literature, Religion, and Postsecular Studies publishes scholarship on the influence of religion on literature and of literature on religion from the sixteenth century onward. Books in the series include studies of religious rhetoric or allegory; of the secularization of religion, ritual, and religious life; and of the emerging identity of postsecular studies and literary criticism.

Apocalypse South: Judgment, Cataclysm, and Resistance in the Regional Imaginary
   Anthony Dyer Hoefer

www.ingramcontent.com/pod-product-compliance
Lightning Source LLC
Chambersburg PA
CBHW020948230426
43666CB00005B/220